Smugg[illegible]
in Hamp[illegible]
and Dorset
1700 – 1850

GEOFFREY MORLEY

COUNTRYSIDE BOOKS
NEWBURY, BERKSHIRE

Also available

Smuggling in The Bristol Channel 1700–1850
Graham Smith

Smuggling in Devon & Cornwall 1700–1850
Mary Waugh

Smuggling in East Anglia 1700–1840
Stan Jarvis

Smuggling in Kent & Sussex 1700–1840
Mary Waugh

Smuggling in Yorkshire 1700–1850
Graham Smith

FIRST PUBLISHED 1983
REPRINTED 1984, 1985, 1987
REVISED and REPRINTED 1990, 1994

Countryside Books
3 Catherine Road, Newbury, Berkshire

ISBN 0 905392 24 8

The cover illustration *Beach Landing*
is from a drawing by Edward Dowden

Designed by Mon Mohan
Produced through MRM Associates Ltd., Reading
Printed in England by J. W. Arrowsmith Ltd., Bristol
Printed on acid-free paper

Contents

Acknowledgements

I am deeply grateful to the following people for the help they have so generously given to me during the writing of this book:
Lord Montagu of Beaulieu; the Honourable William Pease of Lepe House, Exbury; Mr. Robert Bacon, the Agent at Lepe House; Mr. Maldwin Drummond of Cadland Manor; Mr. Brian Buxton of Dibden Purlieu; Mr. M. T. Medlycott of the Manor House, Sandford Orcas; Mr. Sidney Shave of Christchurch; Mr. V. J. Adams of Blandford Forum and the Staff of City of Southampton Reference Library.

I also wish to thank the Conway Maritime Press for permission to use D. Arnold-Foster's book about William Arnold of Cowes, *At War with the Smugglers*; Mr. Clive Hardy for the help provided by both his own *Smuggler's Guide to Purbeck* and his grandfather's *Smuggling Days in Purbeck*; Mr. John Hicks of the Berkshire County Library and Mr. Michael Bulford of Her Majesty's Customs and Excise, London, for permission to make full use of their Gazetteer, which they prepared for the Hampshire County Library's smuggling exhibition, *Contraband*; Mrs. K. Merle Chacksfield of Romsey for the help provided by her book *Smuggling Days*; Mr. Allen White for the assistance afforded by his book *Eighteenth Century Smuggling in Christchurch*; Mr. Graham Smith, the Librarian and Archivist of Her Majesty's Customs and Excise, for permission to draw on his work *Something to Declare: 1,000 Years of the Customs and Excise*, as well as his article on Warren Lisle, which appeared in the *Dorset* magazine; and Mr. Eric Jones Evans for leave to use facts from his article in the *Hampshire* magazine on Tom Johnson.

For their permission to use the photographs of, and their provision of the items from their Museums, I am very grateful to the Curators of the following: the Dorset County Museum, Dorchester, Russell-Cotes Art Gallery and Museum, Bournemouth, and the

Red House Museum, Christchurch. For their assistance with other illustrations I am also in the debt of Mr. C. Lynne; the Librarian of the National Maritime Museum, Greenwich; Miss M. Holmes, the County Archivist of Dorset; Mrs. B. Holland of The Queen's Head Hotel, Burley; Mr. M. Edgington, Reference Librarian of the Dorset County Library, the Lansdowne, Bournemouth; Mr. P. Bourke of Chettle House, Chettle; the Borough of Poole Museum Service; the Curator of the Art Gallery, Hanley; and Mr. Alan Hay of Her Majesty's Customs and Excise in the Port of Poole, Dorset.

Preface

Many factors made the coasts of Hampshire and Dorset one great entry-port for smuggled goods between the years 1700 and 1850. A glance at the map shows how close the warehouses in which the smugglers bought their contraband were in such places as Roskoff, the Channel Islands, Cherbourg, Le Havre and Dieppe, and how many served the coasts of the two counties. From Cherbourg, for instance, to Bourne Bottom, one of the busiest smuggling beaches and today the heart of the south coast's premier seaside resort, is only seventy-five miles. The prevailing wind here is the south-westerly, which makes sailing across the Channel from England easy, and the ships, fully loaded with contraband from the continent, would have been helped enormously by breezes from up the Channel, just at the time when they were most needed. Certainly the fast galleys so popular in the centre of this area, at Christchurch, would have found rowing out and scudding back with the south-wester on their port side a very fast ride.

Having made the crossing, the smugglers had beaches unsurpassed in any other part of England on which to bring their contraband goods ashore: smoothly shelving, of fine sand, in the main, and sheltered by every sort of bay and cove the Free Trading heart could desire. And then behind these beaches were stretches of land which provided immediate cover for the smugglers getting their goods inland as quickly as possible by wagon, tubman and packhorse to evade pursuit by the forces of the Crown: the vast woodlands of the New Forest and Cranborne Chase, the Great Heath on which Bournemouth now stands, and the rocky mazes of the Isle of Purbeck all made pursuit difficult. And through these fastnesses ran some of the best routeways the Free Traders could have wished for: the wooded ravines of Hampshire west of Southampton Water and the deep chines further west as far as Devon itself. And deeper into England went the ancient paths which had been cut many ages before by the great southward-flowing rivers of England.

G.M.

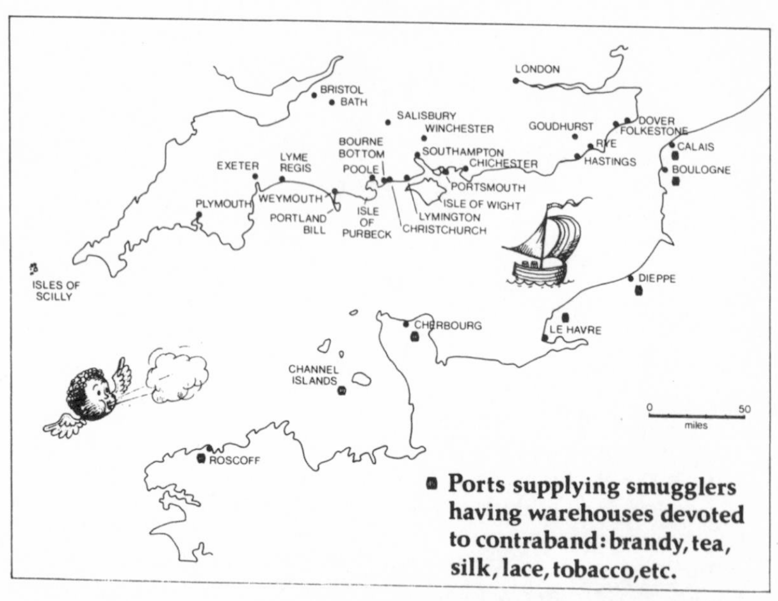

Unloading a Cutter. From a line engraving c.1785.

1
The Smuggling Trade

As early as the year 979 AD import duties were collected from French ships bringing wine and fish up the River Thames to Billingsgate Wharf in London, and there has been a Custom House near the famous fish-market ever since. The potential revenue to be gained from taxing imports to the British Isles was not lost on the Saxon kings of England, but it would be several centuries before import duties became large enough to make smuggling a truly viable alternative.

When William the Conqueror secured the English throne, the flow of French wines to his Norman barons in England became a positive flood. Wine was dutiable, but not in money: the King's Butler, with his tasting-cup on the traditional chain round the neck, selected the best wines from each cargo, and these went straight to the king's cellars. It was not until the reign of King John, when many good ideas were put into practice, that a national Customs Service was set up by the crown for the benefit of the whole country. In 1203 a fixed duty of one fifteenth was levied on all goods coming in and going out of the realm. This was collected at the ports by Collectors, which has survived as a title for the most important Customs official to this day. At the same time, Comptrollers were also appointed to keep accurate accounts of all duties paid, which went directly to the Exchequer.

Nothing has been recorded of smuggling from these early years; but in 1275 King Edward I imposed an export duty on all wool, wool-fells and hides, then England's most valuable products. 'Trounours' were appointed to weigh wool leaving the country, and their main instruments of office were huge scales known as 'The King's Beams', erected outside every Customs House. (One of these can still be seen outside Dorset's finest Customs House at Poole.) In time, these wool duties were gradually increased until the export of wool was forbidden altogether in order to protect the English textile industry. It was at this moment that the 'Owlers' emerged from their creeks and beaches, taking wool, wool-fells and hides across the Channel after sundown: in the 'owl-light', from which they derived the name which stuck to west country smugglers for centuries.

From about 1700 Britain was waging war in some part of the world pretty well continuously, against France, Holland, Spain and, eventually, the American colonists, so that by the mid-eighteenth century overseas war became an accepted way of life. Taxes had to be raised to pay for them, so more and more items were either taxed directly or had Customs duties levied upon them. As Britain's official and unofficial Empire spread across the globe, back home along its trade routes came an ever-increasing supply of new commodities, which the government of the day taxed accordingly. Europe, Africa, the Near and Far East, the West Indies and the Americas, both North and South, all contributed goods which at first were only desirable luxuries but which gradually became necessities. We have only to look at one theatre of imperial wars to appreciate the general pattern. As Britain fought the French for the rich prizes of India, the Treasury needed more and more money to continue the war, and from the ever-expanding Indian possessions, more and more goods were discovered, gathered and shipped home. Meanwhile, the seventeenth and early eighteenth centuries had seen the proliferation of huge country estates and the great houses to go with them: these their noble and *nouveau riche* owners filled with such luxuries as silks, lace, spices, wines, spirits, tea, perfumes, fruits, and so on. The trade routes then had to be defended, requiring an ever-growing fleet which could only be paid for by increased taxes and Customs duties, which were raised on the luxury imports which were being shipped by the same trade routes which had to be defended. By the accession of George III in 1760 there were 800 items on which Customs duty had to be paid; in the following fifty years a further 1,300 were added to the Statute Book.

This, then, was the smuggler's golden age, during which he had these items amongst those worthy of his attention: lace for gloves, 'kerchiefs, dresses and as decoration for linen of all kinds; gloves of silk and leather; silk for dresses and 'kerchiefs; brocade of gold and silver; scented snuff and plain snuff; velvet; straw hats from Leghorn in Italy; dried fruit, especially raisins and figs; tobacco, whisky, brandy, gin, wines, cordials; tea, chocolate, coffee; sugar, spices; dice, playing-cards; soap; coconuts; embroideries; gold, silver and many other metals; pearls, ribbons, calicoes; needlework of all kinds; salt and pepper; coal; sealing-wax; timber, coffin-nails; books, hair-powder, starch, vinegar; wire; golden guineas; newspapers; dispatches; prisoners-of-war and spies.

When duty on these items was imposed, it was said that free trade went out of the window; smugglers took to calling themselves the 'Free Traders', looking upon their activities as those of freedom fighters by whose sole efforts Free Trade, the birthright of every Englishman, was kept alive.

William Cobbett once asked a poor countryman how he lived on two shillings and sixpence (12½p) a week.

'I don't live on it,' was the reply.

'How do you live, then?' inquired Cobbett.

'Why, I poach! It is better to be hanged than to be starved to death!'

Cobbett's countryman might just as well have said, 'I smuggle!' instead. Certainly smuggling had many advantages over poaching: it paid a hundred times better, and smugglers were very unlikely to be caught and beaten to death, shot or maimed by the squire's gamekeepers, or crippled for life by one of their man-traps. When a man was out as a 'Free Trader', he only had a weak Customs service against him most of the time; and even if he was cornered by the Dragoons, he fought well and usually came off best. Even if he was taken alive, and appeared before the local magistrates, it was unlikely that he would be convicted: he was far more likely to be let off, sometimes with an admonishment to the King's men for being too officious, for the gentlemen were in the game at the top level just as the Free Trader was at the lower. But most of the time smugglers were as safe as the Tower of London, for their gangs were so powerful no forces of the crown could face them, leaving large parts of the British coast free for the pursuit of their illegal activities.

Between 1750 and 1840, when smuggling was at its height, the population of England and Wales more than doubled, and to feed it the farmers had to produce increasing quantities of food. As a result, land enclosure — which had been going on by private treaty for some two centuries or more — increased, reaching its peak between 1770 and 1830: six million acres of common land disappeared by Parliamentary Statute in that period, mainly used to produce grain for the armed forces and for the rapidly-expanding industrial towns. During that time grain output more than doubled, thanks to more efficient farming methods.

Demand for grain fluctuated, however, and the weather could play nasty tricks, leading to agricultural depression. During these periods, farm labourers were thrown out of work without warning and without compensation; and usually with little if any form of relief to help them and their families. Their lives were rough and tough: disease, bad sanitation and housing neglected by their landlords were the rule rather than the exception. And the farmers were only too keen to cut their labourers' wages down to the bone whenever they could: the so-called 'Tolpuddle Martyrs' acted as they did not to achieve higher wages, but to restore them to their former level after a wages-cut by the local farmers acting in concert.

A farm worker could slave from sunrise to sunset and still not earn enough to keep himself and his family. There was parish relief, a form of local 'supplementary benefit' supposed to bring families to subsistence level when times were hard, but the amount had been fixed in the sixteenth century: by the 1790s it was totally inadequate. The detested Speenhamland system, adopted by the Parish of Speenhamland in 1795 and swiftly taken up elsewhere, worsened the situation. Instead of fixing a minimum wage, magistrates computed the difference between a man's earnings and the rising price of bread, depending on the number of children he had, making up the shortfall from the local rates. Farmers exploited the system by paying their labourers less than subsistence wages, in the knowledge that the difference would have to be met by all other ratepayers. If workers complained about these low wages, they were sacked; and they could not travel to another part of the country to find work, for the 1662 Law of Settlement forced them to stay in their own parishes where alone they had the right to poor relief.

The redistribution of land after enclosure was always done by the squire, the parson and the richest farmers so that they gained as much new land for themselves as possible. Frequently the small farmer was squeezed out altogether simply because he did not have the documents to prove his ownership. They had two choices: they could stay in the village as wage labourers, or they could move into the mushrooming industrial hells of the new towns to become factory-fodder. Oliver Goldsmith summed their plight up perfectly in the *Deserted Village*, which was published in 1770, in the middle of smuggling's heyday:

Ill fares the land, to hastening ills a prey,
Where wealth accumulates and men decay:
Princes and lords may flourish, or may fade;
A breath can make them, as a breath has made:
But a bold peasantry, their country's pride,
When once destroyed, can never be supplied.

Country labourers seemed to be caught in a cleft stick. Unable to move to where there was work without permanently jeopardizing their right to relief in times of hardship, and unable to protest and campaign for better wages by the Combination Acts imposed by the government frightened by the fire of revolution glowing across the Channel, they could not even resort safely to poaching to feed their families because of the savagery of the Game Laws. What then was left? The answer was very often smuggling, which though illegal and dangerous, was still profitable enough to make it worth the risk.

After Waterloo smuggling had never looked so attractive, nor was it ever found to be so profitable and viable. Cheap labour became immediately available both in town and country, provided by returning ex-servicemen; in the country immediate agricultural depression was the inevitable consequence. The big farmers had done very well indeed out of the wars against Napoleon, but now, with the lucrative war trade gone prices slumped; with plenty of cheap labour on tap, they were even less inclined than before to pay a living wage. One parish would dump its poor over the boundary into the next, and the administration of parish relief grew harsher and more humiliating, so fewer and fewer applied for it. Unrest grew, and from time to time burst out in rick-burnings and machine smashing, as well as the 'Captain Swing' risings, savagely repressed, especially in Hampshire.

One of the vast army of the new poor, more articulate than the rest, put it this way: 'For whom am I to be sober? For whom am I expected to save? For the parish? If I am diligent, shall I have leave to build a cottage? If I am sober, shall I have land for a cow? If I am frugal, shall I have half an acre for potatoes? You offer no motives; you have nothing but a Parish Officer and a Workhouse! Bring me another pot!' For him, drink was one, rather expensive, way out of his hopelessness. Another way was to take to a life of crime: and for those in the counties bordering the English Channel, what can have been more natural than for the crime to be smuggling? Ex-servicemen made splendid smugglers: naval men found themselves back at sea manning the luggers and cutters, while the veteran soldiers made the finest infantry for guarding the convoys of contraband the Gentlemen of the Night had ever had. However, as the Revenue men were themselves reinforced by ships and men released by the Royal Navy, such experienced fighting men could find themselves facing old comrades whom previously they had fought alongside under Nelson and Wellington.

Smuggling also attracted ex-servicemen because they missed the excitement of fighting, and, even more surprisingly, they missed the superiority of service living conditions. The shelter, warmth and food they had been used to could now be ensured by the rewards of smuggling instead.

Thus, as farm labourers' conditions plummeted, the rural crime-rate soared. But while the country Establishment of squires, big farmers and parsons, many of whom were also magistrates, took a firm line with such activities as rick-burning, robbery and poaching, many turned a blind eye to smuggling. Smuggling gave them cheap labour in the fields during the day and keen bringers of contraband during the night. The local gentry benefitted either as Venturers, the men who financed and organized the smuggling runs, or as customers for tea, brandy, tobacco and all the other items provided by the 'Gentlemen of the Night'.

Even though desperate economic conditions were a major factor in the prevalence of smuggling, there would not have been much point in it if there had not been a demand for the smuggled goods. It has already been noted that during the latter half of the eighteenth century, the number of commodities smuggled was enormous, but two of the most ubiquitous were brandy and tea.

Doctor Johnson once said: 'Claret is the liquor for boys; port for men; but he who aspires to be a hero must drink brandy.' In the early fourteenth century brandy was known as *aqua vitae*, or 'water of life', and credited with the ability to keep those who drank it ever young; it was believed to stimulate the heart, protected against the plague and cured colic, dropsy, paralysis, fever, toothache, gout and a hundred other ailments. It was considered so efficacious as a medicine, that centuries passed before brandy was recognized as an enjoyable drink in its own right. Cognac and Armagnac became the most famous producing areas in France, but later brandy was made wherever grapes were grown. The average strength was about eighty degrees of alcohol, but the very best was nearly pure spirit at around ninety-three degrees.

Brandy was issued to both soldiers and sailors to give then 'Dutch courage' before battle. Rum was encouraged to be the drink of both British services to boost the West Indian sugar trade, but certainly up to the Battle of Trafalgar it was brandy that was given as the essential essence of valour and oblivion. As medicine, antiseptic anaesthetic, body warmer after rescue from icy seas, and as the warrior's elixir, brandy held pride of place, and consequently the demand for it in Britain was insatiable, much to the smugglers' delight.

But for the Free Traders, it had one drawback: the liquor they bought from the French was very strong spirit, but it was colourless, and the British liked their brandy with the rich honey colour we know today. A cottage industry grew up as a result in coastal towns and villages, where raw brandy was dosed with burnt sugar, and probably adulterated with water as well, to make it go further.

The spirit kegs used by the smugglers were standard products, stocked specifically for them by the great smuggling warehouses which Continental merchants set up specially to cater for their needs once they realized the extent of the English smuggling trade. The warehouses were centred in the Channel Islands, Roscoff in Brittany, Dunkirk and Fécamp, as well as several other ports. The larger barrel was called an anker, from the Dutch; it held eight and a third Imperial gallons. Its sides were flattened and it was roped in pairs to fit over the backs of pack-horses. The smaller barrel was the handy keg, half the size of the anker, again roped together to fit snugly over the broad shoulders of the tub-carrier, the standard smuggling human 'beast-of-burden' on the south coast.

A keg filled with best brandy could be bought in France for as little as 16s (80p) which compared very favourably with £1.12s.0d (£1.60p) for brandy bought legally with duty paid. The smugglers' price to their English customers for a tub, keg or half-anker was about £1.2s.6d, which allowed a decent profit while still undercutting legally imported liquor.

It was a hard task, however, for a man who had been working in the fields during the day to stagger away from the beach in the dark across rough country for anything up to ten miles, with two forty-five pound kegs thumping up and down on his chest and back. The old smuggler whom Thomas Hardy's father employed as a servant told the young novelist that breathing was very difficult, and many men were deformed for life by their part in the Free Trade. Still, they received anything up to ten shillings (50p) a night, which was far more than they could earn in the fields in a week, and they took home a measure of tea and a bottle of brandy, and were often given a hot meal as well. No wonder many farm-workers took to the work full time and made a profession of it, rising up through the smuggling ranks as the years passed.

Brandy was the smugglers' favourite commodity: it has left its name on places all along the south-west coast where it was stored, either in caves or in the sea-bed itself, such as Brandy Hole in the Pitts Deep stream near Boldre in the New Forest, and Brandy Bay next to Kimmeridge Bay in the Isle of Purbeck.

Like brandy, tea was ideal for smuggling. Again, it was Doctor Johnson who had something relevant to say. In his famous dictionary he describes a smuggler as 'a wretch who, in defiance of justice and the laws, imports or exports goods either contraband or without payment of the customs'. This is particularly hypocritical of Johnson when one remembers that he is as famous for his endless dishes of 'tay' with Boswell and Mrs Thrale as he is for his dictionary. Without smuggling, Johnson might have been deprived of tea, for it was the smugglers who enabled people like the great lexicographer, industrious but not rich, to have their favourite drink at a reasonable price. Doctor Johnson was, to use his own words, 'A hardened and shameless tea-drinker, who has for twenty years diluted his meals with only the infusion of this fascinating plant; whose kettle has scarcely time to cool; who with tea amuses the evening, with tea solaces the midnight, and with tea welcomes the morning.'

Tea was well on the way to becoming Britain's national drink by the end of the seventeenth century. The cheapest tea to be bought legally over the counter of a shop cost seven shillings a pound, almost a week's wages for a labouring man. Smuggled tea, on the other hand, was only two shillings a pound; the reason for this discrepancy was the duty of five shillings a pound imposed by the government as early as 1680. This had little effect on demand for expensive varieties which only the rich could afford anyway, but cheaper tea was still too expensive for the lower orders if bought legally. Tea was smuggled mainly to satisfy the demand at this end of the market, until at the height of the smuggling era over two-thirds of all the tea drunk in the United Kingdom had been supplied by the people's friends: the Free Traders.

China, Darjeeling, Indian, Ceylon, Hyssop, Green and Bohea varieties of tea were all smuggled widely along the south-western coast of England. As the great East Indiamen sailed past the Isles of Scilly, where they usually picked up their pilots, and Cornwall and Devon, they were actually in the habit of selling the tea over the side, like huge, floating grocery shops. It was all done outside territorial waters, of course, especially when the Revenue ships were in the area. Alternatively, the smugglers' agents could go to the warehouses across the Channel. The tea they bought was packaged in waterproof oilskin, 'dollops', as they were called. Once ashore, these 'teabags' were quickly on their way to centres of distribution. Some accounts of tea smuggling from the coast of Hampshire suggest the tea was carried in bigger bags slung from the shoulders of specialist smugglers who walked all the way to London with their contraband under their cloaks. Even more difficult to believe is the claim that the Fleet Prison in London, which specialized in housing convicted debtors, was a tea-storehouse, with smuggler delivery-men supplying the Metropolis from its cells, and prisoners earning a little extra money by keeping Revenue Officers out by force. However, a Parliamentary Committee of Enquiry (in 1736) under the infamous General 'Johnny' Cope did state that London tea smugglers went about their business in gangs of anything up to fifty men, so that not even the City magistrates could deal with them. The London JPs may have realized that if they had, their tea-supplies could have been in jeopardy.

What is certain, however, is that the trade in smuggled tea went on with the acquiescence of most sections of society, even those charged with its moral welfare. The Reverend James Woodforde made this entry in his famous *Diary of a Country Parson* on 29th March 1777: 'Andrews the Smuggler brought me this night about eleven o'clock a bag of Hysson tea, six pounds in weight. He frightened us a little by whistling under the parlour window, just as we were going to bed. I gave him some Geneva, [gin], and paid him for the tea at ten and six per pound ...... £3:3:0.'

How the smugglers went about their business is a complex question. Smuggling goods into Britain was essentially a matter of using the sea, so the ships and boats used by both smugglers and revenue officers were of paramount importance. The Free Traders' basic vessel was the lugger, which could be anything from fifty to 300 tons. The largest of them could carry 3000 half-anker kegs of spirits in their capacious holds, together with up to twelve tons of tea. They were extremely well-armed, many having anything up to fifteen four-pound cannons, easily enabling them to hold off any Revenue Service vessel. Their lug-sail rigs enabled them to outsail many a king's ship by giving them the facility of running very close to the wind and clawing in and out of narrow waterways, such as the Solent and its many rivers, where their adversaries dared not venture for fear of running aground. As for speed, the largest of them was well able to cross the Channel in under eight hours, an essential prerequisite for smuggling contraband to the Hampshire and Dorset coasts.

The luggers were so good at their job that smugglers evolved a system in which smaller, lightly-armed vessels, carrying the bulk of the cargo, were escorted across the sea by the big luggers, a convoy system used long before it was ever put into practice by the Royal Navy and the legitimate British merchant ships. The smugglers did emulate the Royal Navy, however, by putting their own 'marine detachments' on the largest luggers to prevent boarding from the King's ships.

Smugglers also used the cutter, a vessel more generally associated with the Revenue forces. The cutter was a sloop-rigged single-master with a running bowsprit which appeared to 'cut' through the water, hence its name. Originally the cutter carried one or even two square sails, but soon the virtues of jib sails were fully appreciated, working with one square sail, and these ships became so handy and fast — they could touch twelve knots in a good wind — that they were extensively used by Royal Navy, Revenue and smugglers alike.

However, the lugger retained one characteristic which kept its pride of place in the smugglers' favour: its broader beam and lower masts meant that it did not have to have so deep a keel as the cutter, and could therefore be sailed into far shallower water where a pursuing cutter could not penetrate.

One famous smuggling cutter was the *Ranger*, which was built at the shipbuilding village of Cawsand near Plymouth. She mounted twenty-two guns, had a crew of one hundred smugglers, and was so formidable that during the 1780s she could land her goods on the sands of Torbay in broad daylight. Another great smuggling cutter, the *Swift*, lived up to her name on each voyage, depositing 2000 casks of brandy and five tons of tea on the beach at each trip with the result that a year after her launching she had paid for her own building, and continued to bring her owners handsome profits for many years.

Another smuggling vessel was the galley, whose invention has been credited to the resourceful smugglers of Deal in Kent. They probably realized that a high-speed trip across the Channel and back in one night was the best way to beat the Revenue cutters. The fashion spread all along the south coast, and probably linked up with the gigs of the Scilly Isles, which had been used for smuggling as well as pilotage for many years.

Galleys could be anything from thirty to 120 feet in length, and many had a beam of about twenty feet. When chased by the Revenue ships, their habitual tactic was to turn into the eye of the wind and strike their oars deep, so their sailing pursuers could not follow them. Then they made for shallow water, and ran up on to the beach, where the crew would leap out and carry the galley right out of the water. The Kent galleys from Deal and Dover made use of the notoriously dangerous Goodwin Sands on which they would land when the tide fell and left the bars exposed, carrying their craft over to the opposite sides where they would launch and row home, leaving the Revenue cutters helplessly watching far out to sea.

At the other end of the scale from this mighty vessel were the Scilly Isles gigs, still in existence today. Directly a great trading ship was spotted, the gigs' crews would rush for their boats, and the first to reach the big vessel got the piloting contract. The pilot would leap up into the chains, while down from the high decks would be passed the smaller items of contraband, like tea, silk kerchiefs, spice and trinkets, meaning that even for the slower gigs it was not a wasted trip.

Piloting, kelping and fishing — the legal uses to which the gigs were put — were all very well, but the real money was in cross-Channel smuggling. A ten-knot trip over to Guernsey or Roscoff and back, with relays of rowers, was nothing to the smugglers of the Isles of Scilly and the many other villages along the south-west coast of

1. Isles of Scilly Gigs of the type used for high-speed smuggling runs out to merchantmen coming up the Channel, and even across to the Channel Islands and the coast of France.

England which used gigs and galleys. The number of oars in the Scillonian gigs is significant, and supports the idea that they were mainly used for smuggling: in 1721 an Act of Parliament was passed limiting the number of oars any rowing-boat could have to six, which would have had the effect of slowing down the gig crews considerably.

The larger galleys were more like Oxford and Cambridge boat-race eights, whipped through the waters round the coasts of Hampshire and Dorset by as many as twenty sculls. The Collector of Customs at Cowes, William Arnold, told the Commissioners of Customs in London, that 'several of these boats have been seen lately on these coasts, and they have so much the advantage of fast rowing and sailing that we apprehend that but few of the Revenue cutters can come up with them.' The reference to sailing indicates that even the smallest gig could sport a little mast at the extreme stern to take a light, but very useful, lugsail. One of the cutter captains had an addition to make to the Collector's comments, comparing the pursuit of a galley by a cutter to 'sending a cow after a hare'.

After the luggers, cutters and galleys came the smallest smuggling craft, the home-made punts and skiffs, tub-boats and scows, which were often the vessels of small-time smugglers who liked to run up a crude little tub-boat on the banks of a New Forest stream, the Stour or the Avon, and come down to the coast to dabble speculatively in 'The Free Trade'.

Contraband goods had, of course, to be transported from shore to ship and from ship to customer. Most smugglers developed a smoothly-running system for getting the ships filled on the other side of the Channel, and an even smoother and more complex one for getting those goods to their customers. There were variations in their methods, dictated by local conditions along the southern coast, but basically their general approach was the same.

Before examining these methods, a more general point must be made: English smuggling was divided into two distinct Ages, the Golden and the Scientific, divided at 1815 by the outcome of the Battle of Waterloo. Before 1815, smugglers had only to contend with the inefficient forces of the Revenue Service, making their task relatively easy. After 1815, the Royal Navy was freed from wartime duties to work closely with the Revenue forces to fight smuggling, so the smugglers had to be more cunning and the game became more dangerous. This fact, combined with the setting up of the official Coastguard service in 1831, meant that smuggling inevitably went into gradual decline.

The Revenue Service really started in 1698 when 299 Riding Officers were appointed by the Crown to stop 'owlers' smuggling wool *out* of England. By 1713 the Riding Officers had been given some military muscle by the stationing of troops of Dragoons at strategic points along the south coast. The Dragoons remained, working uneasily with the Revenue men until the Coastguard service became effective. The troops were useful in their way, for, as mounted infantrymen, their tactic of riding hard to where they were needed and then dismounting to fight on foot was judged ideal for combatting the smugglers on cliffs, in woods and on the beaches.

The Customs Commissioners had no very high opinion of their Riding Officers: it was said they cost too much, gave little return in results of smugglers and goods seized for the salaries they were paid, only rode out on their own business, which was often indirectly to do with smuggling on their own account, and wrote up their Journals in such a way that they 'seemed busier than they were'. The Commissioners believed many of them were actually smugglers' agents, and that their Journals were a fabrication from beginning to end. Their illegal duties added another dimension to the title Collector, for they were believed to collect the money which financed the smugglers' runs. The honest Riding Officers seem to have had neither the courage nor the resolve, nor probably the resources, to face the large gangs of smugglers.

The post of Riding Officer was, however, highly prized, and there were always far more applicants than there were appointments available. The reason was that, though the salary was low, seizures meant 'prize-money' or a reward. In spite of working alone, being hated by their local communities, tolerating terrible conditions and wickedly long hours in the saddle and writing up the inescapable Journal at the end of each interminable day, the Customs Board never had to advertise for Riding Officers. The Journals of Officers in the Christchurch to Poole area give a good sense of the character of the job. Abraham Pike, for instance, made very few seizures in 1803 and 1804, captured no smugglers, and the phrase 'No success' runs through each page like a monotonous refrain. Mr Joshua Jeans, one of Mr Pike's predecessors in Christchurch, did nothing at all, let alone appear, during the notorious Battle of Mudeford in 1784; while in 1747 not a single Revenue man of any rank showed up in Poole while the terrible Hawkhurst Gang raided the Customs House. Clearly, both these occasions were examples of the Riding Officer being too frightened, too deeply in league with the smugglers themselves or too thoroughly bribed beforehand.

It was not only the ranks of the Riding Officers which were suspect: it was said that the entire Customs Service was riddled with inefficiency and corruption. The highest posts were filled by nepotism and government supporters from the most recent election. The chief Officers, the Collectors of Customs, were often men who had just retired from some career very different from the Customs Service, or they were sometimes bankrupts receiving a helping hand from the other old boys in the network. Experience of and interest in the work of the Board, was, therefore, frequently lacking: what they had in common was the idea that money was to be made out of their new profession. Like many civil service posts of the eighteenth and early nineteenth century, the position of Customs Officer was a sinecure to be milked for whatever it could give.

Along the coasts there was little system: regular patrolling was avoided, ostensibly to deny the smugglers too clear a picture of the Riding Officers' whereabouts, and they worked on hints, rumours and reports of smugglers working, all of which were usually too little and certainly too late. In this inefficient and, for the smugglers, 'Golden Age', the Riding Officers were the first line of the Customs' land-defence. In theory they each had a beat of four miles, but it was usually much more: Abraham Pike's was sixteen. Everything depended on the Riding Officer's horse, which had to be purchased out of the Officer's own pocket, although the annual salary was only £42.

Riding Officers were often too old for the job, which required great stamina and strength; many were simply too lazy, and many were corrupt. Despised by the people amongst whom they lived and worked, seen as agents of a hated government, they were constantly chivvied by letters from remote and demanding superiors whom they very rarely saw. It must be admitted that they had nothing to lose by being lax in their duties and closing their eyes to the smugglers' activities. They may not have been the best of the King's Officers, they may not have been the best of men, though some were very fine servants of the Crown; but who can blame them when they were constantly reminded of the penalties of over-zealousness by incidents such as that which involved Mr Critchell of Ringwood, who was beaten almost to death when he challenged a band of mounted smugglers in the middle of Burley one day; or that which involved Mr Bursey of Milford who, after answering a knock on his door one dark night, was attacked and left lying across his own threshold, in front of his wife and children, with frightful head injuries from which he also died. An alternative strategy for smugglers to get rid of a zealous Riding Officer without killing him was to bind and gag him while the goods were being run; or he could be caught and bundled aboard a lugger and dumped in France, where, during the Napoleonic wars, there was a poor lookout for an Officer wearing a uniform marking him as a servant of King George.

By 1813 there were 2,100 Customs Acts on the Statute Book, and smuggling was at its height. Two years later the French wars were all over, and the smuggling picture began to change immediately. In 1816 the Royal Navy took over the Revenue cutters, and in the very next year it began the task of blockading the coast of England, a change from years of practice blockading the coast of France. Their vice-like grip had an immediate effect: huge amounts of contraband were seized as they were being run ashore, or within territorial waters. They included 370,000 gallons of gin and brandy, 42,000 yards of silk, 36,000 packs of playing-cards, 21,000 Indian silk 'kerchiefs, 19,000 pounds of tea, 3,000 pounds of snuff and 875 smuggling ships of various types.

In 1831 came the two measures which spelt the end of smuggling within a decade: the Royal Navy began using its own ships as well as those of the Revenue Service; and the Coastguard came into being as a fully-fledged service. Meanwhile, many items began to be freed from duty, culminating in the Corn Law Acts in 1848 when 450 items previously dutiable were removed from the Statute Book and England officially entered the Free Trade era, and smuggling ceased to be a profitable undertaking on its former scale.

Once the Royal Navy had taken over the Revenue cutters, smugglers found themselves in deep trouble. The ships were sailed better than the Revenue crews, and their surveillance both at sea and on land was far more efficient. Smugglers seemed unable to move without the Navy knowing about it, even on the beaches and in the ports they had previously thought so safe.

Clearly, new methods would be needed if the contraband was to be brought ashore as it had been before the great changes had come about. Above all, what was needed now was ingenuity, and the smugglers soon showed that they could supply this commodity as well as all the others which had been their stock-in-trade for years. Thus began the Scientific Age of English smuggling.

The Royal Navy pounced on anything that looked even remotely like a smuggling ship, so smugglers began to use a new subterfuge. A perfectly innocent cargo would be brought into Portsmouth, Southampton, Christchurch or Poole in a legitimate merchant ship and unloaded on to the quay right under the very noses of the King's men, whether Customs, Royal Navy or Coastguard, and if they were lucky the smugglers would get their contraband away from the port in the normal modes of transport: carriers' wagons or packhorses. The secret was, of course, that the forbidden goods were hidden inside the legitimate goods. Barrels were fitted with false bottoms, tops and even sides; spars which carried sails at sea were bored out; baled goods had secret centres; coils of rope which were never uncoiled were contraband-containers; sails were brought ashore bundled up with goods inside; and the vessels themselves had secret compartments constructed all over them. Even the oars in the ships' boats became elongated brandy-casks, and were carried innocently ashore past the ever-watchful Coastguards.

Tobacco was particularly malleable to the smugglers' needs, for it could be plaited into ropes as actual strands alongside the innocent hemp. Foodstuffs apparently not used on a voyage were hollowed out and made to accept such forbidden goods as silk 'kerchiefs and gloves: one smuggling captain stuffed several beautiful lengths of silk into the turkey he carried ashore after one trip. Hams were also hollowed out, lined with calico, and then filled with compressed silk; the hole was then skilfully plugged and camouflaged. Weird garments were evolved for the smuggling of tea: capes, jackets and even drawers all with padding which was composed of elongated tea-bags. There are countless other examples of ingenious hiding places for many different types of contraband. Methods of getting the tubs of spirits and gin ashore were revised, for no longer could luggers anchor off the old favourite beaches with impunity. The smugglers formed either great necklaces or rafts which, by careful adjustment of weight, could be made to float either below the surface of the sea or, when necessary, to sink to the bottom. Floating halfway between surface and sea-bottom, the raft was towed into such places as Poole Harbour, past the quay and its watching Coastguards and Customs men, and on up into the reaches of the upper harbour where it was hauled into the shallows and there left until dark, when it would be taken apart and loaded into wagons. If the ship towing the raft was challenged, the raft was cut free and either left to the mercy of the sea, or weighted and dropped offshore, after a bearing had been taken and its position noted. Then, 'when the coast was clear', a smaller boat would be sent to collect it.

Both smugglers and Coastguards used the same method to find such cargoes on the sea bed. They would drag grapnels of different types along the seabed until they hooked on to the kegs and their linking lines. A variety of tools was developed by local blacksmiths, among them the grappling-iron, the plain grapnel, the sand-creeper and one known as the centipede.

Disposal of contraband goods once landed also required cunning and organization. First of all, there had to be someone who could finance the purchase of the cargo. These entrepreneurs called themselves Venturers like their counterparts in legitimate trade, the Merchant-venturers of Poole, or Southampton or, most famous of all, of Bristol. The money might come from their own pockets, or may have been made up from shares, the amount and collection of which was organized by the Venturer; and it was also he who, most likely, provided the Agent, whose job it was to go round to the shopkeepers, farmers, parsons and other moderately wealthy people, collecting their shares. It was often the local squire, a principal landowner with or without title, who was the Venturer of a particular district; and many used their own Estate Bailiffs to collect when they visited the tenant-farmers, mill or shop on the course of their normal estate duties. Smuggling was so profitable for the Venturer that even if only one run in three was successful, he would consider he was doing very well indeed.

As well as an agent, the Venturer would employ another vital member of the organization: the Clerk, book-man or quill-driver. This man might well be the vestry clerk of the parish church, or the verger, or perhaps the village schoolmaster; and it was his job to keep the accounts of the smuggling set-up in that particular village or area of the coast.

The third most important member of the team was the Captain of the smuggling vessel, in whom the Venturer had to have complete trust. Whether the Venturer hired it, or owned it alone, or whether it was one of several others which formed his smuggling fleet, he would have made sure the crew were the finest seamen and navigators wages could buy. Some captains owned their own ships, and were, in fact, both captain and Venturer in one and the same person.

The first step in an 'enterprise' would have involved the captain taking the agent across the Channel to buy contraband goods on behalf of the Venturer. Before setting out, the agent and captain would work out the all-important time of return and place of landing, both of which had to be fixed to the minute. This would have been done either on board the smuggling ship or in one of the many waterside inns which thronged the quays and beaches all along the coast, especially in its bigger ports such as Christchurch and Poole, as well as in smaller villages such as Mudeford and Bourne Mouth, (present-day Bournemouth). There may have been some captains who were so well trusted by the Venturers that they handled the purchase direct; but the character of the times seems to indicate that a Venturer preferred to have his own man taken across by the captain. Clearly, there were variations in this procedure, but as this was the most secret part of smuggling, naturally nothing has ever been written down about it.

The ship would then proceed to the Channel Islands, where the biggest warehouses used by the smugglers had been set up, or perhaps Roscoff or Cherbourg, for the French government actively encouraged English smugglers; merchants from many countries had settled in France specifically to cater to their needs. The agent would then make for his favourite warehouse to choose the goods. They would already be specially packed: spirits in roped kegs, tea in waterproof packets, and tobacco well compressed so that it would take up the least room and be proof against the sea at the same time. Once bought, the agent would watch over the cargo until it was loaded on board. Supervision of loading was particularly important after 1816 when secret compartments received the goods which otherwise would be found by the ever-probing Coastguards.

We know that pursuit and capture at sea while making the crossing were not unknown; but so inefficient were the king's men, and so skilful and determined were the sea-smugglers, that more cargoes got through than did not. Just as vital as the ability to fight his way through opposition at sea was the smuggling captain's skill in making the right landfall. To be a good 'spotsman' was every contraband captain's aim: this meant that he could arrive at the right spot on the coastal map every trip; and having arrived he would send out a blue flash as a signal, which would be answered by the lookout's 'flink', a flash from a spout-lantern which told him his voyage had been a complete success and that the coast was clear. Clearly, a captain who gained a reputation as a good spotsman would be much in demand.

2. A spout lantern. Held in the crook of the left arm, the signaller's right hand covered the end of the spout, and then was removed to show a pin-point flash of light to the incoming lugger.

After the sea-voyage, came the landing, and this third stage of the goods' journey was in the hands of a man called a Lander. He was the smugglers' beachmaster, responsible both to his chief, the Venturer, and to the Captain, for getting the cargo ashore and then immediately away along the routes inland, which led either to dumps and hides or immediately to the selling-points nearest to the coast.

The lander selected and recruited the smugglers, choosing them for their strength, their knowledge of the local country, their loyalty to the organization or gang, their obedience, their stamina over long distances of tough going, and their ability to keep their mouths shut about the plans for the Run, both before and after the event. The money which made the dangerous trade worthwhile to the men who carried the goods inland — field-labourers, herdsmen, country craftsmen, discharged or disabled soldiers and sailors, — was far greater than the amounts they earned during the working day.

The smugglers' convoys were protected by squads of batmen, who formed flanking escorts and scouted ahead and behind for Revenue men or Dragoons. Since the penalty for carrying a firearm was death, batmen were armed at first with great clubs made of ash or holly, but as the smuggling became more violent on both sides, guns and blade-weapons were increasingly used.

Having been informed by the Venturer the date, time and place of the next landing, the lander would decide how many horses, wagons, tubmen, batmen and packhorses he would need to shift that particular volume of contraband off the beach. Wagons and horses were supplied by farmers who lived within a belt about ten miles deep from the shore, and the lander only needed to leave a note at the stable-door telling the farmer the numbers required for the following night, and the doors would be left unlocked. Few farmers were brave enough to ignore such an instruction: burning of barns, ricks and homesteads were the common penalties; and in some areas reprisals took the form of killing not only of livestock but even members of the farmers' families. These were rarely used, but everyone knew they could be in extreme cases of non-co-operation with the smugglers. It was all part of the terror tactics used to encourage people to work with them, while at the same time discouraging informers. When the teams of horses and wagons were back in stable and barn, kegs and tea-packets would be left for the farmer's fee, together with any goods ordered from the smugglers. It is said that the farmers around Christchurch supplied special muffled harness when their vehicles and horses were needed: rope-traces instead of leather, felt horseshoes, and even leather washers for the wagons.

Timing was, of course, of the essence for the Lander. First, he had to summon his forces quickly but without alerting the authorities. It is said that a milkmaid went round the streets of Christchurch with two pails of milk suspended from a yoke; on the surface of the milk floated small wooden balls of varying numbers, which told the initiated at what time and where the run was going to be that night. Strange as it may sound, it seems as good a scheme as any to pass on such essential but confidential information.

When he had got his forces mustered, the Lander had to conceal them if he suspected the Customs men — known variously as Philistines, Gobloos, Landsharks or Shinglepickers — and their accomplices the Dragoons, were likely to be troublesome that night. A barn was the best place, but it had to be near the sea. Again, at Christchurch the smugglers were very fortunate for they could use the great earth banks of Double Dykes at Hengistbury Head as a unique hide for any number of horses, wagons and men. The Lander needed to have his men ready before the expected time of the smuggling lugger's arrival 'in the offing', but he did not want them in position more than half-an-hour early since most would bring something with them 'to keep out the cold', so a long wait might result in drunkenness and noise.

However he arranged it, the Lander would certainly send his signaller to a high point near the landing-place with his spout-lantern, with an ordinary tinder box. The signaller would be chosen for the sharpness of his eyes, and he would peer into the blackness watching for the single blue light from the lugger's lantern which showed it had arrived in the offing. Immediately the blue showed, out would go the single light from the spout-lantern, shown by simply removing the hand from the end of the spout which had been pointed out to sea where the ship was expected. This would tell the captain that he was 'on the spot' and that 'the coast was clear', both smuggling terms which have since passed into the English language. Along the cliffs of Boscombe, behind Bourne Mouth or even Purbeck, where cargoes were landed in full daylight, during smuggling's Golden Age, the bracken and gorse were simply fired as the signal that all was well and the contraband could be brought straight in.

It was bad enough if the captain arrived late, for the waiting smugglers would be approaching the stage where their noise would only be equalled by their inability to do a good night's work; but it was worse if he was too early. Having shown his 'blue' and received no answering 'flink' from the expected spout-lantern, he would have to stand offshore, unwilling to anchor in case he was surprised by a Revenue cutter, just 'jilling about' with flapping sails and a very little way on the vessel. This was when the smuggling ship was at its most vulnerable, particularly if it had come into a narrow bay with little room for manoeuvre. Bourne Bottom, the site of the present Bournemouth Pier, saw several occasions when irate captains who had turned up to find no one to receive their cargo ran the stuff on to the shore in their own boats and left it there. When one remembers that the smugglers' favourite weather was the worst the winters in these parts could fling on to these shores, it is no wonder that when these 'good spotsmen' were captured by the king's ships, they were drafted immediately into the Royal Navy, especially during the Napoleonic Wars, for their unique skills were highly valued by the regular and senior Service.

Once the Captain had got his 'flink' from the signaller, however, he made his way gingerly in to the shore, noting carefully the state of the tide and the slope of the beach, which in many places could not be predicted from day to day. If the tide was coming in and rising, and

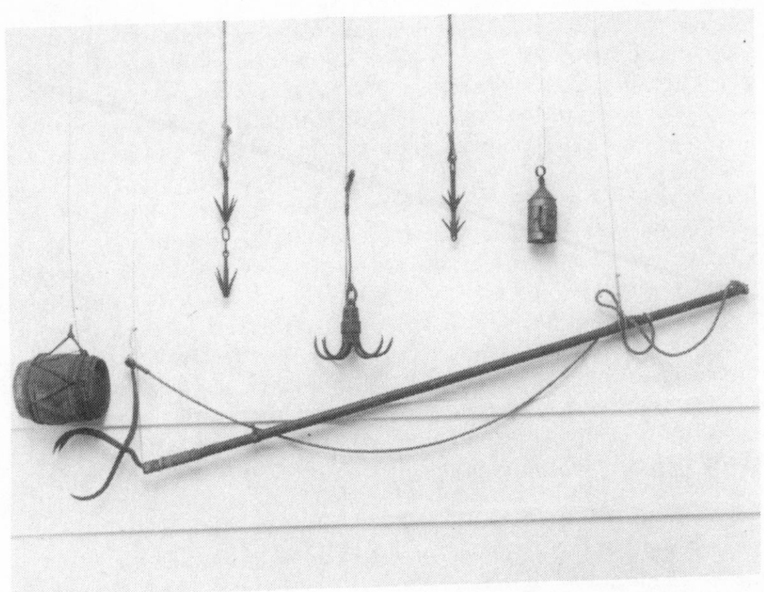

3. Smuggling hardware. Top row: linked grapnel, sometimes called a centipede; ordinary grapnel, which functioned as an anchor as well; grapnel on one bar, and a smugglers' lantern, used before the spout lantern was invented. Bottom row: spirit keg, with wire harness and ropes, a pair of which would have been slung over the shoulders of each 'tubman'; and smugglers' grab, or grapple, with rope-operated jaws, used for getting spirit-tubs out of shallow water, such as ponds, or the sea at low tide, after hiding them from the Revenue Officers. These last two items and the large grapnel are on display in the Dorset County Museum, Dorchester.

the beach had a steep slope, then he would run the lugger straight in, and, directly the bow dug into the sand or shingle, he would drop a kedge anchor over the stern. The lander would have been watching all this meticulously, and even as the ship touched the beach, he would have his men into the surf forming a human chain from the tide line out to the ship's waist, from which the kegs and the waterproof packets would be rapidly handed down to by the crew.

As the ship touched the shingle, the Captain would order a cable, known as a warp, to be brought from the kedge-anchor along the deck to the forward windlass, and the second the last packet or keg was over the side, he would give the order for the windlass to turn in order to pull the ship's bow off the beach. As the vessel pivoted on its own length, the sails, which would never at any time have been fully lowered, would be whipped aloft and the anchor lifted while the wind filled the sails and set the ship in motion. The lugger would be up and away in a matter of seconds. If, however, the tide was against them or if the captain found his path in to the beach was too shallow for his heavily-laden craft, he would anchor a little way off shore and order his tub-boats out. These were roomy little rowing-boats designed to take the kegs and the packets ashore. Often the lander would also have tub-boats waiting if he thought this sort of situation might develop, his professional anticipation helping the Captain at a crucial point in the run. If the Captain was in a hurry and it was a mixed cargo, tub-boats would be used to take in the dry goods, but the kegs of spirits would be lashed to a 'tub-line' in pairs and towed ashore by one of the boats. Here it would be grabbed by the lander's men and hauled in through the surf like Seine-net fishermen bringing in the salmon. If the cargo was entirely composed of kegs, then this method would most probably be employed; as each pair reached the shore it would be severed from the tub-line by one swift slash of a smuggler's knife.

The Lander's final task was to get the goods off the beach as smartly as possible. As he liked to vary not only the landing beaches, but also the locations of the first storage dumps, the distance to be covered by tubmen, wagons or packhorses on the night's first stage also varied in length. Above all things, regular routines had to be avoided for the secret of success was to keep the King's men guessing. Tubmen did the fast, short stints across broken ground and through dense woods where wagons and even packhorses could not go, when the dump was not too far from the shore. Besides, tubmen attracted less attention than convoys of rumbling wagons, but woe betide the tub-carrier who dropped a keg, or stumbled and burst one open: when he found out, the penalties exacted by the Lander could be severe.

2
Portsmouth, Southampton and the East Hampshire Coast

From the eastern side of Southampton Water to the Hampshire border stretch Portsmouth and Langstone Harbours, a heavily indented coast ideal for smuggling gangs. Langstone Harbour had its own gang, the members of which were nearly all fishermen, and their speciality seems to have been rafting in the kegs under tow by one of their apparently innocent fishing-smacks. As was usual with this method, the raft of goods, floating just beneath the surface, was weighted to sink, so it could be cut loose if the Revenue men appeared on the scene. The spot would be noted by bearings so that the smugglers could return when all was quiet to drag the kegs up with the ubiquitous grapnel. Cattle-herds were driven along the shore to obliterate smugglers' footprints after a run had been made. Rumours of ghosts and hauntings were used in several places to frighten off any inquisitive person: Pook Lane, at Warblington, is said to have been dubbed Spook Lane in smuggling days, for it led inland a long way and was a vital route for goods being brought in.

Langstone Mill and the two inns, the Royal Oak and the Ship, were the smugglers' haunts, and it is probable that a tunnel used to connect all three hides. The Mill was both water-mill and wind-mill, and the tower of the latter must have been an invaluable lookout-post and signal tower for the Langstone Gang in its heyday. After the establishment of the Coastguards one of their ships, optimistically named the *Griper*, was moored almost permanently in the Harbour so that a close watch could be kept on the gang, but it is said that so efficient had its methods become by that time that none of the smugglers was caught.

In the great Harbour and Naval Base of Portsmouth, the main concern of the Customs Officers was with the cargoes being brought in by regular trading ships. But they had to deal with smugglers as well, and the burden of this double watch often proved impossible to carry. The situation was aggravated by the many other duties which were not directly concerned with the Revenue Service but which these Officers had to carry out in a great port.

One of these duties was that of Quarantine Officer: the master of every ship entering the port had to be interviewed before coming in. The merchant ship would be hailed by a Customs cutter at sea and then the bizarre task of handing up the Quarantine Testament would take place. This volume, encased in copper, and attached to a sea line, was taken by the Master, who would swear that he had no infectious diseases on board. Whether the Master admitted to them or not, the Quarantine Officer was protected from possible infection from a contaminated Testament by the Master throwing it into the sea to be hauled through the water back to the Revenue cutter. The sea-water was supposed to kill any germs which may have been adhering to it. Several of these bizarre books are still in existence, and they show there was some concept of contagion even in those unscientific times. The post of Quarantine Officer was no light duty, for an Officer who absconded or allowed ships, persons or goods to escape from quarantine, was liable to the death penalty.

Revenue Officers in Portsmouth Harbour also had the job of protecting wrecks and their crews from local wreckers. This must have been a difficult task: the extent of the inhuman practice of luring boats to founder is shrouded in shamefaced mystery, for no coastal area liked to admit that the business of wrecking went on in its confines. Certainly far more of it went on than is generally realized, and it was closely allied to smuggling.

The enforcement of the Navigation Laws which dealt with the registration of ships, and the collection of Light Dues for Trinity House's light ships and houses, were also the responsibility of the Customs Officers of all ports of the kingdom, as well as a list of duties which were far removed from the prevention of smuggling. All of these interfered with the task which is usually thought of as the sole concern of the underpaid and overworked Revenue men.

The prevention of smuggling in Portsmouth Harbour was closely linked to that in Southampton and Cowes on the Isle of Wight, especially in operations at sea in which the Service's cutters and cruisers were involved. Portsmouth's position made her the centre of operations, superior to both Southampton and Chichester, guarding them both as well as herself on the east side of Southampton Water. The western approaches were looked after by the Collector of Cowes, particularly well after William Arnold's appointment there in 1777.

One of the greatest problems faced by the Portsmouth Revenue Officers was posed by the convoys of East Indiamen bringing in their huge cargoes of tea which, in time of war, lay off Spithead where their escorts of Royal Navy ships left them. Usually half a dozen Officers had to be posted on each of these merchantmen to ensure that the tea was not sold over the side to the small smuggling boats which tried to come out to them. This concentration of the Officers naturally weakened the watch on the rest of the coast.

Towards the end of the eighteenth century, the Customs Officers of Portsmouth were being stretched to the very limits of their capacity, for the local smugglers were growing progressively more daring and cunning, and the many miles of coastline within the several harbours in their charge were very difficult to cover adequately. In 1783, the year before the 'Battle' of Mudeford, a Customs boat was lying in wait for a rowing-boat from the Isle of Wight which was known to be planning a run on to the shore near Eastney Fort. Before the King's vessel could intercept the smugglers, the lander's party fired the bracken and gorse on land and the Island's vessel turned out to sea and made back for home. The Customs boat gave chase, of course, but, as usually happened, could not catch her quarry because the ten oars took her through the water at an enormous speed. Furious, the King's vessel itself turned back, and made up for her failure by catching a single smuggler from the landing party, one Edward Stigant.

The same thing happened all over again the following night, but this time the Customs men managed to catch more of the smugglers on the shore. A few days later the chief Customs Officer got word that another large galley was intending to land near another fort, the Cumberland. Watch was kept by both land and water, and eventually over sixty smugglers turned up, disguised with masks and blackened faces, and all armed with clubs and cutlasses. Soldiers were summoned and the smugglers fled, but not before several were captured: these received light sentences because fever had broken out in the prison to which they should have been sent.

Hayling Island, between Langstone and Chichester Harbours, had a smuggling coast all the way round, and apparently boasted not just one, but several different gangs of contrabandists. There are so many smuggling tales around here, comic, tragic and merely routine, that a separate book would be needed to do them all justice. Suffice it to say that from the Customs Officers' point of view, policing Hayling must have been a nightmare within a nightmare, and one can only feel both admiration and sympathy for the King's men who had the misfortune to be posted to the Portsmouth Collection.

One of Hampshire's most notorious smugglers was Thomas Johnstone. Johnstone was born on the coast near Lymington in 1772, and like many other famous smugglers, he came from a smuggling family, and like the legendary Isaac Gulliver himself, he was himself a smuggler's son. Johnstone Senior was ostensibly a fisherman, and began taking Tom out fishing with him at the age of nine. By the time the boy reached twelve, his father had died but the lad was able to handle any type of vessel, and it was said knew well the whole coast from Suffolk to Cornwall. In fact, he was very soon in demand as a pilot in the Channel. It was this unequalled knowledge and experience that marked him out from other smugglers all through his long and varied career.

At the age of fifteen he began his career as a smuggler, and it was not very long before his colleagues recognized him as one of the bravest and most ingenious recruits who had ever entered their ranks. His seamanship marked him out even amongst those superlative sailors, the sea-smugglers.

Large stature seemed to be a *sine qua non* for those aspiring to high position in smuggling, for like his Dorset counterpart, Isaac Gulliver, Tom was broad-shouldered and stood well over six feet. He was also noticeably handsome, with brilliant blue eyes and a mop of dark, curly hair. Young as he was, he soon took command of his own gang, for both men and women loved him, and his ships' crews positively worshipped him, finding his keen sense of humour one of his most endearing qualities.

In addition to this multiplicity of natural gifts, Tom Johnstone was apparently a talented actor, with a flair for personal make-up. On several occasions, when he found himself in a tight corner, he was able to change his appearance to such good effect that he was able to avoid detection by the Revenue Officers when they were hot on his trail. The only other famous smuggler who used disguise in something of the same manner was Gulliver, when he hid from the Preventers in Wimborne Market disguised as a shepherd.

Tom early showed all the qualities of a zealous patriot, for when the French wars broke out in 1793 all he wanted to do was to fight them at sea, his natural element. He chose to go to war in a privateer, not as a sailor in the Royal Navy. The ship, a sloop, was called the *Three Friends*, and operated from Gosport. Unfortunately, after a period of success, the privateer was captured by the French after a stiff fight, and Tom found himself in a French prison.

He must have let his captors know that he was a smuggler by profession, for they released him in return for his agreement to take dispatches to a spy by means of a smuggling lugger bound for Southampton. Ill-luck struck again when this ship was intercepted and boarded by H.M.S. *Defiance*, during which action Tom was wounded in the arm. However, he managed to slip the package to the

Midshipman commanding the boarding-party, telling him to give it to his captain, for it would be of great interest to the government. The smuggler was allowed to continue to Southampton, but yet again misfortune struck Tom when he was seized by a Press Gang immediately after stepping ashore. He fought his way out of its clutches and escaped to Sussex, and, realizing that he was now a deserter from the Royal Navy with a price on his head, he decided to return to smuggling full time and in the biggest possible way.

He soon gathered yet another gang around himself and his trade prospered. It was during this highly successful period of his career that he met Sir Robert Goodhurst, who persuaded him to take back to France on one of his trips a certain French General who had agreed to spy for the British Government as a condition of his release. Johnstone successfully landed the Frenchman on his native shore, returned to England, but was promptly taken prisoner by the Riding Officers of Customs at Winchelsea while in the very act of landing a huge consignment of contraband. Tom and his ship's mate were taken to the New Gaol in London to await their trial; but prison was anathema to him, and he bribed his gaolers in order to escape. He managed to cross the sea to Flushing, now with a £500 price on his head.

Johnstone must have returned to England after a few months' residence in Holland, for in the following year he was volunteering to pilot a British force preparing to invade that country. The combined operation was a complete success, thanks to his pilotage. As a result Sir Ralph Abercrombie, the Commander, secured him a free pardon, to which Abercrombie added a personal letter of thanks and a fee of £1000.

While staying in Holland Tom had fallen in love with the wife of Colonel Cornelius Ten Brink, who had extended the hospitality of his own house to the Englishman. Frederika Ten Brink left her husband and came to England with Johnstone, and they set up house in London. Soon Tom was running up huge bills, and in two years had amassed debts of over eleven thousand pounds. Surprisingly, he did not turn to smuggling as a means of raising funds, and the only explanation seems to be that he was afraid to leave Frederika even for a day, for she had many ardent admirers in London society.

The most noble of these was the Marquess of Townwood, and he may have had something to do with Johnstone's arrest for debt in 1802. Tom was flung into the Fleet Prison, the ancient debtors' gaol. In court not only his debts, but also the fact that he was a pardoned deserter from the Royal Navy as well as a notorious smuggler were brought out. However, with a little help from his friends, 'Captain Johnson', as he was now known, escaped from a very secure cell with a double door and made his way undetected to the high outer wall of the prison, where the traditional rope-ladder was awaiting him. By nightfall a swift chaise-and-four had taken him to the coast near Brighton where he boarded a smuggling lugger which took him across to Calais.

In France he was taken to the house of a French smuggling colleague, where a wound he had suffered in making his escape over the Fleet's wall was tended, and he was nursed back to eventual fitness. It was while in this house that he received a visit from a French officer, who pointed out to him all the factors which would make a return to his native land very inadvisable: there was a price on his head as an escaped debtor, a felon, and his debts were still undischarged. The officer then informed him that he would be allowed to remain safe in France if he would agree to do a little smuggling on behalf of no less a person than the Emperor Napoleon himself. Even though France and England were still at war, Tom agreed, and in due course he was sent by the French authorities to his old refuge, Flushing, where he was informed that the French were going to put him on the 'Guinea Run'.

At the end of the eighteenth century the price of gold had soared through devaluation and the effects of war. The French government was willing to pay up to £1.10s.0d for every gold guinea brough over to France from England. Flushing was the centre of this Guinea Trade, to which the English smugglers were said to have taken across between ten and twelve thousand guineas *each week*, piercing the Royal Navy's strict blockade as they did so. Napoleon used this gold to buy arms outside France and to pay his vast army, and English banks were involved in the treacherous traffic.

Although it may seem unpatriotic to smuggle gold in time of war, the lower classes from which most of the smugglers came had a very ambivalent attitude to the government and the war which it was waging in their name. They hated their political masters and yet, at the same time, rejoiced in the victories won in that same government's name. Men did not go willingly into the Royal Navy, but had to be pressed; but once in they fought and died apparently gladly for such leaders as Nelson and Wellington. While Wellington called his men the scum of the earth, Nelson dared not let his sailors ashore between commissions for they would never return to serve him voluntarily.

When he was a prisoner on St Helena, Napoleon himself told his captors: 'I did not receive money direct from Spain: I got bills upon Vera Cruz, which certain agents sent by circuitous routes, by Amsterdam, Hamburg and other places to London, as I had no direct communication. The bills were discounted by merchants in London, to whom ten per cent was paid as their reward. Bills were then given by them upon different bankers in Europe for the greatest part of the amount, and the remainder in gold, which last was brought over to France by the English smugglers, Even for the equipping of my last expedition after my return from Elba a great part of the money was raised in London. The smugglers did great mischief to your government. During the war all the information I received from England came through the smugglers. They are people who have courage and ability to do anything for money. They had at first a part of Dunkirk allotted to them. At one time there were upwards of five hundred of them in Dunkirk. I had every information I wanted from them. They brought over newspapers and despatches from the spies we had in London. They took over spies from France ... They assisted French prisoners to escape from England ... They are,' ended the ex-Emperor, lapsing into his native Corsican, '"*genti terribili*"!'

The Guinea Run, upon which Tom Johnstone was soon to find himself embarking, demanded a very special type of vessel, very fast and well able to escape pursuit by the fastest cutters the King's men could put against it, for, especially when pursued by ships of the Royal Navy, guinea-smugglers would be shown little mercy once caught at their shameful trade. So a galley was evolved, over forty feet in length and with a beam of around seven feet. Two dozen to forty rowers were used, and these men could get their rate of striking up to such a pitch that nine or even ten knots could be maintained under ideal conditions. When spotted and pursued by the enemy, they could escape by turning into the wind, so that the king's sailing-ship had to abandon the chase; or they could set a course at an angle to that which the wind dictated to their pursuers. Deal, Dover and Folkestone were the ports where some of the finest of these galleys were made and sailed from to such counterparts as Calais, Dieppe and, of course, Flushing. A very strong tradition adds Christchurch to these other ports with Cherbourg as the French opposite number, a mere eighty miles away, a distance which could be covered in a long night's row. When the weather held fair, these galleys made runs every night, even continuing as often as they could when the weather broke. It is said that the golden guineas were carried by the smugglers in money-belts.

When Captain Johnstone had been at the Guinea Trade a good few weeks, he realized that he was well on the way to recouping his lost fortunes; but then in May of 1803 the French suddenly announced that they had enough English guineas to be going on with, and the frail Peace of Amiens which had been in existence since 1802 came to an end as they resumed fighting with the Allies. One cannot feel much sympathy with Tom in this new predicament, halfway to a fortune: before, his reverses had been bad luck or bad management: this time it seemed like a just reward for a traitor. Now he was an enemy in an enemy's land, unable to return home to enjoy his ill-gotten gains because he was a wanted man there, and also because the French refused to let him leave. He was once more a prisoner, and it was in this second captivity that he was again approached by the French government. Napoleon needed a Chief Pilot to guide his invasion fleet to the English shore, and he had heard of Tom's reputation, as well as his triumph when acting in the same rôle for Sir Ralph Abercrombie on the expedition to Holland. The Emperor of the French could offer Tom a reward uniquely suited to the Captain's needs: a free pardon to be enjoyed in an England under French rule which would ensure him complete immunity from the law of his native land. There would also, so said the French, be a huge fee when the job was done.

When the Emperor made the offer in a personal interview with the English smuggler, Tom is said to have told him that although it was true he was a smuggler, he was, at the same time, a true lover of his country and not a traitor. What Napoleon actually said in reply is not recorded. Whatever he said, the meeting resulted in Tom being flung into prison once again.

It took nine months for Tom to work out a method of escape, but at last he did, giving his gaolers the slip and diving into Flushing Harbour when he saw an American flush-decked schooner, the *Lafayette*, tied up alongside the quay, newly arrived from New Orleans. The Americans were all for handing him back to their allies the French, but somehow he managed to prevent this and smooth-talked them into signing him on as an extra hand for their return voyage.

Once in New Orleans he gained the position of clerk in the British Consulate by saying he was an out-of-work English Channel Pilot, which was, of course, true up to a point; but there was not a great deal of call for such sailors at that time in America. It was not long before he sailed back to England in the frigate H.M.S. *Roebuck*, with another free pardon in his pocket. This came about because he had been requested as an assistant by the American inventor, Robert Fulton. Tom had met Fulton in France just before he had gone on the Guinea Run, when Fulton was in Calais working on the development of the steam engine for the French government.

He joined Fulton at his new office in Dover, where the American was now working on explosive devices for the Royal Navy to use against his former employers, the French. The smuggler in Johnstone must have found nothing strange in this topsy-turvy partnership for the two men got on famously and steamed ahead in developing charges which would blow French ships out of the water when they least expected it. By 1806 their infernal devices were ready, and an English fleet under Admiral Lord St Vincent set sail for Brest with Tom as Chief Pilot and explosives expert combined. Once in sight of the French Brest Squadron, Tom was to lead in the swimmers with the devices to be attached underwater to the hulls of the French men-of-war.

Quite what went wrong has never been revealed, but the attack turned out a fiasco. Lord St Vincent had no word of blame for Captain Johnstone, who, he told his masters at the Admiralty, was only prevented from doing what he was expected by the vigilance of the enemy. Not surprisingly, Tom then went back to smuggling, but not because he was tired of working for the Royal Navy. In 1809 he again offered his services as Chief Pilot and explosives expert to the expedition against the Walcheren Islands of Holland. Once with the fleet in Flushing Harbour he entered the water towing yet another of the indefatigable Fulton's nasty mechanisms to the sea-wall of the main fort, where he lodged it and then retired out of range to watch the huge explosion which set off the enemy's main powder magazine. For this performance, he was awarded an annual pension of £100 for life.

When the French wars finally came to an end, the Lords of the Admiralty offered Captain Johnstone command of H.M.S. *Fox*, a Revenue cutter based at Plymouth. He was one of many smugglers taken on by the forces of the Crown to combat their former brothers of the Trade, for it was government policy to use those who knew their methods best to seek out the smugglers; Customs practice was also being followed in basing Tom as far as possible away from the part of the coast along which he had plied his Trade in former days. As one would expect, he was a very successful Revenue Captain, being experienced, ingenious and entirely ruthless when it came to hunting the smugglers down. The hatred the smugglers felt towards Tom was enormous and they very soon had a contract out on him, with the result that he was ordered not to leave the *Fox* when in the port of Plymouth. He once disobeyed, and was set upon so fiercely by local smugglers that he was very nearly blinded by a most savage cutlass-blow in the fray which followed.

Not surprisingly, his Navy service only lasted two years, for the rôle of poacher turned gamekeeper was not worth the risks, and he obtained an honourable discharge with the pension of a post-captain. He was now forty-four, he was receiving two fat pensions, and he probably had quite a sum saved, so he decided to retire to a little house near the River Thames in London and settle down in connubial bliss with the daughter of a minor Somerset squire, who bore him three fine children.

But a man with such an eventful past as Tom Johnstone could not have expected to be left in complete peace for long, particularly when that past had included an episode in the service of Napoleon

Bonaparte. It was soon after the former Emperor's incarceration on the Isle of St Helena that Tom's house in Vauxhall Bridge Road, a not unfashionable address, was discreetly visited by a number of French gentlemen. They had, they told him, a plan to free his former master, and it involved rescuing Bonaparte and taking him in a submarine across the Atlantic to America where he would be safe. The £40,000 they offered Tom as his fee for captaining the submarine may explain why he even bothered to listen to this incredibly crazy scheme; perhaps he hoped they would give him at least part of it before he actually entered the submarine, and he would be able to abscond with it.

4. The submarine *Nautilus*, designed and built by the American inventor Robert Fulton, in which Tom Johnstone was to rescue the Emperor Napoleon I from St. Helena.

Submarines were a new invention: the vessel in question had just been devised by Tom's old friend, Robert Fulton, and was called the *Nautilus*. A hundred feet long, it was constructed of iron with a copper skin, and while on the surface was propelled by a sail which could be folded away, and by a hand-cranked propeller under the water. The vessel would travel on the surface at a good six knots, and if English ships appeared would be able to dive to avoid detection.

Amazingly, Johnstone actually agreed to captain the *Nautilus*, and somehow the submarine was brought across the Channel and up the River Thames. Of course, there may have been other explanations apart from sheer greed which made him join this ludicrous venture; but in fact he did not have to put them to the test, for on 5th May, 1821, the former Emperor died on St Helena.

Johnstone decided to put the submarine up for sale. He had to wait a full year before he was called upon at his Thames-side residence by a group from the Spanish Marine Ministry. After the usual preliminaries, he conducted them down through his garden and on to the *Nautilus* moored in the river. He explained that as he had no crew, the Spanish officials would have to crew the boat themselves; and after settling them at the hand cranks and instructing them in what they had to do, the weird craft moved out into mid-stream and made for Blackwall, passing under London Bridge on the way. Then Tom announced that in order to demonstrate the submarine's full capability he was going to submerge. To the accompaniment, no doubt, of much rolling of the eyes, down they went. All was well for some yards as the Spaniards cranked away with a will, congratulating each other on having backed an obvious winner this time; but all too soon the *Nautilus* ran full tilt into the anchor cables of a moored vessel, which Tom had been unable to make out as he peered from his conning-tower into the filthy water of the River Thames. Turning to see the Spaniards crossing themselves and muttering their final prayers, he pulled out his watch and somehow conveyed to them that they had two minutes of life left unless they cranked in the opposite direction in order to free the submarine's nose from the cables. This the crew did, and the *Nautilus* lurched to the surface, but the portholes in the conning-tower gave way under the water pressure, and water poured in. Luckily, they all managed to escape from the doomed craft, and the Spaniards withdrew from the purchase of the submarine.

Captain Thomas Johnstone, known affectionately by a generation as the Hampshire Smuggler, eventually died in his house by the Thames in March, 1839. He could not have asked for a better end, considering how violent a career he had had. Although smuggling was his bread-and-butter, he should also be remembered as a great Channel Pilot, and an intrepid underwater warfare expert, one of the first Britain produced.

Inland from Portsmouth and Langstone Harbours there are innumerable villages with smuggling connections, each one small in itself, but all indicating the north-bound routes by which the smugglers took their goods once they were well away from the coast. Lanes, Roman roads and ordinary roads were all used; a study of those frequented gives a clear impression that their main concern was to get the contraband goods as quickly as possible north and east towards London.

Just below Droxford, for instance, on a route which runs due north from Portchester, lies Soberton in the Meon Valley, where a vault in the church of St Peter and St Paul was used for hiding contraband. Its entrance is just by the chancel door, and it seems to have been specially made for that purpose, for the vault has never been assigned to the remains of any definite family.

Just to the east of Winchester, about fourteen miles from the two harbours, are several receiving depots for smuggled goods. Cheriton, just below the Alresfords, in the valley of the River Itchen, had a remote farm called East Down, from which close watch could be kept for approaching Revenue men, which was the main depôt. There is some evidence to indicate that Cheriton was on a special gin-smuggling route, for many bottles from Holland have been found in almost all the cottages dating from the smuggling age in the area. It is certainly possible that there were such specialized routes.

Ropley, four and a half miles from Cheriton to the north-west, had many storage facilities amongst its farms and cottages. On one occasion a party of Revenue Officers called on the squire, who was also the local magistrate, and informed him that they had come to search specific cottages in his village. The Lord of the Manor invited them to take a glass of brandy, of which he had a good store from obvious suppliers, and while he plied them with the excellent spirit, his agent hastily went round to all the cottages on the Officers' list warning the residents to get everything incriminating into the many secret cupboards and cellars which had been constructed especially for such an emergency. When the Revenue men eventually left the squire's hospitality they found 'nothing for the Service', which was the official phrase used in their Journals for a fruitless search.

About three miles to the north of Ropley, just beyond the misleadingly named Dry Hill, lies Medstead, which gained a reputation as a dêpot for the storing and distribution of lace, silk and brandy. It is said that the smugglers had a large cave here, possibly under the earthwork which lies just to the north. A tumulus and an ancient abbey are also to be found on the map of this district, and if the Hampshire smugglers around here were anything like their counterparts in West Dorset, these ancient places may also have had their uses for the concealment of contraband. There were also several small manor houses in the area, providing hiding places as well as good customers of the local gangs.

Northwest of Medstead is Preston Candover, on the main road to Basingstoke, a village unique in having two wells which were used as dumps. One of them is said to have had a cavity at its head into which a wagon and a full team of horses could be driven when the need arose, a marvellous hide, if it was true. Just to the west of Preston Candover lies Micheldever Forest, as well as the Roman road linking Winchester and Basingstoke, and these two features must have been well used by the smugglers. Becket's Down may have been used as an open-air market where the smugglers set out their stalls of contraband for the country-folk from miles around to come and browse and buy at their leisure; its position made it easy to give early warning of the approach of any unwelcome visitors, such as Revenue men or Dragoons. Goods going up-country through this area must have found their way to Winchester, for the clergy of the Cathedral and the masters at the great school were probably on the smugglers' list of favoured customers in the eighteenth century.

Smugglers also operated from the east side of Southampton Water and from the port itself. The situation of Hamble at the mouth of the river of that name is similar to that of Lymington, and, indeed, the two towns have much in common. Hamble, like Beaulieu further west, was one of the first towns to have Dragoons quartered there, indicating that it was regarded as a place which needed stiff policing. This happened in 1723, when the authorities decided that ten Dragoons, a fairly large party, were necessary if smuggling was to be kept in check. This is not surprising, for the map shows that the two rivers, the Beaulieu and the Hamble, extended the smugglers' highways far inland, and these were continued by roads to which the contrabandists transferred their goods from the small boats which they used on such waterways.

Hamble was also the home of a well-known smuggler named Sturgess who operated in this area; he came under the watchful eye of William Arnold, the great Collector of Cowes, for his extensive smuggling activity. But for all Arnold's vigilance, Sturgess was able to acquire in 1783 a splendid new cutter of 220 tons, heavily armed with twenty guns. Sturgess named her the *Favourite*. With such formidable ships in the hands of the smugglers, it is no wonder that the efforts of the Customs Officers of the Solent and Spithead to contain the smugglers of the area were described as 'a positive war' by a later writer.

Netley, with its huge Abbey and little Tudor castle, must have been a popular place with the smugglers of Southampton Water. There was ample storage space in the cellars and vaults of the Abbey; and the castle ceased to be garrisoned in 1627, after which point it was free to be used as a smugglers' watch-post, signal-station and, after its development as a gentleman's residence, as a selling-point for the finest contraband brought up Southampton Water. Here the local smuggler-chief was a man named Russell, (as with Smuggler Sturgess of Hamble, the official records do not supply his Christian name) who is said to have decoyed the Preventive Officer away from one his runs

5. An Officer of Light Dragoons, one of the smugglers' most feared opponents.

at a favourite landing spot by ordering another lugger to come in with a load of what appeared to be kegs, but which, when examined by the King's Officer as they lay stacked up on the shore, turned out to be straw replicas of brandy barrels. So much ridicule was heaped upon the head of the wretched Officer by the local people that news of the farce reached his masters in the Customs House at Southampton, and they moved him to another district, though some sources say that he was dismissed the Service altogether. Whether Russell was the resident of Netley Castle or not we do not know, for its ownership is shrouded in mystery until more recent times.

As one would expect of so ancient and important a port, Customs Officials were established at Southampton very early in her history. In 1203 King John appointed two Southampton citizens to look after the revenues from duties levied on cargoes landed and taken out of the port. These two men were assisted by a clerk who did the actual accounts. In the year 1205 Southampton was third in the Revenue tables of all the ports in England.

There was some trouble in 1398, the last year of the chaotic reign of Richard II, for by this time the Customs Service in Southampton had reached such a state that an inquiry was held into corruption in the port. The Collector of the time was accused of allowing wool and other exports to be shipped out without imposing duties on them. Things improved rapidly, for in the year 1423, early in the reign of King Henry VI, one of the Southampton Customs Officials refused to be bribed by a Genoese merchant who wanted to get away with a cargo of wool without paying duty. The Official suffered for it: he was shanghaied by the Genoese, taken in their ship down Southampton Water, and dumped on the Isle of Wight.

In the the year 1473 it was Venetian merchants who were bribing the Customs Officers of Southampton to let their huge cargoes past, giving butts of wine and Venetian florins in their efforts to corrupt the King's men. Apparently this sort of thing began to work, and Florentine merchants went so far as to invite the whole City Council to dinner to show their gratitude for the understanding way they had let cargo after cargo past without having a groat paid in duty on them.

By the eighteenth century, the smugglers of Southampton were proving that they were a very ruthless lot: in 1733 there was an affray in the port in which Customs Officers were beaten up by smugglers wielding huge holly clubs and ferocious whips. One of the King's Officers was knocked senseless and died two days later from the wounds he suffered to his head. There was some reason for the smugglers of Southampton being so ruthless: they were finding, as the eighteenth century went on, that smuggling in the area was increasingly difficult. It was easy for the Revenue boats to close in on their luggers in the narrows of Southampton Water, especially when they were on a tack which had taken them close in to the shore. Southampton smuggling was, therefore, not a large-scale affair: a couple bottles of gin and the occasional bale of silk were brought in by members of ships' crews in much the same way that these deeds are done today at ports and airports. No doubt there was much traffic by small boats going out to ships at anchor offshore and along the quays.

And no doubt there was a counterpart to Mrs MacLane of Gosport who, like Little Buttercup (or rather Mrs Cripps, to give her proper name) in *H.M.S. Pinafore*, was what was vulgarly termed a 'bumboat woman', rowing out to the ships both of the merchant and Royal Navies in order to sell all the little things that sailors need. Mrs MacLane specialized in 'ribbons and laces, to set off the faces of pretty young sweethearts and wives', but she had a sideline, too. Just what this was came to the surface one day when there was a sudden storm in Gosport Harbour, and her wherry capsized in the confusion. When the rescue-boats got to her, it is said, she was found floating serenely with the aid of the air-filled bladders under her skirt which, once on board a ship carrying smuggling sailors in its crew, she was able to fill with gin and brandy.

Southampton was the headquarters of the Collection, covering a district which extended to Portsmouth to the east and Christchurch to the west; and it was in its Custom House that the Court of Award sat every three months to look into and settle the claims made by Customs and Excise Officers, as well as informers, on the seizures of contraband and smugglers' vessels which had been made by the efforts of these claimants. Seized goods were all auctioned off and the money made shared out among Officers and men of the Preventive Services: the officer in charge of a successful operation received twenty-five shares at one end of the scale, while the lowest rating at the other got six shares. An informer was awarded half the value of the goods seized, so it did pay to grass on the smugglers; but informers needed a good amount as capital, for they almost always had to leave their home district and start life up somewhere else. Smugglers were notorious in their pursuit of those who had betrayed them, frequently resorting to torture and murder in revenge.

Round the head of Southampton Water lies Marchwood. Formerly known by the ancient name of Kingsland, Marchwood had a beacon on the hill of that name for the purpose of warning 'the rangers of Beaulieu' when the Spanish Armada hove in sight. Another connection with Beaulieu was provided in smuggling days by the cargoes of contraband which were landed straight on to Crackmore Hard, and transported by pack-horses which wore their shoes reversed in order to confuse the Revenue Officers of Southampton. Their destination was a house near the present-day Beaulieu Road Station on the edge of the heathland. Somewhere on the shore are the ruins of an ice-house, belonging to some manor-house now disappeared, but which must have been attractive as a possible dump for smugglers who could not pause very long, but who had contraband to leave for the local squire. Like Pokesdown in Bournemouth, the name Pooks Green, a little inland from Beaulieu, indicates ancient barrows, for place names based on the name of Puck usually imply the presence of tumuli or other prehistoric monuments. They were places avoided by superstititious local people, making them ideal undisturbed locations for contraband.

Not long ago, during rebuilding work on several of the older cottages of Marchwood, many hides were found behind matchboarding and under false floors; several rotten casks which must once have held good brandy and gin were also uncovered by the local workmen. It is not often that actual casks, rather than bottles, are found; barrels, being made of wood with metal hoops, tend to rot, or to have been broken up for firewood. The whereabouts of a few are known, outside museums such as those at Dorchester and Carisbroke on the Isle of Wight, and to the smuggling-history enthusiast they are collectors' items.

The Marchwood Magazine was built in the middle of the last century, and its strange red-brick buildings of barrack-block and guardrooms with their colonnades of cast-iron pillars, are still standing today. As late as 1873 a crew of smugglers with an amazing talent for survival was intercepted off the Magazine by a Customs cutter from Southampton just as they were bringing in a cargo of contraband to the Marchwood shore. It is not known just what was in their boat to make it worthwhile smuggling at this late date.

One of the odd facts about this strange shore is that there seem to be no smuggling stories about Hythe. However, Ipley Manor, two and a half miles into the New Forest from the Hythe shore, and a little further north of Beaulieu itself, was notorious as a sanctuary for criminals of various kinds. There is obviously an interesting story here: what sort of criminals: murderers, spies, poachers, smugglers? The rumours fit in well with this area, which must have been constantly crossed and re-crossed by smugglers going about their unlawful business.

Though the oil refinery's present sprawl makes it difficult to believe, Fawley was a hotbed of smuggling two centuries ago. This was another inland location where caves were used by the smugglers, for in Sprat's Down Wood there were several, one of which is still accessible. One of the cottages in the wood was once visited by the local Revenue Officer, apparently on a social call, for the old couple who lived there had come to look on him as a friend. However, he turned out to be more fiend than friend, for on hearing his heels ring hollow on the floor flagstones, he summoned aid and searched until he had found the entrance to the cottagers' contraband cellar. Friends or no, he soon had them bundled off to Winchester Gaol for the underground room was stuffed full of recently run goods.

Ashlett Creek at Fawley was much used by the smugglers, and Cadland Manor House provided a first delivery-point for the brandy, wine and other luxuries they brought up through the Solent or across from the Isle of Wight. The Cadland Manor of those times was the first house which disappeared when the Fawley oil refinery was built on its lands, to re-appear in its present form on the shore of Stanswood Bay, facing the Isle of Wight.

Calshot Castle, another of Henry VIII's gun-forts, had a garrison in pre-smuggling days which saw the profit to be made out of imposing unofficial tolls on vessels entering Southampton Water. The captains of the ships which were stopped saw the wisdom of doing so for none knew better than they how completely the guns of Calshot Castle controlled the very narrow waterway, only just over a mile across. Customs Officers were eventually installed in the castle, but they must have had the profit motive firmly to the fore like their predecessors on this remote spit, for there is only one incident recorded of their ever having made a seizure of smuggled goods, and the proceedings following this were dropped when the Chief Customs Officer of Calshot accepted a bribe in the form of the daughter of one of the smugglers involved. She was probably accompanied by a hefty dowry.

3
The Isle of Wight

Since the beginning of England's history, the Isle of Wight has been of vital importance strategically because of its proximity to France and to Southampton Water, with its great port. The Wight, to give it its old name, featured at the top of the battle-plans of the commanders of all three threatening Spanish Armadas, for the King of Spain gave them secret orders to take the island as their base of operations before attempting the assault on the mainland. Earlier in the same century the islanders saw themselves as living 'in a frontier place', vulnerable and closer to England's enemies than any other part of the realm. The Dons never managed to invade, but in the reign of King Henry VIII the French had succeeded in doing so.

Henry declared war on them in 1544 and took Boulogne; so they made for Portsmouth, then, as now, the Royal Navy's main base and the home port of his unfortunate flagship, the *Mary Rose*. The English fleet came out to meet the foe, and just off the harbour the great seven-hundred ton carrack suddenly heeled over and sank. The French had 220 ships and galleys carrying 6000 troops, but in the narrow seaway of Spithead they were unable to achieve a conclusive victory when the battle was joined; so, being baulked of taking the English fleet, the French seemed to have decided that they would have the Isle of Wight instead.

They landed 2000 men, but the islanders were ready for them, having been reinforced by thousands of men from the mainland of Hampshire. A battle raged for two full days, and the invaders were beaten back to their ships, killed or taken prisoner. To ensure that nothing so destructive of national pride ever happened again, Henry built his famous gun-forts along the Channel coast, from Sandown to Pendennis, and ordered each parish to maintain an armoury stocking everything from bows and arrows to heavy cannon.

The Isle of Wight was an obvious forward base for traffic to and from the Continent for English smugglers of the eighteenth and early nineteenth centuries. They brought their very welcome contraband to the great houses of the island — Nunwell, Arreton Manor, Appledurcombe and Carisbroke Castle — and to the farms, inns and cottages of the scattered villages; but they also used the island as a convenient staging-post, a main dumping depôt where contraband could be stock piled reasonably safely, before being taken on across Spithead and the Solent and up Southampton Water to the coasts of Hampshire and Dorset in whatever quantities, and at whatever times and tides the smugglers chose.

For the lugger captain coming in to St Catherine's Point, the most southerly land of the island, there are problems in the form of long ledges of submarine rocks continuing the land southwards under the sea. But once he got to the west of the Point, places like Blackgang Chine with its deep gorge cutting through the towering cliffs reaching 400 feet, and the very useful sea-mark of St Catherine's Tower, offered him obvious landing-places. Continuing west along this coast, the many chines all welcomed the smuggler, even though the beaches are narrow and the slopes up through the gorges are steep: Walpen Chine, Ladder Chine, Branes Chine, Grange Chine, Chilton Chine, Brook Chine, Shippard's Chine and Compton Chine, as well as the fine Freshwater Bay and, finally Scratchell's Bay at the Needles.

The many ridges of submarine rocks did offer some advantage to smuggling captains: there were not many Revenue or Royal Navy skippers who would follow them into the southern coast of the Isle of Wight, for they knew they could never hope to be as well acquainted with the submerged rocks as the smuggling luggers with their own pilots on board. Standing on the high cliffs by Blackgang looking south in a south-westerly gale, it is possible to appreciate what a terrible seaway this is, for the long stretches of white water over the ridges disappear into the mist as if they continue right out into the Channel almost as far as France itself. Atherstone, Niton Chale Brook and Ventnor, as well as Blackgang, all have their ledges running south, and it was between these that the sea-smugglers had to steer.

If local traditions are anything to go by, then Rookley was the focal point where the smugglers' paths inland from the south-western and south-eastern coasts met; the first, and probably the main, dump for the newly-run contraband may have been here. Rookley was probably a smugglers' garrison, all approaches to it guarded night and day, and a place where no Revenue man dared to go.

The Headquarters of the Customs Board was in the island's main port, Cowes. In September, 1777, William Arnold took up his appointment of Collector of Customs. Arnold was probably the finest

Officer the Service had ever had, and his gifts were sorely needed on the island. The smugglers themselves must have watched with some consternation the beginning of his long and highly successful period in the office of Collector.

The tablet on William Arnold's house in West Cowes informs the present-day visitor that it was the birthplace of Doctor Arnold, Headmaster of Rugby from 1826 to 1842; he was William Arnold's son. However in the context of smuggling history, it may be of more interest to imagine William Arnold commuting across the River Medina forty years earlier to his office in the Customs House in East Cowes each day. What was so special about this Collector? First, he had complete integrity: he was incorruptible in an age when bribery was the way of life, especially in the Customs Service. Secondly, he had a single-minded devotion to his duty, working long hours and even paying for several vital cutters to fight the smugglers out of his own pocket, when official funds were not forthcoming.

Late eighteenth century administrations were constantly trying to reduce the drain on the exchequer during the Wars of American Independence. When Arnold started at Cowes he found the Revenue cutters had been withdrawn from the station. He was soon writing to his masters, the Board of Customs, warning them of the dangers he had found facing him. Fast galleys were actually being built in the port of Cowes specifically for smuggling; and the smugglers themselves had become daring in their huge gangs, which were well armed and used disguises to protect the identities of their members as they freely ran their goods and beat up any Revenue Officers who tried to prevent them. His main feeling was one of powerlessness, especially as he watched the smuggling craft actually leaving the port to take contraband over to the Hampshire shores for he had no cutter under his command to intercept them.

Arnold had been appointed as the local representative of the government, amongst the ship-owners and builders, the merchant captains and the Royal Naval officers, and the civil authorities of the Isle of Wight, a very busy and important waterway and coast. He was, in Shakespeare's words, 'a great oneyer' in the isle, and very soon he was known, liked, respected and accepted by all the local landowners, officers, and magistrates. In addition, he was also Deputy Postmaster of the Island, and, a few years later, the Collecter of Light Dues for Trinity House.

William Arnold might have expected the end of the war with the American colonies to bring him more money with which to mount a proper operation against the smugglers, but this was not the case. In 1783 he wrote even more strongly than before to his masters telling them how smuggling had increased to an alarming degree, and that it was now 'principally carried on in large armed cutters and luggers from two or three hundred tons burden, with which the Revenue cruisers are not able to contend. It is no unusual thing for them to land their goods in open day under the protection of their guns, sometimes in sight of Revenue cutters whom they will not suffer to come near or board them.'

Arnold went on to make clear to the Customs Commissioners that these large vessels were escorting convoys of smaller cargo-carriers: 'They keep off until towards night when they run in and land their cargoes at places where gangs of smugglers sometimes to the number of two or three hundred meet them.' The Free Traders, claimed Arnold, now had a system of pricing their goods according to the distances they had had to bring them.

His remedy was an extension of the Hovering Act to three leagues, and his letter had the effect of his being offered more Officers to assist him, but he roundly told his masters that it was ships and experienced men he needed, not a few more land-based men. Specifically, he wanted a cutter at Cowes; and a Royal Naval frigate to patrol Studland Bay, with a cutter to serve her, all to work directly under his orders.

The Board of Customs ignored all his requests. Arnold saw there was no other course open to him but to fit out his own boat. For this he requested the Commissioners' permission, and when it was granted he persuaded his brother-in-law to join him in the finances and hired the *Swan*, a well-known local cutter. He took on a first-class local crew and appointed George Sarmon, a Cowes cutter specialist, as commander.

In spite of this auspicious start, just a month after commissioning, the *Swan* foundered in a ferocious gale which caught her between the Needles and Hurst Castle, a notoriously dangerous waterway. She was completely wrecked and Arnold had surprisingly failed to insure her. Then came the good news: the Admiralty changed its collective mind and sent the cutter *Expedition* to that very same waterway.

Expedition lived up to her name and was soon bringing into Cowes seized contraband and the ships which had tried to smuggle it ashore from Hurst to Christchurch; and when the Admiralty heard of her success they sent a sloop as well, just as Arnold had suggested some time earlier. H.M.S. *Orestes* was a three hundred tons, eighteen gun, yellow-painted sloop-of-war, of welcome shallow draught, and with huge sweeps which could get her into shallows where the smugglers would never expect her to go. Arnold got on well with her commander, Captain Ellis, as he did with most men and all officers of the Royal Navy. *Orestes* took over the Studland Bay station and immediately was in action with a formidable smuggling cutter of over

200 tons and a massive armament of twenty six-pounders. This ship was trying to land 2,000 gallons of brandy and gin and nine tons of tea on the pebble beach leading to Hurst Castle, but this was prevented by the sloop; a running fight ensued in which the smugglers' skill and guts showed clearly that while a mere Revenue cutter, whether privately or government financed, would have had no chance against them, *Orestes* was able to capture their cutter and brought her into Cowes.

This miniature sea-battle was soon followed by an even bloodier battle between the *Orestes'* boats, which she had lowered to get at the enemy in shallow waters, and an even larger smuggling cutter, this time mounting twenty-two guns. Arnold was able to tell the Commissioners of his successes, and not without a feeling that his ideas had been shown to be the best, for this second smuggler had, as he put it, been more like a pirate ship than a mere smuggler!

In 1784 the Board of Customs sent him a new cutter as a present, and he named her *Swan II*, using the ten six-pounders which he had rescued from the first *Swan*. George Sarmon was made commander again, and soon she had a consort, the cutter *Speedwell*, which Arnold hired from her owner Henry Roberts. They were soon joined by the *Laurel* of Poole, and the lugger *Diligence* from Weymouth. Now, thanks to Arnold's foresight, the coast was properly policed by a squadron of fine ships.

By 1786 Arnold's untiring efforts were making life very difficult indeed for the smugglers of the Isle of Wight. Even the gangs led by such notorious smugglers as John Streeter were broken by his crusade against them. None of the big smuggling ships, which had so alarmed him when he had first come to Cowes, now dared to show themselves in his waters. However, the smaller fry were still a nuisance, especially those still using the island's beaches and chines to the east and south. Arnold tightened the land patrols by his Riding Officers, making sure every part of the coast was visited, paying particular attention to the fort commanding Sandown Bay, making sure its garrison was alert and well-practised in the use of the fine complement of guns mounted there. The notorious stretch of coast from St. Catherine's Point to the Needles was put under very tight surveillance: Chale Bay came in for particular attention, for with the terrible tide-race off Rocken End which stretched to Atherfield Point, it had always been the haunt of wreckers who preyed on the endless succession of ships which came to grief there. The incredibly steep cliffs made it exceedingly difficult to police from the land, but Arnold managed it, even bringing the notorious Ladder Chine under his control by means of skilful deployment and supervision of his Revenue Officers, whom he personally visited and encouraged.

After his successful war against the smugglers, Arnold was also involved in the wars against Napoleon, and, as one would expect, he showed as much vigour and ingenuity here as he did against his smuggling fellow-countrymen. He died very unexpectedly while on duty in March of 1801 at the tragically early age of fifty-five, his end without doubt hastened by overwork. He was buried in Whippingham Churchyard, and his memorial tablet sums up a remarkable man and a unique Customs Officer: *'Sacred to the memory of William Arnold, Esq., late Collector of H.M. Customs in the Port of Cowes, Isle of Wight: a man who, by his amiable, as well as by his faithful, discharge of his duty in his public station and private character justly entitled him to the warmest esteem and affection of all who were permanently or occasionally associated with him in business, society or domestic ties.'*

The villages of the Isle of Wight all seem to have their smuggling connections. Bembridge smugglers used their fourteen feet gigs to cross to Cherbourg and Harfleur, each boat bringing back twenty tubs, good cargo for a modest place, where the profits from the trade were often put into bricks and mortar: many of the rows of Bembridge cottages were paid for by smuggling. The windmill must have been a useful day-mark for them, returning loaded to the gunwhales with contraband, as well as a lookout.

Binstead Churchyard, only five miles from Bembridge, contains the grave of Thomas Sivell who, in 1785, at the age of sixty-five was shot dead on his smuggling boat when being chased by a Revenue cutter in the Solent. His efforts to escape had included ditching his cargo of thirty barrels of gin and thirty-eight of brandy, as well as several casks of tea, but all to no avail. He was one of the victims of William Arnold's hard line with the smugglers of the Island.

A few years later, further south at Sandown Bay saw a unique combined operation between a Customs cutter, an Excise cutter and a Royal Naval frigate, who managed to corner a smuggling lugger, the *Kite*. The habitual rivalry between the three services was not entirely absent, however, for the three captains took some time to agree a concerted plan of action, and by the time they actually reached the *Kite* she was in the process of getting the stuff ashore. Only sixty gallons of brandy were still aboard, the rest having been whipped away by the highly efficient lander and his gang.

A visitor to Niton, the most southerly village on the Isle of Wight in smuggling days, was struck by the fishermen who never seemed to go out fishing but always had plenty of money at their disposal; and he also noticed that most of the men had a string of aliases which they frequently used, a characteristic of their brothers of Mudeford. Ralph

Stone was one of the names used by the Niton Gang's leader. Each village had its smuggling-chief who used the men of the settlement as his gang. St. Helen's, which lies across Brading Harbour from Bembridge, was ruled by Dick Dawes, a hard-drinking man who was more famous for his daughter's deeds than his own. She was the notorious Sophie Dawes, the so-called 'Queen of Chantilly' and her birth in 1792 is commemorated on the cottage overlooking the village green of St. Helen's. Sophie became the mistress of the Duc de Bourbon and caused considerable scandal in the turbulent world of post-Napoleonic France.

Mottistone, about halfway between St. Catherine's Point and the Needles, has a fine Norman church which must have been useful as a sea mark as well as a good lookout and store, the functions of many church towers all along these smuggling coasts. The churchyard has a large family tomb, which, like that at Kinson on the mainland, was used for hiding contraband. The notorious Mottistone Gang also had the use of several large caves in the cliffs just above the beach; but it was the cottages nearest the sea which were used for the vital signal system which gave instructions and advice to the large smuggling luggers as they nosed their way to these dangerous, desolate coasts. Small windows cut high up in walls looking out to sea were the 'eyes' from which the lookouts kept watch, and in which the signal lanterns were placed and flashed in the agreed codes of the smugglers. From such slits and peepholes these lights could easily be removed when the Philistines, as the Revenue men were known, had been spotted coming to the cottages along the roads on the landward side.

Brook, just east of Freshwater, was another smuggling village. Brook Ledge and Brook Chine were both great attractions for the incoming smuggling ships and the local lander. Here the men used seaweed carts to get the goods up from the beach; relics of those days such as brandy kegs and wine-flagons have been found in the village. Even a glass-bottomed peep-bucket, used by the smugglers when searching for a crop of kegs underwater which had had to be weighted and sunk, has been seen comparatively recently, though no one knows its exact location now.

The story is still told in Brook of how the Chief Riding Officer of Customs of the area habitually rode a fine white horse on his ceaseless patrols along these cliffs, which range from a few feet to several hundreds in height, sheer in many places. One evening a landing-party was using the Purbeck method of swaying brandy-kegs up their vertical cliff by means of ropes anchored to a stout nine-inch post driven hard into the cliff top. They had lookouts posted as a matter of course, but one of them must have been rather dim, for he saw a figure on a horse cantering along the perilous edge of the cliff and, because the animal was black, and he was watching for the Chief Riding Officer on his white horse, he did not grasp that this was their hated enemy until the Officer was upon them. The Revenue man had switched horses, whether by intention or simply because his white horse could not be used is not known. Whatever the reason for the change the hoisting party was well and truly caught. The smugglers, like a good number of their fellows from Brook, landed in Winchester Jail, where they served out their sentences, for this was before the Isle of Wight had prisons of its own.

A little further east, and slightly inland on the main road of these parts, is Brighstone. This is the home of an islander whose grandfather was a smuggler, caught in the act one night but who did not finish up in Winchester Jail. Instead he was passed into the Royal Navy, a reminder of the welcome given to some smugglers by the Senior Service for their expert seamanship. This also emphasizes the Isle of Wight's function in the overall pattern of smuggling along the coasts of Hampshire and Dorset: the biggest contraband ships would land their goods on the southern shores, in spite of the extremely hazardous sea approaches, towering cliffs, and difficult inland paths. These cargoes were then split up into manageable loads and transported by pack-horse and farm-cart across the island to the northern shores, or to *caches* more or less halfway across the island; the smugglers' agents would then arrange their destinations and the timings of their despatch across the narrow waters of the Solent. Clearly, most of the goods were sent across to the shores west of Southampton Water, but some must have been risked up Southampton Water itself, and even into the very dangerous waters of the harbour of Portsmouth and those further east. This was a very daring route, but the smugglers were known for daring which bordered on the foolhardy; and it is no wonder that William Arnold wrote of his chagrin at seeing smuggling boats actually leaving his own port of Cowes for the mainland under his very nose before he had equipped himself with sufficient cutters to be able to prevent them. One can imagine goods being taken over in this way using the smallest of rowing skiffs by the enterprising boatmen of Cowes, men who were respected ship-builders and repairers, who passed the time of day with the new Collector, and then grinned behind his back as they went off to arrange the next contraband-carrying trip.

It is not really surprising that the Isle of Wight Customs Officers could be cruel in their efforts to stop this insolent traffic. In the churchyard at Binstead near Ryde, is the headstone to the grave of Thomas Sivell who was shot dead by Customs Officers who stopped and boarded his sloop, the scene being vividly carved by the local memorial mason whose sympathies must have been entirely with the unfortunate man, to judge by the vigour of the sculpting. It is by no means certain that Thomas Sivell was a smuggler, but the Customs Officers clearly suspected that his sloop was carrying contraband; and the resistance which his crew must have put up when boarded would indicate that they had something to hide.

4
Lymington and the West Hampshire coast

Across the Solent from the Wight lies Lymington, the port for the ferry to Yarmouth. Daniel Defoe found the town had no trade with other countries, its waterfront teeming with smugglers and all sorts of desperadoes. Contraband was smuggled over by the everyday ferry-boats from the Island, and this, together with the stuff coming in by the smugglers' own craft, went up the Lymington River to Boldre, Brockenhurst, Lyndhurst, Cadnam and depots beyond, most of them well into the New Forest. So active were the Lymington smugglers in their heyday that one of the town's leading ladies, the future bride of the poet Robert Southey, complained bitterly that she was awoken practically every night by the noisy smugglers passing under her windows. They cared for no one, not even the Dragoons stationed in the town: who, no doubt, were well bribed anyway. In fact, the lady's cottage was burgled one night but she heard nothing suspicious until it was too late, because the noise of the smugglers, and their brothers-in-arms, the poachers, was so commonplace in her ears. By the 1820s, the smugglers had such a hold on Lymington that the town's magistrates were said to have sworn in the most notorious of them as Special Constables in order to ensure that some sort of order was kept among their own kind.

With this sort of domination by the smugglers, it was inevitable that Lymington should, like Christchurch, be riddled with their tunnels. Some people now doubt that they actually went to the trouble and cost of such excavations just for the Trade, which apparently could not last. But at the time, smugglers had no reason to doubt the continuing profit to be made from the Trade, so digging tunnels would have seemed worth the effort.

The cellars of two of the biggest inns in Lymington, the Londesborough Hotel (known in smuggling days as the Nag's Head) and the Angel Inn, are joined by a tunnel which still runs under the

High Street, its mouth just discernible at the Nag's Head end. The subterranean passage has been bricked up, in common with other smugglers' tunnels, but from the pattern of the brickwork it can be seen to have been of comfortable size, and obviously built for a busy trade. The Lymington system does not stop there: from the Angel the tunnel makes its way down the hill, passing under the present Police Station, to reach its outlet in the bank of the Lymington River. It is clear that the Free Traders came up the river from the sea, moored at the tunnel's mouth, and either stacked their goods there, or climbed up the hill under the main street; or perhaps the method was like that used in Poole, and ropes were ready for them when they arrived with hooks at the ends to which they just affixed their kegs and packets. We shall never know for sure the exact methods used by either the Lymington smugglers or many others; but we can be sure that one section of the Lymington smugglers eventually went too far. They were the Ambrose Hole Gang, the place being just outside the town on the Forest edge. Not content with smuggling, they went on to burglary and even murder. The affair was well hushed-up in the Lymington area, and the only fact that can be ascertained is that the soldiers had to be used to clean the gang out of their nest with a fierce little battle in which much blood was shed on both sides. Afterwards, a huge haul of loot, both smuggled and robbed, was found inside Ambrose Hole, in addition to a well in which, so it is claimed, around thirty bodies were discovered, victims of the gang.

The regular Lymington smugglers kept going with the Trade as long as they could; and they were, in fact, members of the very select band who decided to turn the new-fangled railway to their advantage. Using their age-old craft of catching and mongering, they began a lucrative trade sending hampers of good Solent fish up to London, with a layer of brandy kegs underneath. There is a Customs House right next to Billingsgate Fish Market, so the interest of the Excise men was not unexpected. They raided the fishmonger's shop and found not only the brandy kegs, but a letter from Lymington asking for the placing of further orders of brandied fish; the Excise men tipped off their colleagues in the south, who promptly raided the fishing-smuggler's cottage, where they were met by a shower consisting of bucketfuls of 'filth too disgusting to be described'. The smuggler was arrested by the reeking Excise men, but had to be released eventually as the Mayor of Lymington intervened and accused them of getting a confession from him by trickery. Again the smugglers of the town had had a helping hand from the magistracy, for Lymington, like Christchurch, was nothing if not a complete smuggling town.

A legitimate lugger once put into the port of Lymington and down its gangplank trooped a number of English passengers who summoned the Harbour Master and asked him to call the town's doctor at once. The reason was that the captain of the ship had died on the way over from France, and they wished to see him properly laid to rest. The doctor examined the deceased and duly signed the death certificate; then the passengers called the Lymington undertaker and made it clear that they wished to pay for a fitting funeral for their late commander. The hearse was backed up the quay and the coffin was reverently laid inside. Then, drawn by the black horses with their sable plumes nodding, the impressive cortège left the port, both crew and passengers falling in sombrely behind, to be joined by the Harbour Master and a number of Customs Officers. The procession passed through Lymington, but most of the walking mourners stopped at the Angel Inn and went inside to drink a last bumper to their late captain. The Customs men were particularly well looked after in the way of drink by the passengers, and for a good reason: the undertaker's men in charge of the hearse whipped up the horses as the outskirts of the town were reached, for they were in on the plot. Very soon the coffin was being opened in a dark New Forest dell, where it was soon emptied of the many bottles of best brandy which it contained. So the good doctor must have been a party to the deception of the Customs Officers as well.

Just one more macabre smuggling tale may be recounted here. Just to the east of the wide mouth of the Lymington River lies Pylewell House, with its complementary Pylewell Home Farm nearby, which was a well-known smuggling-dump. So busy was this as a contraband-store that some people claim today the eerie sound of brandy-barrels can be heard as they are rolled across the upper floors by the ghostly fingers of long-dead Lymington smugglers.

Between Pylewell House and Needs Oare Point the smugglers found an ideally flat coast on which to land their goods. The wide mud-flats stretching far out into the Solent were death-traps to Customs ships, but perfect refuges and protection to the smugglers who knew the tides and the inlets between them. Here the wild-fowling punts were greatly used to take the stuff from the luggers; and when the water ran out and the mud began, locally-made pattens, or platform shoes, were worn so that the mud was no trouble to the local smugglers. If the landguard of Customs men closed in on the smugglers as they drew near the firm ground, they simply pressed their kegs down into the mud and returned for them later.

Just inland from Pitts Deep, the deepest part of which, known as Brandy Hole, was a favourite place for sinking tubs when necessary, lies Sowley Pond, no doubt also used as an underwater depot, especially when the local Riding Officer was out and about. The Forge Hammer Inn used to be near the Pond. After the establishment of the Coastguard, it was approached by a group of the Guard after having been named as a smugglers' dump in a report. While the Officers were still a little way from the inn, the landlady came out, buttonholed one of them, and loudly demanded that the man should settle his outstanding bar-account, using rather bad language as she did so. While this was going on, much to the amusement of the poor man's colleagues, the smugglers in the inn were hastily removing the illegal goods, which were indeed cached in the huge inn chimney, out through the back door and away over the heath to a convenient copse in the New Forest. A pre-determined whistle signal told the landlady that the coast was clear, and so she ceased her harangue and let the Coastguards enter her inn.

The Beaulieu River was a busy entry for the smugglers; its difficult entrance and tortuous course made pursuit difficult for the forces of the Crown. Traffic must have been more or less continuous across the Solent from Newtown and its fine harbour, and the whole shore eastwards to Gurnard and even West Cowes on the Isle of Wight. The three mile crossing was child's play to the smalltime smugglers of this side of the Island, for they could use their rowing-skiffs as tub-boats as if the island were a huge smuggling lugger anchored just off the coast of the mainland. Several hards along the Beaulieu River and most of the farms were involved in the traffic, but the famous Buckler's Hard was the smugglers' main goal. One of the cottages, now the Chapel in the village, was apparently the local headquarters for the Free Traders, where accounts were kept and settled, future ventures planned, and where busy Gentlemen rested in congenial surroundings and recovered from the effects of harsh winter weather. Not only the village inn, called the New Inn, but also the Master-builder's House and all the cottages were on the smugglers' list of deliveries. With their services so much in demand, and the ships which were built here so vital to the work of the Royal Navy, the contrabandists must have moved about the village with complete confidence. Shipwrights, carpenters, riggers and labourers all needed what they brought, and when a ship was to be launched the elaborate ceremonies and celebrations must have made even more business for them. One can imagine, especially on looking into the Master-builder's Office which is now so vividly re-reconstructed, Henry Adams, the Master-builder from 1749 to 1790, entertaining the local patriotic gentry and the Royal Naval Officers who had come to represent the Senior Service.

Right up the river to Beaulieu there are variously-named copses coming down to the water's edge, fine hiding-places for the smugglers' goods; and then comes Palace House, which in smuggling days was only sporadically occupied. This suited the Gentlemen of the Night very well, and they may have used it as a lookout over the surrounding countryside, for a staircase can still be seen going up through the heart of the house to the roof, just under which lay a secret chapel. When Palace House was occupied, the smugglers made sure that the unwelcome residents kept well within doors by increasing the moanings, eerie cries and monkish plainsong with which they were in the habit of frightening anyone who came too close to the great Abbey ruins. Rumour has it that there was a special brandy depôt in the cellars of the ruined Abbey where the fine cognac was rendered fit for English tastes. Not only did the Free Traders of Beaulieu use the monks' cellars but also their pilgrims' road, which struck out west across the New Forest for Ringwood and beyond, passing through such places as Pilley and Boldre.

The village of Beaulieu was one of the first along this coast to receive a small troop of Dragoons for billeting when the government finally got round to deploying them. Smuggling must have been extremely active here, even though it was well inland, thanks to the great facility of the Beaulieu River. Later, when smuggling had reached its peak, the newly-formed Coastguard high command also designated the village a hotbed of the Trade, for nine Officers were stationed on the west side of the river's mouth, and eight on the east, thereby effectively sealing one of the most used smugglers' entries into this country.

Immediately opposite the port of Cowes lies Stanswood Bay, possibly one of the busiest for smugglers in the whole of the British Isles. The smuggling ships must have come to it up the Solent from both east and west, as well as across the two and a half miles from Cowes itself, for William Arnold himself reported seeing them carrying contraband when he took up his appointment.

This whole corner of the Waterside, as it is known, was like a peninsula, cut off from the rest of the country, for no road was built down its length until 1924; and places like Hythe and Ashlett were supplied by water, so bad were the land communications. This made it ideal country for smuggling, the forces of the Crown being very unwilling to penetrate what was, in effect, a wilderness; their attitude to it was the same as that which they held towards the New Forest, of which this is the eastern flank. The sixteen miles from the shore of Stanswood Bay to the vast contraband markets in Southampton were nothing to the Free Traders, for they would have had the use of the teams and wagons from the many farms of the area; and even if they had used tub-carriers, it was but two of their normal stages.

A very wide shingle beach occupies most of the shore between Stone Point, just east of Lepe, and Calshot, and about halfway along its length is Bourne Gap, which, like its namesake, Bourne Bottom further west, was a favourite landing-place for the local smugglers. Very likely they knew that wherever there was a 'bourn' there would be a shallow valley cutting down to the beach up through which they could easily carry their contraband. The Bourne on Stanswood Bay had a wide inlet, and was quite a decent little harbour before it silted up and could no longer be used after 1703. Its marshy valley contained Little Stanswood Farm, a mill and a few cottages which must have been an important smuggling settlement, the miller being a vital distributor. There was a dump for contraband at the southern edge of Badminston Common, probably in a cave which has since collapsed, and no doubt Mopley Pond was also used when things got too hot and the Preventers were close on the smugglers' heels. In Sprat's Down Wood there were three smugglers' caves, one of which survives. The hamlet of Sprat's Down is even today called 'Lazy Town', a name which it gained in the smuggling age because the people there ran goods all night and slept all day, a phenomenon which was also noted by a visitor to Niton on the Isle of Wight. Once again, a glance at the map will show how hectic the smuggling trade must have been in this corner of the county with Southampton Water and the Solent giving smugglers two shores on which to receive goods.

Just to the north-west of the present Cadland Manor House is a group of cottages known as Nelson's Place. The story goes that Nelson himself once came ashore here to visit his old friend Mr. Drummond at the earlier Cadland Manor House, which then stood on the site of the Fawley oil refinery. The great sailor stopped for a warming drink, to get the Solent chill out of his bones, at the White Horse Inn, now two cottages, and ordered the finest French brandy. Of course, the landlord was easily able to supply this, as he was, together with Mr. Drummond of Cadland and the local farmers, a very good customer of the local smugglers. To commemorate this visit, the hamlet was dubbed Nelson's Place, and today the old inn bears the legend 'Nelson drank here', the sign erected by the present Mr. Drummond of the rebuilt Cadland Manor House.

A short distance to the east, in the corner of this remote part of Hampshire lie Eaglehurst and Luttrell's Tower. The height of the tower is 110 feet and it stands on a thirty-foot cliff, known as Eagle's Cliff. Its three storeys are served by a spiral staircase which goes right up to the roof with its distinctive battlements, from which the view is breathtaking, extending as it does over Southampton, Portsmouth, the Isle of Wight and the New Forest. St. Catherine's Chapel tower on top of its 773 foot hill at the southernmost tip of the Isle of Wight can easily be seen, as well as every other extremity of the island.

What a command-post, what a lookout, and what a signal-station this great folly would have made for a smuggler-chief of the high

6. Luttrell's Tower at Eaglehurst near Calshot, Hampshire.

Trade days of the eighteenth century! Although it may seem too ostentatious, it did indeed serve all three purposes for its designer and builder, Temple Simon Luttrell. The house behind is known as Eaglehurst, and looking at the two together one imagines that the Tower was built to provide the residents in the house with an eye-catching view, but this is not so. Although the date of construction is uncertain, Luttrell's Folly must have been built between 1730 and 1750.

The life of its builder is shrouded in mystery. Descended from a well-known Irish family, his date of birth is unknown, although it is said that he died in 1803 in a French prison. This fact links neatly with the strong tradition that Luttrell was a very special sort of smuggler who concentrated on the very finest French brandy, bringing it over through a highly-efficient organization of which his tower was the grand pivot, his main customers being the Royal family and the very highest members of English society.

Luttrell's death in a French jail is, perhaps, the most intriguing fact of the few which we have. Did he go over to the continent in order to select his wines and spirits personally, using a peerless sense of taste in order to please his highly-placed customers? Was he caught on one of these trips by the French, who had suddenly realized his emiment connections and background? Did they hold him as a *prominente* prisoner, to be used as a bargaining counter in the war with England? Or was he a government agent, a latter-day Sir Percy Blakeney getting enemies of Napoleon's régime out of the country of their birth along the secret pipeline of which the sea-smugglers were such an important part? We shall probably never know, but such lack of information makes him all the more fascinatingly romantic.

What is clear is that Luttrell's Tower was used as a prominent mark which helped ships, both innocent and smuggling, to navigate the Solent's difficult waters, and it showed the contrabandists where to make for the shore. Once they had come in, and landing was under way, they could be sure that the local lander, perhaps Luttrell himself, would soon get the goods hidden, for he had built a tunnel from the tower to beach on which the stuff was landed. The tower itself would have had a good large cellar; and there was further accommodation in the three caves at Sprat's Down Wood, which would have been well looked after by the men of 'Lazy Town', who were almost certainly Luttrell's smuggling fraternity. It is possible that the tower's cellar was also connected by tunnels to the Sprat's Down caves and others on Badminston Common. Once the coast and hinterland were clear, the contraband was taken on to such places as Southampton in hay-carts from the nearby farms, and so on to London.

Luttrell's Folly must have been rather like a marine control-tower, from the top of which Luttrell himself, or his deputy, watched for his smuggling ships and, by a system of well-devised signals, told them to come in to land or to hold off, as the proximity or distance of the King's forces dictated.

Luttrell must have had a very detailed signal-code, but on one occasion things went awry. One of the Riding Officers stationed at Calshot Castle somehow got into the tower and surrounded it with his men. He waited until night fell and a smuggling lugger was nosing its way in to Eaglehurst cliffs: then he sent the signal indicating that the coast was clear and all was safe for a landing. In came the ship, the landing-party made ready to bring the contraband ashore, and at that moment the King's Officer blew his whistle. His posse of men rushed out and ambushed a fine haul of both sea and land smugglers, as well as a good part of their cargo of fine brandy.

The Eaglehurst estate was later bought by the Earl of Cavan, who had been a General in the Peninsular Wars under Wellington, his appointment being that of second-in-command to Sir Ralph Abercrombie, Tom Johnstone's commander. Cavan bought the estate in order to build his home on it; and, like William Stuart Rose, the

Christchurch Member of Parliament, he was influenced by the tents he had lived in while on campaign in the Iberian Peninsula. When he designed his future home, he decided on the form of a military tented encampment, with not one, but several, tent-like buildings to make up the whole house. As a result Eaglehurst House seems to have the General's tent as its central block, and the tents of his subordinate staff-officers flanking it to form of the rest of this strange and fascinating building. But unique as Eaglehurst House undoubtedly is, it does not surpass the great Tower of Temple Simon Luttrell.

5
Hurst Castle, Milford and Mudeford

Hurst Castle, at the end of the shingle spit known as Hurst Beach, became a smugglers' nest very early in the game. Unlike Sandown Fort on the Isle of Wight which William Arnold found quite competent to keep Sandown Bay free of smugglers, he was less happy about Hurst: in one of his many letters he stated clearly that it was notorious as a favourite resort of smugglers from the Isle of Wight. There was in fact a Preventive Station at Hurst from quite early on, but this, along with the other evidence, indicates that the government's forces at Hurst were in league with the smugglers throughout the whole of its history.

Of course, it is remote: even today one reaches it with some difficulty, by boat from Keyhaven or by hard trudge along the pebbles of Hurst Beach. Its strategic importance is obvious: it sealed off the mouth of the Solent, for its guns could control the open water, less than a mile across to its opposite numbers on the Island, Yarmouth Castle and Sconce Point, a sconce being an earthwork for cannon. Built during King Henry VIII's programme of fortress-building using stones of Beaulieu Abbey, Hurst was completed in 1544. It was immensely strong, with a central twelve-sided tower which was enclosed by a curtain wall on which were placed three semi-circular bastions. Like most coastal defences, it was neglected in the reign of Queen Elizabeth I, but in 1608 it was surveyed, as were many of the other forts along the coasts, and extensive repairs were undertaken. In 1635, as if in preparation for the fast-approaching Civil Wars, the brass cannon were at last replaced by iron guns.

Under the command of the government of Cromwell, King Charles I was lodged at Hurst on his way from Carisbroke Castle on the Isle of Wight to London, where he stood trial and faced eventual execution. When informed that he was being taken to Hurst Castle, King Charles's reply was: 'Indeed, you could not have named a worse place!' His fears were given more substance when he was greeted at the castle gate by the Captain of Hurst, a huge, forbidding, black-bearded fellow, who frowned horribly upon him as he fingered his basket-hilted sword. King Charles was convinced that his enemies meant to do away with him in Hurst, its position and remoteness admirably suiting it for grim deeds. The same qualities suited smuggling, too: apparently actually standing in the waters of the Solent themselves, the smugglers' lookouts on the castle's upper platform could see any enemies approaching, whether Revenue men, Dragoons, Coastguards or King's ships, and take the appropriate steps to meet them.

King Charles spent three very uncomfortable weeks at Hurst, walking daily upon the beach or the roof for exercise, and watching the Parliamentary Squadron patrolling offshore on the watch for any rescue-attempt by sea from Ireland, France, or Holland. When his son became King Charles II with the Restoration of 1660, he wanted Hurst Castle to be dismantled, no doubt remembering what his father had suffered there. But his advisers persuaded him against the idea, and by 1675 it was restored to full garrison and armament, in which state it remained until well after the Second World War.

It may have been a lonely posting for soldiers, but they could not have lacked for comforts and luxuries of the more internal kind, for clearly they worked very well in a business partnership with the smugglers. As early as 1682 Customs Officers were being refused permission by the garrison to enter, let alone search, the castle after they had been told it was a smugglers' centre. In 1700 Hurst was chosen by the government as the prison for anyone convicted under the Act for the Further Preventing of the Growth of Popery, and in that year a priest named Father Atkinson was brought to the castle, and remained a prisoner there, perhaps the only one, until his death thirty years later. Inside the castle can still be seen the stone slab which Father Atkinson used as a bed, and on which, so it is said, he slept with nothing more than a blanket under him. There have inevitably been reports of hauntings by Father Atkinson's ghost.

William Arnold's concern about Hurst was heightened when one of his captains returned with a captured smugglers' ship to tell his Collector that Hurst Castle was definitely being used by the notorious John Streeter, one of the leading figures in the infamous Battle of Mudeford of 1784. Arnold had proof that small smuggling craft from Christchurch and Mudeford regularly gathered at Hurst, under the protection of the castle's guns, either for the collection of contraband stored there, or to form convoys escorted by the big armed luggers bound across the Channel. So it could well have been that Streeter had the Captain of Hurst under his thumb as well as much of this part of the smuggling coast.

However, as the Napoleonic wars reached their height, in 1803 full-scale preparations were made to receive and repel invasion forces. These included the strengthening of Hurst Castle and its garrison. It was the chance for the government, the Customs Board and the armed forces to clear out the rats' nest of smugglers once and for all, and we hear nothing more of the castle's use by them.

7. Milford Church, with its typically squat tower, much favoured as a lookout and contraband-hide in both Hampshire and Dorset.

Westward along the coast lie Milford and Milford-on-sea. Here was another very popular landing-place, the first on this stretch of open beaches with cliffs behind, but out of range of friendly forts such as Hurst Castle. Milford 'bunny', the ravine running up through the low cliffs, is no more than a steep-sided lane, but its luxuriant trees must have made it a very convenient smugglers' path, especially as it leads straight up to the All Saints Church, with its squat tower, very like that of Kinson, 'the smugglers' church'. The high lancet windows at the very top of the tower may well have had a lantern placed in them for seaward signalling, though the manor-house would seem a more convenient lookout, as it is partly between the church and the sea. Milford must have been pretty active with the contraband trade, for a

Riding Officer, under the Chief at Christchurch, actually lived here to keep an eye on the place. It was a dangerous posting, as Mr. Bursey, one of the Riding Officers of Milford, found out on the night on which he was roused by a loud knock on his door. He looked out of his cottage window and saw two men, who told him that a large cache of contraband had just been discovered in a barn not far from the village. They said they would lead him to it if he gave them ten pounds there and then. Bursey smelled a rat immediately, for it was common knowledge that informers were always given half the value of any contraband they reported, by law. One can only assume that he knew the men enough to trust them, for he opened his front door and, without having armed himself, stepped outside to join them.

The next morning he was found by his wife lying across the threshold dead as the result of many terrible injuries to his head. It is a mystery why the smugglers did this to him but one explanation may be that the local smugglers blamed him for bringing about the Battle of Milford Green in 1786 by setting up an ambush or summoning the military. The details are completely unknown, but there is no doubt that a large gang of smugglers was set upon by a force of Revenue Officers and the Lancashire Militia, which was stationed at Lymington, and that in the pitched battle which followed many casualties were sustained on both sides. It seems to be one of those incidents which was hushed up by the local people because they were ashamed that it had happened in their locality at all. A point it does illustrate, however, is the use of military units from far distant parts of the country so that there would be no fear of local connections and sympathies preventing the soldiers doing their duty when ordered in pursuit of the smugglers.

The next 'bunny' or ravine along the coast is that of Becton, slanting in an unusual north-westerly direction as it cuts up into what is now Barton Golf Course and Barton Common. Once there was a large manor house here, but it was burnt to the ground in about 1750 in a conflagration which is said to have been started in the cellars by a spark from a careless smuggler's pipe falling into a newly-broached brandy-keg.

When the planners moved Dorset's county boundary to the east to take in not only Bournemouth but also Christchurch, they little knew that they were choosing a famous smuggler's path as their line of demarcation. Chewton is the next Bunny, cut through the gradually rising cliffs by the little Walkford Brook along which the county boundary runs as far as the railway-line. Its depth, its luxurious trees and bushes, and the distance it penetrates inland made it one of the finest smugglers' tracks along this part of the coast.

On the right side of the Bunny just after its mouth is Naish Farm, now a holiday caravan park. From the old farmhouse the smugglers had clear views of the Solent, the Isle of Wight, Christchurch Bay and beyond, so like Hurst Castle, nothing could approach them without their being aware of the threat well in advance; and they must have used it as a signal-station, as they did all of their best lookouts. The farm still has a tunnel connecting it with Chewton Bunny itself, which must have been very useful for smugglers coming up from the beach to dump their goods immediately on landing, when they knew the Revenue men were liable to be at the farm; and equally useful to the farming-smugglers who were surprised by a dawn raid by the 'Shingle-pickers' who wanted to search for contraband because they knew a run had been made. Naish Farm must have been high on the standard list of 'suspected places', a phrase often used in Riding Officers' journals.

Chewton Bunny becomes Chewton Glen after it passes under the present Christchurch Road: this may have been a Victorian device to tidy up the coarse local name to something more pleasing to the refined ears of the local gentry, both resident and visiting on holiday. This would have been judged necessary when the house now known as the Chewton Glen Hotel was let out to such distinguished Victorians as Captain Frederick Marryat, who, about a hundred years ago, came here and wrote his most famous novel: *The Children of the New Forest*. Born in 1792, he entered the Royal Navy as Midshipman and saw service throughout the Napoleonic Wars, rising to the rank of captain and receiving the Legion of Honour from the King of the French. He retired from the Navy in 1830 and began a career as a novelist, soon making his name with sea-yarns such as *Masterman Ready* and *Mr. Midshipman Easy*. A third novel, *The Three Midshipmen*, describes life in a Royal Navy cutter engaged in the war against the smugglers along this coast, and for this he drew on his own experiences of the winter of 1821, when he assisted the local Revenue cutters in his own ship, H.M.S. *Rosario*. In 1822 he wrote a long letter to the First Lord of the Admiralty recommending several improvements in the government's methods of combatting smuggling.

He came to Chewton Glen in 1847 and he must have been very interested in the smugglers' convoys which passed through the Bunny-Glen right under the windows of his house, even though the Trade must have been falling off somewhat at this stage.

The Walkford Brook, which was responsible for cutting out Chewton Bunny, extends well into the New Forest, and the smugglers must have led their pack-ponies along the stream's bed, an excellent long-distance smuggling path, well sheltered from weather and spying eyes by the overhanging trees. One of their main goals was Wootton, where in a forest cottage lived four ladies whose speciality was storing smuggled silks and laces. They probably unpacked them there and prepared them for the next stage of their journey to the shops in the neighbourhood. It may have been that certain dumps specialized in particular commodities, so that when a smuggler was given a particular article on the beach and told to take it along a certain route, he knew exactly where he was to drop it off.

One night Customs Officers knocked at the ladies' door searching for contraband just landed by the smugglers at Chewton Bunny. The ladies let them in and the whole cottage was meticulously searched, but nothing illegal was found. When the Officers had left, the ladies were able to undress themselves and unwrap the lengths of silk and pieces of fine lace with which they had swaddled themselves directly they had received warning of the Officers' approach through the smugglers' network.

Even the beach itself at Chewton Bunny favoured the smugglers, for as the waters of the Walkford Brook seeped down, they formed deadly quicksands from the foot of the cliffs to the sea's edge and only those who knew the beach very well indeed would dare use it at night. Local landers were therefore protected from sudden attacks no matter from which quarter they came.

The nearest inn to Chewton Bunny in smuggling days would have been the Cat and Fiddle Inn at Hinton Admiral, now on the A35 road, and the successive landlords must have thanked Providence often for their proximity to that wonderful landing-place. It is only just over a mile and a half as the crow flies from the inn, and just a little more along the route taken by a tubman carrying brandy and gin. He would have come a short way up the Bunny and then have turned left on to one of the many paths across Chewton Common. Several of these exist today, and where residents' dogs are walked in the twilight now, the Free Traders would have tramped 200 years ago on their way to the ancient Cat and Fiddle which was not only their first paying customer, but one of their most important dumps, situated as it is on the very edge of the New Forest.

Friar's Cliff and Highcliffe have always been what the second name suggests: cliffs too high to scale easily and with no convenient bunnies, chines or combes. Here Lord Bute's huge house must have taken much of the smugglers' contraband; and the beach below it was the scene of one of the strangest smuggling stories ever told. Richard Newman was one of the assistant Riding Officers of Customs at the turn of the last century, a valued lieutenant of Abraham Pike, the Chief Riding Officer of Christchurch. In the year 1799, Mr. Newman, an extremely keen and zealous Officer, was struck by an idea for catching smugglers red-handed which was no less brilliant than it was unusual. He had been much exercised in his mind by the way the smugglers could never be caught in the actual act of landing their illicit cargoes, the stage in the operations at which the Customs men always tried to take them, for then the guilt of the Free Traders could be proved beyond all possible doubt in court.

Determined to capture some smugglers at work or perish in the attempt, Mr. Newman took several Customs Officers and ordered them to dig themselves slit-trenches just above the tide-line, well spaced out, from which each occupant could watch the sea. These 'graves', as the men immediately dubbed them, were dug from Chewton Bunny to Mudeford, so that the entire sweep of this part of Christchurch Bay could be kept under the closest possible watch. Each man was fully armed with cutlass, pistol and the all-important musket, exactly the same weapons later given to the Coastguards when their Service came into being several years later, for Newman had ambush in mind, not merely passive observation. When each Officer was safely in his 'grave', Newman went along the length of the beach carefully covering each with a layer of sand and arranging a rather charming mask and headdress of seaweed for each of his long-suffering colleagues.

For many nights the Preventive Officers lay entombed under the orders of their unorthodox superior, and there is little doubt that Mr. Newman was there with them in his own strategically placed pit, obeying the first principle for a good commanding-officer in not asking his men to do anything that he himself is not willing to do also. It is significant that he died at a prematurely early age from illness contracted from exposure while pursuing his duty in the foulest of weathers.

At last it happened: a lugger nosed cautiously into the bay, and the delighted Mr. Newman knew that it had all been worthwhile. He was slightly anxious that no land-smugglers were on the beach to welcome their sea-going mates, suspecting that they had had wind of what the Revenue men were doing on the beach every night; but the ship came on and soon the crew had stacked their own cargo of brandy-kegs neatly on the beach, having decided that they could not afford to wait for their longshore brothers. The sea-borne Free Traders then rowed smartly back to their lugger, set sail and were soon well out of Christchurch Bay.

Newman must have been sorely tempted to give the signal to attack to his hidden henchmen, but it was the local land-based smugglers he was after, so he held his hand. He had not long to wait: a short while later the local lander appeared with his gang. Newman let them start on the job, and then, rising majestically to his sodden, freezing feet, he literally blew the whistle on them. His men also rose stiffly to their icy feet and gave the smugglers the fright of their lives. The entire gang fled from the beach leaving the tubs in their haste.

It was a seizure of goods rather than an arrest of red-handed smugglers, so Mr. Newman cannot have felt too pleased. However, he must have consoled himself with the contraband he had caught, and the next day he had the kegs loaded on wagons from Christchurch and sent off to be lodged in His Majesty's Warehouse in the Customs House at Poole. He must have been a little light-headed through the endless nights of waiting and watching, because he sent no more escort with the valuable consignment than the two grooms from the inn which had supplied the wagons.

Off went the convoy, into Christchurch, through the town, across the River Stour at Iford, and then out on to the Great Heath where Bournemouth now stands. It was a very hot day, and when the wagoners stopped for the midday break they decided that His Majesty's Board of Customs would not mind if they refreshed themselves with a little sample of what was in the barrels. They discovered that it was a very fine French brandy, and the more they had, the more they wanted. They ate as they drank, and then they set off reluctantly on the last leg of the journey to Poole. It was not long before they were sleeping soundly, the reins slack in their hands, and the horses going it alone.

Fortunately the horses knew the road very well, but rather than face the long pull up the hill to the heights above Poole, they decided that, what with the heat and the flies, they had had enough for one hot summer's day. Cool stables back in Christchurch called, so they turned off the main road, into a side track which led eventually back onto that same main road. A few hours later they arrived back home, the brandy safe and the wagoners sound asleep.

What Mr. Newman said on hearing of this is not recorded, neither is the reaction of his master, the Chief Riding Officer of Customs in Christchurch, but they could draw some comfort from the fact that the brandy cargo was intact, or at least almost so.

Along the beach just before Mudeford the roofs of two strangely-shaped houses can be glimpsed. The circular roof belongs to 'Gundimore', a weird residence built by William Stuart Rose, Member of Parliament for Christchurch in the 1790s. He was a poet and traveller who had fallen in love with Persian tents, and he called this permanent version of his beloved shelter after a poem full of Eastern romance which he himself had written. Friend of poets and novelists, he would have received brandy, gin and tea delivered straight to his door by smugglers without even having to leave the beach, for in those days there was no promenade. In the same way the fishermen-smugglers of Mudeford would have not had far to come to deliver the finest Christchurch salmon immediately after netting.

Sir Walter Scott came here for a holiday in 1807 and wrote a great deal of his famous poem *Marmion*, dedicating it to Lord Montagu, but prefacing it with a verse-letter to his host in which he praised his poem *Gundimore*, just as he must have commended the strange house of the same name where he had spent so many happy and productive hours.

A year after Waterloo, Coleridge, writer of such famous poems as *The Ancient Mariner*, gratefully accepted Rose's invitation to a holiday at Gundimore. No doubt Rose plied his tormented guest with plenty of contraband gin and brandy in an effort to persuade him that they were less harmful than opium. Perhaps Coleridge himself asked the smugglers who dealt with the East India trading ships, whether they could find him any opium: we do not know for sure.

Robert Southey came over frequently to Gundimore from his cottage in nearby Burton, and the talk of poetry would have lasted far into the night as they looked out of the French windows across the placid waters of the Solent to the lovely vision of the Isle of Wight; and it is even possible that Louis Phillipe, the exiled King of the French, the guest of Gustavus Brander at Priory House, Christchurch, was entertained by the hospitable Mr Rose, with the help of the goods supplied by his smuggling friends of Mudeford.

Further along the promenade at Mudeford Quay car-park is the site of the bloody Battle of Mudeford which took place in 1784, for the beach that preceded the car park was an ideal landing-spot.

In July 1784, the sloop-of-war H.M.S. *Orestes* had taken up station in Studland Bay, mainly as a result of William Arnold's many requests to the Board of Customs. On 14th July she was cruising off Yarmouth, Isle of Wight, on watch for smugglers' ships, when a cutter approached which informed her captain that two smuggling luggers, commanded by William May and William Parrott, were due off the mouth of Christchurch Harbour at Mudeford, and that they were loaded with a huge double cargo of tea and brandy bought in the Channel Islands. By the time *Orestes* had arrived off Beerpan Rocks at Hengistbury Head, with her escort of two Revenue cutters, it was six in the morning and the luggers were already anchored a few yards out from the beach.

Through his telescope, the commander of *Orestes*, Captain Ellis, R.N., could see the smugglers ferrying in casks and packets by rowing-boat from Mudeford, and that, as far as he could judge, about 300 people, ships' crews and residents from Mudeford, Stanpit and even Christchurch itself, were as busy as ants helping to bring on shore the huge illicit cargo and load it into well over fifty wagons drawn by nearly 300 horses.

8. The Site of the Battle of Mudeford 1784.

On seeing the little flotilla of King's ships bearing towards the beach, the smugglers on board the luggers ran their ships as far up the shingle as they could and then started stripping them of sails, spars and all other portable equipment. Captain Ellis snapped his telescope shut and immediately ordered away a cutting-out expedition in six ships' boats with fully armed crews. He was determined to destroy the smugglers' luggers even if it was too late to seize their cargo, for the wagons were now moving off. In command of the cutting-out operation was the sailing-master of *Orestes*, William Allen.

As his six boats rowed up to the sterns of the luggers, Mr. Allen stood up in the sternsheets and loudly called on the smugglers still on board to surrender in the name of the King. It was a brave action, but at the same time foolhardy, for the smugglers' reaction was predictable: a tremendous volley of small-arms fire came from the ships, the beach, and from a breastwork the smugglers had scraped up in the sand-dunes for just such a purpose.

Nothing daunted, the King's men came on in, beached their boats, and flinging themselves into cover, immediately returned the enemy's fire. Seeing them land, the smugglers withdrew to the Haven House Inn and its stables, from the windows and doors of which they kept a constant and well-directed fire. Meanwhile, the King's men were boarding the luggers, making sure they had no more smugglers aboard, and making them their own.

When they had done this, they were able to count the cost, and it was high: many sailors had suffered wounds, and, worst of all, Mr. Allen himself, a young man of only twenty-five, had been mortally struck. His first wound had been from a musket-ball in the thigh, but a second had pierced his right side, gone through his liver, and then penetrated his stomach.

When Captain Ellis saw his cutting-out expedition held down by the smugglers' small-arms fire, he decided it was time to use his large arms. Balls from his cannon hit the tower of the Priory Church at Christchurch, so it was said, and a chain-shot wrapped itself round one of the tall chimneys of the Haven House Inn, afterwards kept for a while as a relic by the landlord.

The Battle of Mudeford is supposed to have lasted, on and off, from six o'clock until nine o'clock at night. The smugglers fought ferociously, doing their traditional job of keeping off the King's men while the contraband was removed. During the latter part of the eighteenth century, smugglers almost always fought like tigers when cornered, but there may have been a legal reason for their resistance on this occasion. It is possible that they had heard that an Act of Oblivion was about to be passed which would pardon them and forget their past misdeeds, but such an Act was merely a prelude to a much stronger Act for the Prevention of Smuggling. It seems a rather unlikely thesis: far more likely is the fact that they fought long and fiercely because they were hard men and positively resented the rather unsporting manner in which the Revenue Service and the Royal Navy had joined forces, working with an unusual harmony which boded ill for them. It should also be remembered that the double cargo they had saved from the King's men was enormous: 120,000 gallons of spirits and between thirty and forty tons of tea!

All the Customs and Naval forces took away were the two luggers and their boats, many wounded sailors, and the corpse of William Allen. He was buried at Cowes with full Naval honours, the escort being the ship's company of all the king's vessels in the engagement, the Officers acting as pall-bearers, and the cortège being led by *Orestes'* marines, marching with arms reversed. Many people at the funeral wept openly, for William Allen had been a fine officer, loved and respected by all who knew him.

9. Cutters in action: smugglers chased by the Revenue men. From a line engraving c.1785.

At the inquest a verdict was brought in of 'Wilful murder against a person or persons unknown, but that William May and William Parrott, the two reputed masters of the smuggling vessels, were aiding, abetting, assisting and comforting the said murderer or murderers'. The hunt for the killers was on, and at the end of the month a notice appeared in the *Salisbury Journal* offering the very large reward of £200 for information leading to their arrest. In February of the following year Henry Voss, George Coombes and Jonathan Edwards were charged at Winchester Assizes with being implicated in the murder, but as William Allen had died actually *on* the tide-line, the trial would have to take place in the High Court of Admiralty in London.

The two captains, May and Parrott, were also implicated but they escaped the long arm of the law. The evidence for the prosecution showed how Parrott had fired a musket or blunderbuss from the inn at the Officers' boats and that May had done the same, but it could not be *proved* whether he had fired before or after the King's men had fired at him. The evidence showed that the smugglers had a whole arsenal of weapons, and that they must have had free run of the inn, for they fired from bedroom windows as well as downstairs windows and doors.

The upshot of the trial was that Voss and Edwards were acquitted of both felony and murder, but Coombes was convicted on both counts. His jailers were ordered 'to convey under safe custody the said George Coombes unto the gallows set and placed in the public stream in the River of Thames within the flush of the sea and water and jurisdiction of our Admiralty before the bank called Wapping on Monday the 23rd day of January. The said George Coombes, at the influx of the sea and water, there you are to hang by the neck until he shall be dead according to the maritime customs observed ..... And that you are immediately after the execution to take the body of the said George Coombes to be hung in chains at some conspicuous place on the coast of Kent or Essex.... Given under the Great Seal of the High Court of Admiralty.' The Court also gave orders that the body was to be dissected and anatomized.

So on the morning of his execution George Coombes was led out from Newgate Gaol by the Admiralty's Officers, the leader of whom carried their unique mace which was in the form of a silver oar. Coombes' behaviour was exemplary, and after he was dead the orders were changed. His body was brought back to Mudeford and hung in an iron cage from a gibbet on Haven Point, because the crime for which he had died had been committed in that place.

But he did not hang there long: his smuggling mates cut him down and he was given secret Christian burial by a sympathetic parson. The Battle of Mudeford had resulted in death and a huge cargo lost to the Revenue forces, but only one smuggler paid the price: the others implicated had melted away into the mists of Christchurch Harbour. It may well be asked: if George Coombes had been tried at Christchurch or even Winchester, would he have been found guilty, or would he have been acquitted by a jury sympathetic to the smugglers' cause, as so many were along this southern coast?

There is another interesting question to be raised over the Battle of Mudeford. Where were the Christchurch Riding Officers of Customs? The Supervisor of Riding Officers at Christchurch in the year 1784 was Joshua Jeans, a native son of a Customs Officer who became Mayor four times. In spite of this background, on reading the full report of the battle, the Commissioners in London decided that Jeans might well be implicated in some way, so they sent a Mr. Monday, a Customs General Surveyor, or Inspector, to look into the matter.

His report, completed in May of 1786, revealed that Jeans had on several occasions before July, 1784, failed to support and assist his subordinate Riding Officers, and had actively discouraged them from doing what they saw to be their duty on a number of other occasions, even after the Collector of Cowes and the Customer of Lymington, superior Officers to both themselves and Jeans, had strictly ordered them to attend more thoroughly to their duty. Just before the Battle of Mudeford these keen and conscientious junior Riding Officers had actually seen the smugglers' wagons being driven through the town of Christchurch and out to Mudeford, obviously for the purpose of meeting a huge consignment of contraband expected on the coast. They had told their Supervisor, Jeans, of their suspicions, and had asked him what steps he thought they should take to counter the threat on their strip of the coast. Jeans replied that he thought they ought to go home to bed, for that was what he was going to do.

As he delved deeper into Jeans' past doings, Mr. Monday found that he had actually been *forbidding* his Officers to enter in their official Journals the names and descriptions of smuggling vessels which they had seen. He had, Monday discovered, laid a particularly strong embargo on any reference being made to what had happened on that day in July when Mr. Allen had been killed. He had, moreover, gone so far as to order them to keep away from Mudeford, and to take no notice of what went on there if they heard anything 'for the Service'.

Directly the Commissioners had read Mr. Monday's report, Joshua Jeans was dismissed from his post at Christchurch and drummed out of the Customs Service altogether. But worse followed: even his zealous junior Officers, Newsam, Reeks and Bursey, had been bribed immediately after the Battle of Mudeford with a hundred kegs of brandy to let a part of the double cargo pass them as the smugglers took it into the New Forest. Bursey was dismissed the Service like his chief, but the charge of collusion with the smugglers, though proved against him, could not be substantiated in the cases of Newsam and Reeks. However, they remained under strong suspicion, and were told by the Commissioners that they would have to pay the strictest attention to their duties, making sure that their conduct was above reproach if this business was to be overlooked.

Across the Run, where the waters of the Rivers Stour and Avon debouch from Christchurch Harbour into the sea, opposite the Haven House Hotel, stands the Black House, on Gervis Point. Today it contains flats for holiday makers, but its squat, dark and ugly appearance is a constant reminder of its unpleasant past. No one knows for certain when it was built: perhaps at the same time as the inn opposite, or possibly by Dutch settlers who came to Mudeford in the sixteenth century. Its ground floor was formerly one great room, used in the past both as a boat-building shed and sail-loft. There is a strong tradition that during the Napoleonic wars the infamous guinea-boats were constructed here; and another that it owes its depressing black colour and name to the fire one day lit by Revenue men to smoke smugglers or guinea-boat builders out into the open to be arrested.

When the Battle of Mudeford took place, the inn was run by Mrs. Hannah Siller, who took over from her husband on his death in 1780. She came from an old innkeeping family: her grandfather had kept the Lamb at Holfleet near Winkton, on the road from Christchurch to Bransgore, and he had also owned Holfleet Farm. Hannah's Aunt Mary had married William Mist, one of the Officers of Excise at Wareham.

Hannah was apparently a fine girl, handsome of feature and with a crowning glory of raven black hair which was the envy of other girls for miles around. She married John Siller, landlord of the Haven House Inn, at Christchurch Priory. The ceremony was probably attended by several smugglers, including her brother, Tom, a smuggler from Canford from whose house twenty-six gallons of brandy and twenty-six of rum had recently been seized.

After her widowing, and when the Battle of Mudeford was some months past, Hannah moved to the Ship in Distress in Stanpit, between Mudeford and Purewell. On the large-scale Ordnance Survey map her name is immortalized in the name 'Mother Siller's Channel' running between Grimbury Marsh and Pound Hill, and from the head of this waterway a path leads up to the Ship in Distress through Stanpit Marsh, now a famous nature reserve. It was not long after her tenancy began that she became known as "the protecting angel of all smugglers", a title to which she could well have laid claim when she was at the Haven House Inn. John Streeter, one of the leading figures in the Battle of Mudeford, had ridden up to her door and ordered all her patrons down to the beach to assist the crews of the two luggers to clear them of all sails and equipment, which she then allowed to be stored in her outhouses. Not surprisingly, she was a witness at the trial which followed the Battle.

In the 'Golden Age' of smuggling, before the Coastguard was formed and took its grip on the Harbour entrance at Mudeford, cargoes were brought straight in through the Run, across the harbour and up through Mother Siller's Channel by day or night. It was relatively simple to keep the Revenue men away from either side of the Run, and once in the harbour the smugglers were safe, so long as they were not going on up to the actual quay. When a consignment reached her inn, Hannah Siller bought what she needed and served the smugglers with what they needed, and then they would go on inland along the network of routes. One of the inns they called at next would have been the ancient Fisherman's Haunt at Winkton; then the Lamb at Holfleet, no doubt still in the hands of Hannah's own family; then, following the road into Bransgore, which in those days was still within the confines of the New Forest, they would reach the Three Tuns. From there the Free Traders would go up Thorney Hill and into the Forest fastness of Burley, where they would call at the Queen's Head.

Widow Siller fell in love with Billy Coombs, one of her patrons at the Ship in Distress. Billy was the Captain of the *John and Susannah*, a swift smuggling lugger of 100 tons, well armed with fourteen cannon, which was often used as a privateer. As he left on yet another smuggling run, he won from Hannah her declaration of love for him; he promised her that when he returned they would be married, he would give up smuggling and privateering, and he would become landlord of the Ship in Distress. As a pledge of good will, he left with her a packet of his personal papers.

Unfortunately, the widow's curiosity got the better of her one night after he had been away some time, and she went through his documents. There, among the promissory-notes and bills, she found a love-letter sent to Billy by a young lady of Hamble, another nest of smugglers, and Billy's home-port. The girl looked forward to his return there, especially as he had promised to marry her on that happy occasion, after which he would settle down and lead a sober life.

Not unnaturally, Hannah Siller became distraught when she read this, and decided to inform on Billy Coombs to the Preventers, letting them know when and where he was expected to return. When Captain Coombs sailed blithely into Christchurch Bay he found the *Osprey* waiting for him. Very soon the two ships were exchanging broadsides in a duel which lasted three hours, but in the end the *John and Susannah* was battered and dismasted, and someone on board hauled down the colours in token of surrender. Unfortunately, this was done without Billy's orders, and his men continued firing for some time afterwards. This was considered such a serious breach of the rules of battle, that when he and his crew were all under lock and key, he was brought to trial and the death penalty was passed upon him. He was hanged, in fact, at Stoney Pointe, Lepe, just across Southampton Water from his home in Hamble.

John Streeter was another notorious smuggler involved in the Battle of Mudeford. Streeter married Rose Button, a local girl, at Christchurch Priory in the year 1773, settled down and worked hard, and by 1779, at the age of 29, was the proud owner of a fine ship, named the *Phoenix*, which he used for the purpose of smuggling.

One day he came in to Christchurch Quay with a cargo of grain from further along the coast, and was just tying up when the Revenue 'rummage-crew' descended on his ship, giving her a thorough search. Streeter showed great surprise when the Officers found little barrels of brandy, rum and gin hidden under the grain, and stoutly asserted that the staff of the granary must have put them there, knowing he was sailing to an acknowledged smuggling-port. He claimed to know nothing whatever about the lower part of his cargo, being an honest coasting merchant. The Customs men seized both cargo and boat, and, in order to get his vessel back, Streeter eventually admitted his guilt and was fined. But they kept the *Phoenix*, in spite of his vigorous attempts to sue the men who had 'rummaged' him.

John Streeter's enforced change of occupation from smuggler to landsman led him into a very profitable offshoot of smuggling, the tobacco trade. By 1784 he had become the owner of a tobacco and snuff manufactory in Stanpit near Christchurch, next to the Ship in Distress. It was an ideal situation, for his supplies of highly-compressed tobacco from the great cross-Channel warehouses could be brought by the same smugglers who supplied Hannah Sillers and used her Channel.

However, the Revenue 'Landsharks' would not let him alone: they were convinced he was carrying on a fraudulent trade of some sort. He had set up the manufactory legally enough, buying several hogsheads of tobacco in London, using the proper certificates. But that was as far as Streeter's legality went: all succeeding consignments of the weed were brought to the back door by old mates in the Trade. Streeter dampened it and parcelled it up in the manufactory, ready for shipping all over the country, very probably using the stage-coaches carrying the Royal Mails which passed through Christchurch, where they halted at the Old George Inn in Castle Street. This late development in the transport of contraband was particularly useful to the smugglers, for the mail-coaches carried their own armed guards, as well as all the protection that their prestige implied. So successful were Streeter and the other illicit tobacconists in the area that the legitimate sellers of snuff and plug complained to the authorities that their sales had diminished to practically nothing. Desultory efforts were made to catch Streeter and the others out, but it was not until 1786 that he was at last arrested for his part in the Battle of Mudeford, tried, sentenced and lodged in Winchester Jail. They could not keep a man like Streeter down for long: he escaped, most probably sprung by some of his many friends in the game, and spent the rest of his life as an outlaw, living principally in Guernsey, but returning to his old haunts round Christchurch, once disguised as a woman when he was in imminent danger of being spotted. He had left his wife in his house at Stanpit, and the tobacco and snuff manufactory still functioned, presumably under her direction, but with intervals of inactivity when the authorities grew too interested. He probably looked after purchases of tobacco in the Channel Islands so it is not surprising that he returned from time to time when the coast was clear; it is more surprising that he not only managed to father several children but had them christened in the Priory Church of Christchurch. We do not know whether he appeared on these occasions in his rightful place as father, but clearly the Vicar of Christchurch winked an eye at the business.

Perhaps the strangest part of this little story is its ending: John Streeter eventually bought another house in Stanpit and lived there quietly and apparently unmolested by the authorities until his death in 1824 at the age of 74. Just how he managed this is not known: perhaps he performed some signal service to the state during the wars against the French, or perhaps he had disguised himself sufficiently well to fool the Revenue men, or possibly they had lost all interest in him by that time. What is certain is that snuff-boxes, if not the snuff to go in them, continued to be made in Stanpit for many years after his death.

6
Christchurch: Portrait of a Smuggling Town

There was a port at Hengistbury Head in Neolithic times, which continued in business right up to the rule of the Saxon kings, during which time Christchurch was established. Built at the confluence of two great rivers, the Dorset Stour and the Hampshire Avon, the tongue of land between the two streams was called in Anglo-Saxon '*Tweox thaem eam*', meaning 'between the waters', which became corrupted to Twynham. At first, the rivers carried invaders' war-ships, later traders' vessels, well inland; and later still roads were built in their valleys. Even from early days Christchurch was known as the Port of Wiltshire.

Debouching into Christchurch Bay through the narrow gullet now known as the Run, Christchurch Harbour has many times been seen as having greater commercial and military potential than the townspeople really desired. For instance, in 1762 the Government, needing yet another port on the south coast capable of taking large merchant-ships as well as vessels of the Royal Navy, commissioned John Smeaton, the well-known builder of the third and most successful of the Eddystone Lighthouses, to prepare a plan for the improvement of Christchurch Harbour. He was asked to pay particular attention to the deepening and widening of its exit and solving the problems presented by the constantly shifting sandbars.

Smeaton's report disappointed the Government, for he began: 'I cannot flatter the inhabitants ever to expect a harbour at Christ-church of any great depth or capacity....' However the 'inhabitants' had neither the need nor the desire for a deep-water port, because, by this date, they had established an industry which enjoyed the finest facilities along the south coast, and that was smuggling. They wanted no meddling Government dredging their harbour and straightening its entrance so that Revenue cutters or Royal Navy sloops could pursue their swift-sailing luggers and fast galleys into their own private haven, boats which had been specially designed for these waters.

The fact is that there can have been few other ports in the country so suitable for smuggling in the period from about 1700 to around 1840. As well as the river routes, Christchurch is flanked by fine, sandy, gently-shelving beaches, almost totally free of rocks. There is the New Forest to the north-east, and Cranborne Chase to the north-west, great wooded fastnesses in which the fleeing smugglers were safe from pursuit, able to sell their contraband goods in peace. Along the coast to the west stretched the 'Great Heath', wild 'tawny ground', barren and desolate, criss-crossed with tracks, pitted with holes and ponds, difficult ground over which to pursue the Gentlemen of the Night as they hurried their newly-landed cargoes away from the beaches. Through these three tracts of land, the smugglers passed along routes leading to great markets in Winchester, and so to London; to Salisbury, Bath, and even Bristol. On the way were their intermediate market-places, often open-air, such as the one in Ridley Wood near Picket Post, as well as hundreds of houses belonging to regular customers, the farms, vicarages and mansions of the landed gentry of Hampshire, Wiltshire, Dorset and Somerset, as well as the homes of humbler customers.

The other great factor which helped to make Christchurch the capital of this contraband coast was its position on the Engish Channel. At the apex of the two great bays of Christchurch and Poole, it lies relatively close to France, the Channel Islands and Holland, each of which had ports catering almost exclusively for the English smugglers' needs.

It was also simple to seal off the town from the landward side. The two rivers, Avon and Stour, lent their winter floods to aid them, for it was during this season the smugglers made most of their runs. The medieval bridge over the River Avon was only sixteen feet at its widest in smuggling's heyday; while that spanning the River Stour at Iford to the west was wider but frequently out of repair, and its approaches were difficult through narrow, twisting lanes. Both bridges could be blocked to keep out both Revenue men and pursuing soldiers by such means as a haywain skilfully wedged between the parapets, or a flock of sheep which proved suddenly impossible to manage.

Christchurch was in fact the seat of a Supervisor of Customs, with four Officers under him; after 1795, he was also supported by cavalry stationed in the newly-built Christchurch Barracks. These 'Philistines', as the townsfolk called them, needed watching, but this must have been fairly easy: round-the-clock surveillance of the Riding Officer's residence at Number Ten, Bridge Street would have

10. Number Ten, Bridge Street, Christchurch, the residence of the Supervisor and Chief Riding Officer of Customs.

presented no problems, for practically the whole population was in on the game. From the top of the huge tower of the Priory Church the panorama of town, sea and country could be kept under constant watch; the Revenue men's whereabouts could be indicated to smugglers in the streets by turning the huge golden salmon, Christchurch's famous weather-cock, in the Officer's direction.

The first picture of Christchurch's smugglers comes from the pen of a man who went to school in Christchurch between the years 1776 and 1780. His name was Richard Warner, and his testimony is of the highest quality, for he eventually took Holy Orders, and became the official historian of the City of Bath.

From 1662 until 1869 Christchurch Grammar School was housed in St. Michael's Loft, which runs over the Priory Church's Lady Chapel. Richard Warner's Latin and Greek lessons were sometimes interrupted by the sight, from his 'aerial schoolroom', as he called it, of the town's smugglers coming home after a successful landing of 'the stuff' on the beach below Hengistbury Head: 'With the assistance of a tolerable glass ... I have myself, more than once, seen a procession of twenty or thirty wagons loaded with kegs of spirits, an armed man sitting at the front and tail of each, surrounded by a troop or two or three hundred horsemen, every one carrying on his enormous saddle from two to four tubs of spirits, winding deliberately, and with the utmost picturesque and imposing effect, along the skirts of Hengistbury Head, on their way towards the wild country to the north-west of Christchurch, the point of their separation.

'The Revenue troop, who had always intelligence of the "run", were, it is true, present ..... but with no other views and intentions than those of perfect peace. A flood of homely jokes were poured upon them by the passing ruffians, but these were always accompanied by a present of kegs, greater or less, according to the quantity of the smuggled goods, a voluntary toll, received, as it was conferred, in perfect good humour and with mutual satisfaction.'

That is a very revealing picture of the attitude of the King's Officers towards the daylight smugglers.

The schoolboys not only saw the smugglers of Christchurch coming home but also setting out on their ventures, and they found the sight of one smuggler particularly exciting: '"A celebrated adventurer in contraband articles, he was nicknamed "Slippery" Rogers, from his eel-like faculty of escaping the grasp of his maritime pursuers. The measurement of his noble boat, said to be the longest ever constructed, was almost marvellous, being 120 feet from the tip of her bowsprit to the end of her outrigger. She had a cuddy fore and aft for sleeping-berths, and a large open space amidships for the stowage of two or three thousand ankers of spirits. I must candidly confess that the lads of my school never saw this beautiful vessel starting for her adventurous voyage without giving one cheer for her success. The gallant object was, in truth, not a little adapted to stir the youthful fancy. Her unequalled length and perfect symmetry of form, her thousands of square feet of canvas courting the breeze and swelling to the sun, her forty rowers sweeping the rippled surface of the river with strong, well-measured stroke, their careless mirth, their choral songs and triumphant huzzas, mingled with parting salutes and farewell wishes to their friends on shore, combined to produce an effect that might well have moved the spirit of a much graver personage than an imaginative youth, who had seen only his eleventh or twelfth year.

'The fate, however, of Rogers' magnificent boat formed a striking contrast to the gay picture which I have just delineated. Perfectly heedless of the complexion of the weather, or the appearance of the skies, her desperate crew, usually intoxicated, never hesitated on their homeward voyages to tempt the dangers of the deep at those seasons when every prudent seaman would have remained in port. Indeed, they preferred a run "in thunder, lightning and in rain" as being the more secure at that time from the chase of the Revenue cutters which, under such circumstances, could not keep the sea.

'The adage of "the pitcher and the well ".... was, I presume, as well known to Rogers and his foolhardy shipmates as to the present inhabitants of the globe .... but it does not seem to have made a deeper impression upon them than it usually produces on ourselves. One fatal evening, when the welkin lowered and all around was big with gloom and portent, the crew quitted the port of Le Havre in the height of their accustomed confidence, and deeply laden with their usual freight. As they proceeded, the wind increased and the billows swelled; but the gallant boat still held her way, riding like a Halcyon on the crest of the waves, and twisting as a serpent in the abysses between them. They approached, at length, the shore,

"Where the associates of their lawless trade
Kept watch; and to their fellows off at sea
Gave the known signal;"

but the thunder of a mountainous surf announced that landing was impossible. Heaven, in vain, held out its final warning. The fearless crew pushed madly for the beach, and in a few moments their noble bark was bilged and shattered, and several of themselves, together with the cargo, swallowed by the deep.'

'Slippery' Rogers' lovely galley may well have wrecked itself on Beerpan Rocks, just off Hengistbury Head, for they have been the last call for many fine ships whose wrecks still wait investigation by local divers.

Smugglers, a print of 1799 engraved by J. P. Smith, which shows the typical features of a small landing. (Reproduced by kind permission of Alan Hay)

The smugglers of Christchurch were backed by well-to-do Venturers; they also had important local customers, the 'great oneyers' who entertained on a lavish scale.

Although Kipling tells us that it was always 'Brandy for the Parson', the vicars of Christchurch seem to have had no connection with smuggling, and this is unusual when one considers how strong a hold the Free Trade had in the town, and that practically every church along the coast and for miles inland was used for the hiding of contraband. There is neither written nor oral evidence that the Priory Church was ever used by the smugglers. There are many stories of its being haunted, but ghosts never kept smugglers away from other churches: on the contrary, where there were no *bona fide* spooks, smugglers have been known to don the white sheet and rattle the chains on their own account to scare away prying locals or suspicious Revenue Officers. Possibly the system of tunnels under the town, most of which led to the great church, obviated the need for the smugglers to be seen above ground either in its precincts or its vicinity.

One gets the feeling that they probably used it without the vicar's knowledge or permission. What is certain is that in 1776 the parish clerk asked the then vicar, the Reverend William Jackson, if he considered smuggling a sin, and the priest assured him that whoever smuggled and thereby defrauded the King of his dues committed grievous sin indeed. The clerk rolled his eyes heavenward and replied: 'Then may the Lord have mercy on the poor town of Christchurch, your Reverence, for who is here who has not had a tub?'

If the vicar of Christchurch was not keen on smuggling, there was someone very near him who probably was. To the south of the Priory Church and so close to it that there is scarcely six feet of clearance, stands Priory House, built by a man called Gustavus Brander on land which he purchased from the Church in 1775 and on which had stood the conventual buildings of the actual ancient Priory: its cloisters, guest-house, infirmary and the Prior's lodge.

Brander was a passionately keen antiquarian and he chose to settle in Christchurch not only because he liked the place, but because he wanted to excavate the ancient site at the same time as he dug out the foundations for his new house. Born in Sweden in 1719, he became a merchant, probably in the Baltic timber trade, and worked in London until he inherited his uncle's fortune. He was then able to indulge his passion for the past, patronizing writers, scientists and antiquarians, and eventually becoming a Fellow of both the Society of Antiquaries and even the Royal Society. He kept up his interest in business, for he became a director of a bank, and was eventually asked to become a Trustee of the British Museum.

He was a very pious man, a great philanthropist who believed fervently in the intervention of Providence, not without reason. One night in 1768 his carriage-horses bolted down Temple Lane in London, and shot down three flights of steps leading to the River Thames, not stopping until the river's mud bogged both them and the carriage down. It was low water and Brander and his servants suffered nothing more than a severe shaking. The Council of the City of London ordered a gateway to be erected at Temple Stairs, and Gustavus Brander made sure that his gratitude to Providence was recorded on his memorial tablet in the Priory Church in whose shadow he came to live.

He must have thoroughly enjoyed excavating the conventual buildings' foundations. He unearthed innumerable stone coffins, and, best of all, a pit full of birds' bones, among them those of fighting-cocks which had their spurs still fixed to their legs. From these he deduced that the Canon's quarters must have been built on the site of a Roman temple dedicated to Mars, whose symbol was the cock.

Priory House has an enclosed balcony which would have provided Brander with a lookout-post from which he could see the coast and the sea almost as well as Richard Warner could from his elevated schoolroom, and from which the harbour and quay could have been kept under close observation even in the worst weather. This may have been merely to satisfy the curiosity of an ex-timber-merchant's habitual interest in ships; it may also have been the command-post of a smuggling chief, the 'Godfather' of the local Free Traders.

Gustavus Brander entertained extensively at Priory House. He was obviously a very interesting person himself, and his house must have been a fascinating place, for it drew all the local celebrities, as well as many visitors from London and overseas; in 1807 his guest was no less a person than the exiled King of the French, Louis Philippe.

Priory House was, of course, a treasure-house, with its rooms stuffed with ancient pottery, classical sculpture, fossils from nearby Hordle Cliffs, illuminated manuscripts and missals, Greek and Roman sarcophagi, ancient weapons, tablets of ancient writings, curious prints, and, most precious of all, 'the Iron Chair'. This incredible piece of furniture had a complete record of Roman history wrought upon it, and was supposed to have been the coronation throne of the first German emperors. It had been captured by Sweden's warrior king, Gustavus-Adolphus in the Thirty Years' War and taken back to Sweden, where Brander had purchased it.

To entertain the constant stream of distinguished guests, Brander loaded his table with the best fare and provided only the very finest vintage wines and spirits. One of his closest friends and most frequent guests was Edward Bott, the local lawyer, whose drinking parties were the talk of the neighbourhood, especially when they got out of hand, as they frequently did. With this sort of entertaining Brander almost certainly would have been a very good customer of the smugglers, even if he were not a Free Trader himself.

Another important Christchurch resident was Doctor Arthur Quartley. He was Mayor of Christchurch in 1833, 1836 and 1839, in which year he died in that office. His house, Quartley's, can still be seen in Bridge Street, next to the ancient bridge which for many years bore his name.

His connection with smuggling began one winter's night soon after he had set up in practice. He was awakened by a loud rapping at his front door, and, putting his head out of the window, he saw two horsemen, heavily muffled, below. In a hoarse whisper one of them asked him to come with them as they had urgent work for him outside the town.

Soon he was riding with them along Stony Lane, in complete silence, and at Winkton they turned right, proceeding past the smugglers' inn, the Lamb, at Holfleet, eventually arriving at the little village of Bransgore. The leading horseman drew rein before a small cottage and at last spoke, saying: 'Doctor: there is work for you in there: pray step in.'

Lying badly wounded on the floor Dr. Quartley found a young seaman who, as his friends explained, had been shot in the back by the Revenue men in an affray from which they had brought him back to his home in Bransgore. The doctor went to work, and after he had removed a bullet from the young man's back, he made clear to the smugglers how serious their young friend's condition was and that he was not, on any account, to be moved.

'Well, Tom,' said the smuggler who was obviously the leader, 'do you want to stay here and be hanged, or shall we tip you into the cart and take you deeper into the Forest where you'll be safe?' Clearly, the smugglers must have fought back fiercely, for the danger of hanging seems to indicate that they had wounded, or even killed, a King's Officer, for which the penalty was death.

Dr. Quartley tried to remonstrate, but they ushered him out of the cottage and soon he was on his way back, under their escort, to Christchurch. At the bridge they wished him goodnight, their only words since leaving Bransgore, then wheeled their horses, and were gone.

He had almost forgotten the incident when, as that winter was changing into spring, he was sitting at breakfast one morning. His maid brought him a small barrel which she had discovered on the front doorstep. He opened its stopper to find it was full of the finest French brandy; and chalked on the wood were the words: 'Left here for the doctor's fee.'

Even that was not the end of the matter. Fifteen years later the doctor was dining at Bisterne Manor with his friend Mr. Mills, whose descendants own Bisterne to this day. After a pleasant dinner they went for an evening row on the nearby River Avon. The boat's crew consisted of two of Mr. Mills' gardeners, one of whom paid particular attention to the doctor's comfort, and from his glances Quartley felt he knew him. He said: 'My man, you appear to know me, but I am afraid I cannot recall having made your acquaintance before.'

'Not know me, Your Honour?' grinned the gardener. 'If you please, sir, I be he from whose back you cut out a slug fifteen years ago! Do you remember now?'

Christchurch was well-known as a smuggler's town so came under particular scrutiny by His Majesty's Board of Customs. Southampton was Christchurch's 'mother port', with a Collector of Customs in command. The town was known by the Board as 'a creek .... a place included within the limits of a port .... and at which Officers competent to transact the coast business are stationed by order of the Board of Customs.' Christchurch's chief Customs Officer was entitled 'The Supervisor of Customs and Coast Waiter', the second title meaning that he had to watch over the loading and unloading of merchant ships plying along the coast, record their cargoes and destinations, and give them a 'rummage' every now and again.

His main duty, however, was that of Chief Riding Officer, and he carried this out with the help of four Riding Officers. His residence, Number Ten, Bridge Street, still stands, a tall, elegant but very strongly-built Georgian house. Its vast cellar was the King's Warehouse in Christchurch, in which the Supervisor lodged any contraband goods he had seized from the smugglers; while its roof was designed to provide a lookout-platform from which the Chief Officer could keep the whole of Christchurch under surveillance, roads, rivers, streets, beaches and the bay, as well as the countryside far inland.

In 1942 the Journal of Abraham Pike, Supervisor of Customs and Coast Waiter of Christchurch, for the years 1803 and 1804, was found. There are very few of these official Customs Journals in existence, for most of them were destroyed when the Board's Headquarters was burned down in 1817. It is a fascinating book: to open a double-page entry is to appreciate how busy Abraham Pike was, and what enormous demands were made of him by his masters.

His district extended from Hurst Castle — always a notorious nest of smugglers — to Poole. At the end of each long day in the saddle, he had to record on the left-hand page the exact time he set out from home, where he travelled, what he did, when he returned, the places he visited and at what time, as well as their distances from Christchurch. Like a Naval log, he even had to enter what the weather was doing, including the wind direction.

On the right-hand page Pike had to fill in the real happenings, noting all 'Transactions and Observations' made each day, 'Particularly,' as the page-heading puts it, 'what Officers met, and where; what informations he receives [*sic*] of Goods run, or intended to be run; and what methods he took to prevent the same ...' (This wording is the derivation of the term 'Preventives' to denote the Revenue men.) '.... what Seizures made; what ships he observed on the Coast, and which way they sail; and what Notice of such Ships he gave to the next Officer; what Signals he observed from the Commander of the Cutter; and also whatever happens in the Day, Evening or Night that may be fit for the Commissioners' Knowledge.'

Abraham Pike undoubtedly had one of the hardest jobs in the King's Service, Customs or anything else, but his salary was only £25, with an allowance for fodder for his over-worked horse. Pike's stretch of coast was sixteen miles long, and he patrolled it day and night; winter and summer, without break for holiday or illness, at least not in the two years covered by his Journal. He had to rush to every spot at which the smugglers appeared; he had to watch for their signal-fires by day and their flashing lamps by night; and he had to search every possible hiding-place after a run had been successfully made on to the beach when he had failed to prevent it.

It was hard work, but he did have some help: he worked very closely with his Riding Officers, visiting them regularly and questioning them minutely about all they had seen and heard which might be of the slightest use 'For the Service', checking and signing their journals and taking away their monthly abstracts in order to collate their information with his own before sending the documents on to his master, the Collector of Southampton, who, in turn, passed the information on to the Customs Commissioners in London.

He also worked as closely as he could with the Captain and Mate of the Revenue Cutter, who maintained constant patrol offshore of his stretch of the coast, and with the military: cavalry in the form of Dragoons, and later soldiers of the Royal Horse Artillery, though we hear nothing of their guns.

The Guardroom of Christchurch Barracks, completed in 1795, where the military presence was based, still stands in Barrack Road, a listed building, and of a design familiar to every old soldier, for it was standard throughout the Empire. Surprising though it may seem, there had long been pressure from the few locals who were *not* in sympathy with smuggling for troops to be sent to put the Trade down. In 1770 Richard Hughes, a native of Wick, wrote to the government: 'I beg to inform you that there are two bays on each side of Christchurch that are continually frequented by a most dangerous band of smugglers who appear to hold all the Revenue Laws in open defiance. I venture to recommend that a troop of Dragoons should be sent to Christchurch. At this very moment the smugglers' cutter is lying in Christchurch Bay flying His Majesty's Colours!'

Not even Hughes' final dramatic reference to the Gentlemen provocatively flying the King's Colours moved the sluggish government: it took the outbreak of the Napoleonic Wars to make it order the building of the barracks, so that the soldiers could double their anti-invasion watch with chasing smugglers. Designed to house three troops of cavalry, they were begun in 1792 and completed in three years, being first occupied by the Twentieth Regiment of the Light Dragoons.

But even these reinforcements could not ensure Abraham Pike anything like complete success. The soldiers hated chasing smugglers, with whom they had a lot in common and a lot of sympathy. Most of all they detested being under the orders of a civilian, for although the Supervisor had the power to call for their assistance, he was neither Army nor Navy. The Officers had to take their orders from him, and floundering through mud, rivers, gorse, darkness and the most foul weather, the smugglers' favourite conditions, was not their idea of soldiering. The ordinary troopers were from the same class as the smugglers, and a good deal of bribery took place, nothing being easier than to leave a few kegs of gin and brandy in the Non-Commissioned Officers' billets with a little note appealing to their common brotherhood and suggesting that they be not too zealous in their pursuit. On the occasions when the military *did* corner the smugglers, they always turned at bay and fought with the utmost ferocity, for they had nothing to lose but their lives; and the troopers were always aware that they were being called upon to kill fellow Englishmen. The battles which took place round here were usually bloody affairs: for instance, in 1779 a troop of Dragoons ambushed fifty smugglers in Hook Wood on Cranborne Chase, and in the fight which followed the soldiers lost most of their horses and weapons, and they sustained fearful wounds. All this for twopence a day: no wonder it was easy to cool their martial ardour by bribery.

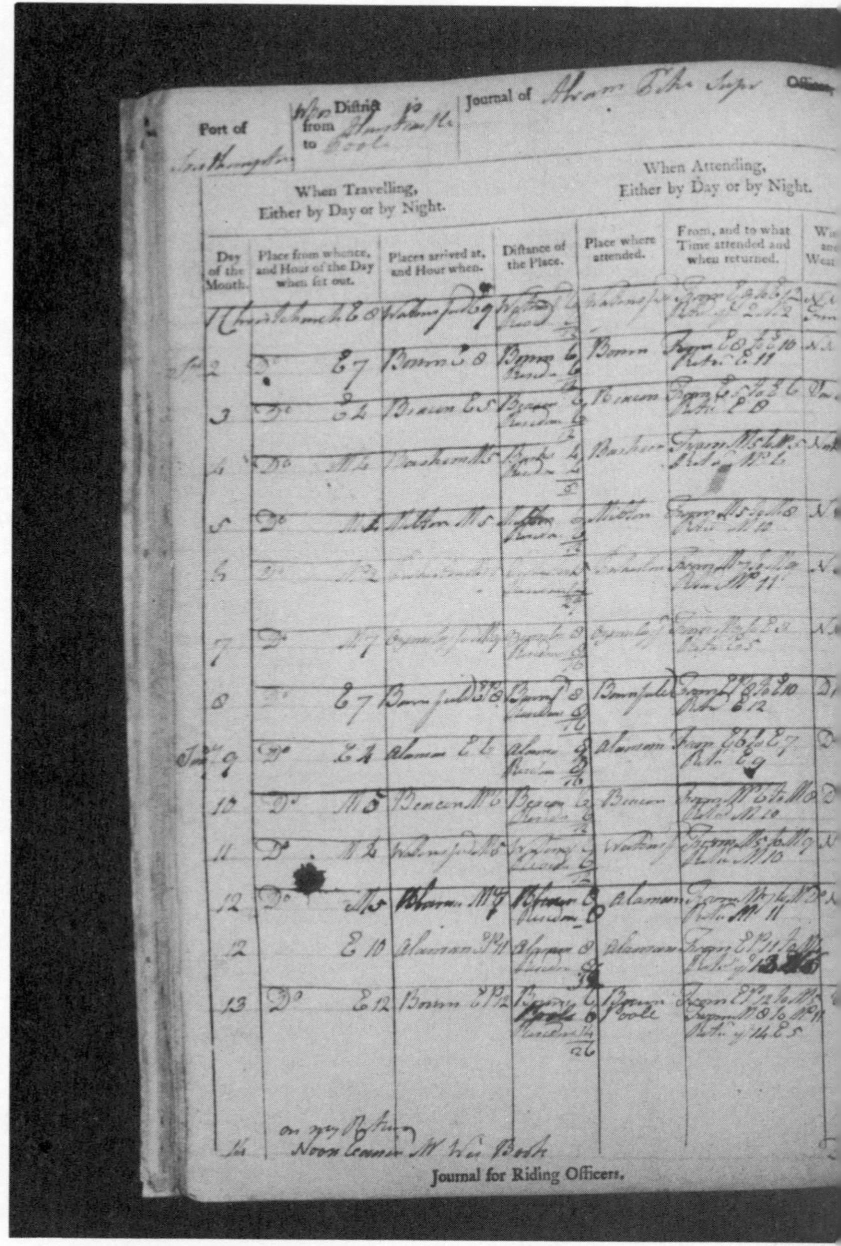

Port of

District from to

Journal of

When Travelling, Either by Day or by Night.

When Attending, Either by Day or by Night.

Day of the Month.	Place from whence, and Hour of the Day when set out.	Places arrived at, and Hour when.	Distance of the Place.	Place where attended.	From, and to what Time attended and when returned.

Journal for Riding Officers.

11. The Journal of Abraham Pike for the month of October 1803.

TRANSACTIONS AND OBSERVATIONS.

[Par]ticularly what Officers met, and where; what Informations he receives of Goods run, or intended to be run; and what Methods he took to prevent the same; what Seizures made; what Ships he observed on the Coast, and which Way they [S]ail; and what Notice of such Ships he gave to the next Officer; what Signals he observed from the Commander of the Cutter; and also whatever happens in the Day, Evening, or Night, that may be fit for the Commissioners Knowledge.

[illegible] on Discoveries the [illegible]

[illegible] with the [illegible] afterwards Surveyed the West coast to [illegible] & [illegible]

Surveyed the East coast to [illegible] & [illegible]

Surveyed the West coast to [illegible] with [illegible] the Month of September [illegible] and Received their Journals for the Month of September [illegible] Signed their Books and Received their Journals for the Month of September [illegible] on Discoveries [illegible] and Compared my officers Journals for the Month of September

Surveyed the West coast to [illegible] from [illegible] Wine and [illegible] and went to the [illegible] on [illegible] Duty [illegible] of Wine and [illegible] from [illegible] for the good of the Service

Went to Bournefield on Discoveries the [illegible]

[illegible] with the Commander of the [illegible] Cutter afterwards Surveyed the West coast to [illegible] & [illegible]

Surveyed the East coast to [illegible] & [illegible] Examined My officers and Signed their Books

Went to [illegible]ford on Discoveries the [illegible]

Surveyed the West coast [illegible] with [illegible] Looking out and [illegible] my officers [illegible]

[illegible] my officers [illegible] the West coast [illegible] Looking out [illegible] and prevented [illegible]

[illegible] with [illegible] Dragoons [illegible] 23 Casks of [illegible] Spirits and [illegible] of Tobacco [illegible] with the above [illegible] 2 Casks of [illegible] of Spirits and [illegible] of Tobacco [illegible]

Abraham Pike did have some successes. On 13th October, 1803, he wrote: 'Set out with Mr. Wise and a party of the Twentieth Regiment of Light Dragoons to Bourne where I found and seized sixty-three casks of foreign spirits and one case of tobacco.' And in February of the following year: 'Surveyed the coast to Bourne. Informed by Mr. Newman that he had seized a wagon and about seventy casks of spirits in a common near Shirley, and that he was afterwards attacked by several persons unknown, and the wagon and goods rescued, and that he had made a private mark on the wagon and could swear to it. I set out with my Riding Officers and a party of the Royal Horse Artillery in pursuit of it to Shirley, Sandford, Kingston and Avon. Searched several suspected place. No success.'

In spite of this disappointment, he was out again the next day searching, with warrants, the houses of one John Tuck of Avon, John Kerley of Kingston, and James Bunce, and in Kerley's yard he found the wagon, seized it after recognizing Mr. Newman's mark, probably made with a cutlass-stroke, and took the wagon and its cargo back to the barracks at Christchurch.

On another occasion his Officers came and told him the smugglers were at work on Bourne Heath. Off he went with them and a party of the Twentieth Light Dragoons and on the Heath he was able to lay hold of sixty-three casks of foreign spirits and one case of tobacco. This time he took the contraband to His Majesty's Warehouse at Poole, where he reported to the Controller of the port.

From his Journal Abraham Pike comes across to us as an incredibly hard-working servant of the Crown, under-valued, and underpaid, fighting a hard, unrelenting war against almost impossible odds, and liked by not many people at all in his district. But he survived to retire, and he stayed in Christchurch with his family, an unusual achievement for a Riding Officer, for most of them took up their appointments late in life, and many died in harness. His tomb has a prominent place in the graveyard of the Priory Church, to the left of the path leading up to the main door. He died on 17th October, 1823, at the age of seventy-two, and he had enjoyed a long retirement, for Customs records tell us that he had 'for many years been superannuated from the Customs'. Not only did he stay in Christchurch but he also gave his son 'Twynham' as a second name, a striking compliment to the town where he did a difficult job faithfully and well, and later was probably liked as well as respected, in spite of his unwelcome profession.

Many places in Christchurch are believed to have smuggling connections. Several inns are known to have had tunnels. Bow House, Number 16, High Street, was formerly an inn with a large cellar which extended under the High Street, as well as a tunnel, very high and wide at its beginning, which led towards Creedy Path, probably piercing the great defensive bank. The Old George has a tunnel, so the landlord says, which runs straight towards the Priory. However, some years ago it had to be bricked up after a small boy went exploring into it and did not return. In Church Street, which leads up to the Priory gates, stands the Eight Bells, now a gift-shop but once an inn famed for its strong beer which was brewed round the back. It has a wealth of smuggling stories connected with it, but we are here only concerned with its tunnel. This leads, like the Old George's, straight towards the Priory, according to the present owner, who had it filled in and the floor raised.

Where there were tunnels, there must also have been hiding-places, large rooms which could be sealed off, unlike conventional cellars. Not all these hiding-places belonged to inns. In Pound Lane, one of the houses which was demolished to make way for new development had a long garden running down to the Mill Stream, the bank of which rose much higher than the level of the garden itself. Into this bank a recess was cut from the garden, about six feet from floor to ceiling, six feet deep and ten feet wide, brick-lined and known as 'the Glory Hole'. During the last war it was used as the air-raid shelter for the residents of Pound Lane; but in smuggling days, it could have been a store for contraband.

A very similar store-place was found at nearby Īford. When a house was being built a few years ago near the New Inn, the workmen struck a brick wall as they were levelling the top of the slope leading down to river-level nearer the bridge. Breaking through this wall, they came upon a tunnel and, following it down, they broke into a subterranean room. On the floor were scattered broken clay-pipes, small brandy-kegs and iron barrel-hoops. In one corner was a hearth with peat ashes still on it, and from it a flue led up through the bank. Before the hearth lay the skeleton of a small dog. The bricks lining the tunnel were very old for they were not kiln-fired but sun-baked, and there were six thousand of them.

Rows of ancient cottages can still be seen in such Christchurch streets as Whitehall and Silver Street. There is a strong belief that in Free Trade days they were all linked by party doors so that wanted goods, or even wanted men, could pass along the row and out of the last door while the Revenue Men or the Military were knocking at the first. Certainly the row of more substantial houses in Church Street between the Eight Bells and the Priory gates were linked together; the Revenue Men may have come to the inn after a successful run with a search warrant, but the wanted barrels would have been taken through the houses to a secret door into the graveyard, possibly to be

12. The Eight Bells, now a gift-shop, but previously a favourite haunt of the smugglers of Christchurch.

dumped in a convenient tomb to await later collection.

Even though the Mill stands at the end of Christchurch Town Quay, to which the Supervisor of Customs came almost every day to check on the coastal shipping using the port, the smugglers must have felt that the double opportunity for efficient delivery of goods to it, and then their equally efficient distribution to the Mill's patrons, must have been well worth any risk. Its proximity to Augustus Brander's house may have been another consideration: although no tunnel has yet been discovered, how easy it would have been for him to construct one when he was excavating the foundations for Priory House.

Place Mill was grinding flour for the good folk of Christchurch in Saxon times, for it is listed in Domesday Book, and it continued to do so up until 1908. In the heyday of the Free Trade all the miller had to do to service a farmer's wants was to place a keg or two of brandy, or a few flat oilskinned packets of tea in the sacks of flour he had just ground. All the farmer had to do by way of payment was to allow the miller to keep the equivalent value of the goods he supplied in grain.

By 1840 Christchurch's major industry was in serious decline. There was nothing the townsfolk could do about it for it was simply a reflection of what was happening all over the British Isles. As has already been explained, the ending of the Napoleonic Wars had meant the release of hundreds of Royal Navy ships and their crews for a concerted war on the smugglers which swept them from the seas, and it was the English Channel which felt this crusade first.

By the time the Coastguard Service was officially established in 1831 even the most stupid Christchurch smuggler must have realized that his industry was finished. The Run at Mudeford was sealed by the setting up of a Coastguard Station there staffed by an Officer and at least ten men. Heavily armed with musket, cutlass and a brace of pistols for each man, and constantly vigilant, they gave the smugglers little chance.

Christchurch's smugglers did not give up easily, however: they devised more and more ingenious methods of hiding their contraband while at sea. Barrels were given false bottoms and spars were hollowed to receive spirits. The 'Stuff' was carried ashore in coils of rope, and in some places tobacco was even woven into ropes and then taken off the ships that way. 'Rafting' of kegs was brought to a fine art, and Christchurch possessed one of the finest exponents of this method in Abe Coakes, the swimming smuggler of Mudeford.

Coakes must have been the local 'gentle giant' to have carried out all the feats with which he is credited. In order to get a cargo of brandy kegs through the entrance to Christchurch Harbour under the very noses of the Coastguard stationed there, the barrels were roped together on board an approaching lugger, about twenty in a string, with cork floats at intervals. The moment of approach was chosen very carefully by the lugger captain for it had to be when high tide was coming into the Run, as the entrance to Christchurch Harbour at Mudeford is known. The night in question would have been what the smugglers called 'a dark', a moonless night, and the sea would rush in with a speed of anything up to ten knots. The ship would approach, apparently making straight for the Run, but, when several hundred yards off, it would sheer away and sail to the east up the Solent. The raft of kegs would have been dropped in exactly the right place, sufficiently far offshore to be invisible, but near enough inshore to catch the tide surging into the Harbour's mouth.

Abe Coakes would have been waiting in the water: now began his task of shepherding the bobbing tubs just below the surface through the Run and on up the shallow Harbour, with its constantly-changing sandbars which fool the most experienced local yachtsmen even today. He would have to negotiate the channel, winding and treacherous, between Grimmery and Brander's Bank, Steepbanks and Samuel's Bank; and Clay Pool where the clear, pellucid waters of the River Avon meet and mingle with the brown, turgid flow of the River Stour, with all the cross-currents this meeting means, before finally reaching the Quay. Place Mill was his first port of call. He would float at least part of his raft right up to the great mill-wheel, where the miller would open the hatch at his knock, and in would go a few more well-run kegs. Rumour has it that Abe Coakes then took the rest of his raft even further up the River Avon, some say as far as Winkton, others to Sopley, but this must strain our credulity too far. Even if he only had Place Mill as his destination, he must have been a marvellous swimmer and a very strong man to guide the incredibly unwieldy mass of barrels and prevent its grounding on the ever-changing bottom.

He must have been a very brave man, too, and he must have loved his work; but his days were numbered. Whereas in smuggling's heyday informers were very hard for Customs men to find, as the 'Trade' declined there were many who saw the government reward of £500 for information resulting in the conviction of a smuggler a securer way of earning money than relying on smuggling itself. After years of swimming past the Coastguards' very noses, someone betrayed him to the Coastguards, and Abe was arrested. The king's men probably needed some convincing that such doings had been going on for so long.

So smuggling eased off, like a bad habit which is, to the victim, delightful, but which he realizes he must give up reluctantly. It was not until 1876 that the last brandy tub was smuggled into Christchurch! It came from, of all places, Lymington, and not in a fast lugger or galley but hidden in a donkey-cart under baskets of fresh vegetables. It was a few days before Christmas and the solitary tub was carefully concealed in the house near Purewell Cross of the man who had smuggled it, where he lived with his son. They must have started their own private Yuletide celebrations a little too early and too keenly, for they were noticed walking with a rather unsteady gait in daylight hours by the local Customs Officer. Knowing that smuggling was almost a thing of the past, the Officer assumed that they must have an illicit still in their house, a practice which had grown up as smuggling declined, and he obtained a warrant and searched the place. He discovered twelve bottles of the best brandy stowed away in the smugglers' kitchen-dresser, the contents of that ultimate keg.

7
Smugglers of the New Forest

From whichever direction the New Forest is approached, its high ground and its walls of trees give warning of a fortress which is also a sanctuary stretching for mile upon mile. It was this feeling of safety soon to be theirs which must have cheered the smugglers as they hurried their illicit goods off any of the beaches from Southampton Water to Poole Harbour, particularly if they were being hard pressed by Revenue men and Dragoons. The men knew that once in the Forest they would be safe, screened by the trees and the gorse.

The New Forest had long been a vast refuge for outlaws: smugglers themselves were outlaws while they were engaged in the Trade, even if the next day they were respectable field-labourers or tradesmen once again; but there must also have been fugitives from justice, deserters from the armed forces and, of course, the deer-poachers, as well as the obvious outcasts: thieves, footpads and highwaymen. Amongst these the smugglers were accepted as brothers, as mates, as 'ackers', just as they were by the same sort of people in the twin stretch of forest, Cranborne Chase, another refuge for the Gentlemen of the Night.

But the New Forest's secure fastness was sometimes penetrated by the forces of the Crown. The smugglers who took Dr. Quartley from Christchurch to attend to their wounded comrade in Bransgore had a pressing sense of urgency in their question as to whether Tom wanted to stay and be hanged or go on and be saved from the noose. Deep in the Forest they would be safe, but Bransgore was only on the edge, and so still a dangerous place. The Free Traders could not call a halt directly they got into the trees either: the Stuff was destined for the farmers, parsonages and big houses of the Forest, just as it was in any other area of this coastal strip. Besides that, there were the towns and cities of Wiltshire and the other more northerly counties beyond, as well as the open-air markets within the Forest itself. The market held regularly in Ridley Wood, below Picket Post, was attended by buyers from all over the Forest as well as those coming from the north, Winchester, Salisbury and even Bristol. It is probable that the smugglers' finer wares, such as lace from Venice, Bruges, Brussels and Valenciennes, brocades from the Middle East, and embroideries from all over the world, were laid out under the great beeches of Ridley Wood. To the right of the path entering the wood will be seen what appears to be a deeply sunken lane; this is something of a mystery for it seems pointless to dig it out next to the obvious way into the wood if it was a hidden path. Of course, it may be natural, a stream bed deeply dug out; but it could also be the remains of a smugglers' cellar where they stored their exotic goods ready for the next market day. It could easily have been roofed, and even brick-lined, for a cellar of this type has been found on the heath which leads down to Ridley Wood from the Burley Street to Picket Post Road.

For smugglers the New Forest was a place of selling-points, but far more a place of transit, and the tracks, trails and roads used by them are still there, in many places untouched since their day. On beginning to explore its depths, a newcomer to the Forest is often surprised by the cart-tracks crossing and weaving in the mud, gravel and sand beneath the trees, sometimes coming together and fusing in a positive Piccadilly Circus of junctions, deep tracks carved into the baked mud in summer, which could only have been made by horse-drawn carts, not by the Forestry Commission's present-day vehicles, for they use the rides which are almost all properly gravelled to sustain the weight of its tree-moving equipment. The condition of the old paths points to a very heavy cart and pack-pony traffic, although the latters' hoofmarks are not so obvious; when one considers the sparseness of the population of the New Forest, one is forced to the conclusion that much of the traffic must have been made by the smugglers.

It is incredible that their tracks are still there in the soil of the Forest, but it is true. The tracks double and re-double, not because the smugglers frequently lost their way, but because they liked to confuse any actual or potential trackers and pursuers. Cranesmoor, just outside Burley, is a perfect example of this sort of tracked waste, though it is heathland: one only need to go deep into any of the Enclosures to find such tracks in profusion under and between the trees.

There are also smugglers' roads, the best example of which is in the vicinity of Burley: Smugglers' Road runs along the ridge from the Burley Street to Crow Road and is clearly marked on the Ordnance Survey map. Like the path entering Ridley Wood, Smugglers' Road has its apparent counterpart in a sunken path paralleling it from the bottom to the top of the ridge. Further along from the car-park on the road to Ringwood at Crow Hill Top, is Knave's Ash, the ancient meeting-place of a number of old roads and tracks mounting from the valley of the River Avon. It was up these that the contraband convoys often came, running along the now-metalled road to join Smugglers' Road, which would have taken the smugglers across to Vereley Hill, Picket Post and Ridley Wood itself. As it follows the high ridge, numerous tracks run along parallel with it, leaving and rejoining it in wide and confusing loops over the wild heath. It is the multiplicity of these ways, similar to that of the deep wooded Forest tracks, which is their striking feature, invaluable to the Gentlement if they were being pursued by the Philistines, for they could turn off their apparent route, twist and turn and double back, until their enemies had been either thoroughly confused and thrown off the scent, or ambushed by the escorting batmen. There are no records of Dragoons being used in this sort of area: one can appreciate why by walking up Smugglers' Road and exploring the surrounding heathland. The deeply sunk lane running alongside the road may well have been man-made by throwing up the huge long earth bank: certainly it is deep enough to hide mounted smugglers on horseback, let alone pack-horses, especially in the height of summer when the bracken is tall.

Knave's Ash may be reached on foot from Smugglers' Road, and the little hamlet is certainly worth a visit. The large cottage was the home of the Warnes, Peter, John, and their sister, Lovey, guardians of this vital route-junction and store. Some people say that it was the site of a gibbet formed from an ancient ash tree, where the corpses of hanged malefactors, highwaymen and murderers, were suspended as a warning to others not to follow their evil ways; certainly both the place's position at the meeting of several ways and, of course, its name, would seem to corroborate this. Across the road from the cottage is a rather sinister circle of fir-trees in the middle of which is a stone bearing the initials 'R.M.' and the date 1828, still well within the smuggling period. This may have been where the gibbet stood; or perhaps it is a grave.

The lady with the delightful name of Lovey Warne was an ingenious smuggler in her own right when she was young. While her brothers kept watch on the cottage and route-junction at Knave's Ash she would trot off on her pony down to Mudeford or Christchurch Quay to indulge in her very specialized form of smuggling. She would board a vessel tied up at either of the two quays, having already had wind that her services would be required on board, where she would enter the captain's cabin, take off all her clothes, and proceed to wind her body in rich silks and priceless lace handed to her by the smuggling captain. She would then carefully dress again, smoothing the fabrics so that they followed the contours of her body as closely as possible, spring on to the cobbles of the quay and trip back to her pony, past the smiling Revenue men, and away to the warehouse-cottage at Crow Hill Top.

The outhouses and extensions which make up this large complex of buildings today show that it was far more than a humble Forester's cottage then. From here the smugglers' convoys would take the goods up the Smugglers' Road across Picket Plain to Ridley Wood, the market-place for their finest wares such as Lovey's specialities, or across the great turnpike road, leading to Winchester and London, to Fritham, from where they would cross No Man's Land and go on to the towns of Wiltshire, particularly Salisbury.

13. Lovey Warne smuggling lace and silks. From an old print.

One day Lovey Warne's luck nearly ran out: she was crossing the quay at Christchurch wrapped in a hidden length of the finest Bombay silk, when one of the local Revenue Officers stopped her and invited her to take a drink with him at the Eight Bells in Church Street. She hesitated, then realized that to refuse might cause suspicion, so graciously accepted the Officer's invitation. Once inside they were soon on the Geneva, or gin, and chatting away like old friends, much to the surpirse of the inn's clients.

It was when she realized his hand was on her knee that Lovey suddenly thought things might be going too far. Shaking off the incipient effects of the gin, she gently but firmly pushed his hand away, but to her horror, back it came again, this time leading his arm, which in a flash was round her waist, which was at that moment wider than Nature intended by reason of the silk wound round it under her dress.

Thoroughly alarmed, Lovey rose with an oath which has, unfortunately, not come down to us, dug her elbow apparently accidentally into the over-familiar Philistine's eye and hurried for the door. The landlady, who had been watching Lovey's predicament with growing anxiety, ran across and asked the Revenue man if he was hurt, seizing his head and demanding to have a good look at his poor eye. Still holding him down on the settle, she ordered her maid to bring her bar-cloth for an improvised cold compress, and by the time he had freed himself from her motherly ministrations, Lovey was nowhere to be seen, having disappeared into the bustling streets of Christchurch.

It had been a close call, and, not surprisingly when she had told her brothers, they said she must never go smuggling on her own account again down to the coast. But they said she could continue to ride her pony leading the pack-pony trains up the Smugglers' Road and across the moors; and she could help them even more by becoming a living danger signal for the whole area west of Burley. So when the Warne brothers, Peter and John, were notified that the Philistines were out on the lookout for smugglers round Burley, they gave word to Lovey, who would wrap herself in a voluminous scarlet cloak and make her way up to the top of Vereley Hill, where she would prominently promenade the whole day long, a living red danger-signal for the smugglers toiling up either from the Avon Valley or from the beaches through such paths as Chewton Glen, which extended almost to Burley itself in those days.

When they saw Lovey on Vereley Hill smugglers knew they had to avoid the Smugglers' Road, and so would take a wide detour round Burley to pass it to the east. She kept up this vital work until well into old age. According to Burley folk, who still talk of her with pride, she was also willing to the end to tuck up her skirts and ride off along the smugglers' paths with an eared bottle of the best brandy hanging from her stout leather belt at each hip.

When there was danger looming at night for the smugglers of Burley, Lovey's job was taken over by Charles and Murphy

Bromfield, who lived in their cottage actually on Vereley Hill. They had a halliard rigged to the top of the highest oak-tree on the Hill, up which they would hoist a specially-made storm-lantern to warn their smuggling brothers of impending trouble from the Customs men. When their oak-tree was felled some years back, the iron staple and ring through which their halliard had run was found still riveted to the highest branch.

The Bromfields' descendants live still in Burley, and the Warnes are commemorated there by Warnes' Lane, a field called Great Warnes, and a bar in the smuggling inn of Burley, the Queen's Head, which has been named 'The Warnes Bar'. Lovey and Peter lived to ripe old ages; but John went down to the coast at Chewton Bunny once too often and was shot by a Revenue man in an affray on the treacherous beach. He survived for some years, but eventually died comparatively young, of the wound which never completely healed. Peter Warne had a beloved pony, a grey, which he used on many a smuggling jaunt down to the sea, an animal so trustworthy that he specified in his will that when he died the pony had to be buried with him, for, as he put it, he would need her to ride on when Judgement Day dawned. When he eventually passed on, his hearse was drawn churchwards by the faithful grey, his friends apparently intent on fulfilling the old smuggler's deathbed wishes to the letter. But the Vicar of Burley refused to countenance anything so thoroughly pagan as pony and master being buried together. Only the master was buried that day: the pony lived on, and when she died at last the Vicar saw to it that she did not gain entrance to the graveyard: she was buried near her master by the clump of fir trees opposite the churchyard gate.

Burley was a very closely-knit community in the smugglers' days, and this was one of the reasons why it was such a haven for them. The Revenue Officers did not like going into the villages of the Forest: Abraham Pike, the Chief Riding Officer of Christchurch was thankful not to have to go that far as his beat's limit of four miles inland only took him to Ossemsley Ford. But Mr. Critchell, his counterpart at Ringwood in whose district Burley lay, had good reason to loathe the village after what happened there on 9th January, 1783, the year before the Battle of Mudeford.

Word reached Mr. Critchell that a huge consignment of brandy, gin and tea had just been delivered to a cottage in Burley, so he immediately called up his Riding Officers and the posse set off across the Forest. Halfway down the village's main street they were alarmed to see a force of mounted men wheeling round the end building with every intention of charging them. Mr. Critchell saw that it was to be a cavalry action even though it was only a New Forest village street and the smugglers were mounted on ponies. But they were at least as well armed as the King's men and obviously quite determined to prevent the taking of their contraband, which, Mr. Critchell realized, must have been in great amount for the smugglers to act so determinedly.

He was also aware that his men, losing their nerves at the ferocity of the smugglers' charge, were wheeling their horses and turning tail. He was left completely alone and was soon surrounded by the shouting smugglers, many of whom dismounted, dragged him from his horse and set about beating him until he was practically dead. Then they re-mounted and returned to the cache of contraband, which they immediately re-loaded on to their New Forest pack-ponies, and took the road out of Burley as fast as possible in case a second Revenue force, or, worse still, the Dragoons from Christchurch, were called out. They left the Chief Riding Officer of Ringwood lying in the road, suffering from dreadful wounds, particularly in the head; and all this in broad daylight.

14. The Queen's Head Inn, Burley, as it was in the late nineteenth century.

The heart of Burley, then as now, was the Queen's Head Inn, and it was here, a few years ago, that a secret room was found during alterations to the building. Situated in part of the ancient inn's cellars, this contraband control-room contained such interesting items as brandy bottles, coins of the period, pistols and cutlasses, and, most intriguing of all, several straw-hats from Leghorn in Italy, a strange but usually very profitable item for smugglers. Whether they had been left there because the smugglers could find no customers for them, we shall never know. From the papers found in the bunker it would seem that here smuggling runs were planned and payment received from the share-holders in these ventures. Perhaps some former landlord was the Venturer of Burley, or perhaps he was the Quill-driver or Writer-man, smuggling terms for accountant. Certainly, he would have been one of the Free Traders' principal customers.

From what we have discovered about the village so far, it will be apparent that this settlement could accurately be described as the smuggling capital of this part of the Forest. One of the last of the Burley smugglers was John King. Born late in the smuggling age, in 1827, he was Free Trading at the age of thirteen after a neighbour, Mr Mussell, asked him if he would like to join him and his son for a bit of smuggling on the coast. In spite of his mother's objections, John went off with the Mussells and a couple of stout New Forest ponies, which were saddled with nothing more sophisticated than a couple of large sacks.

The New Forest's ponies were another of the attractions for the Gentlemen of the Night who smuggled from and into it. Stocky and hardy, hairy and square, the New Forest pony averages eleven hands in height, making it ideal as a pack-animal, and excellent as a fast mount with plenty of stamina. The sparse winter grazing of the New Forest provides it with holly and the soft tips of the young furze, the mask of thick hair on its face protecting it from prickles. There seems to be something of the tough Kalmuck and Tartar breeds about this pony; and though its breed was diluted during the last century by Prince Albert letting his Arab stallion, Zorah, stand in the Forest for the mares' benefit, this would not have decreased its hardiness in smuggling days. Certainly, the smugglers valued the ponies' sure-footedness and great strength, for they were able to load six spirit-kegs on to each pony, and a large number of silk and lace packets into the panniers. With a long leading-rein for each pony-minder, and often cloth shoes to deaden the sound, the ponies of the New Forest made the regular run up from Becton and Chewton Bunny, up to Burley and so on into the Forest.

Few other New Forest villages are as rich in smuggling stories as Burley, but many come close. Boldre, just north of Lymington, could not help but be a smuggling village, for from early days it was an important pilgrims' road across the New Forest from Beaulieu Abbey to Burley, Ringwood and the west. What was good for the pilgrims, as we have seen in the case of the Cat and the Fiddle at Hinton, was usually good enough for the smugglers: Boldre Church was a well-known dump for contraband goods coming from east to west, and also from south to north, for it is on the Lymington River.

Lymington smugglers used both the river and the path which still runs down from the Turf Cutters' Arms to the coast. The huge oven at the Turf Cutters Arms was a certain hiding-place for the Stuff, and in the churchyard there were table-tombs which were used for short-stay contraband.

In smuggling days, the Lymington River was much less silted than it is today, and so much deeper. In the Pitts Deep Stream is Brandy Hole, so named from the frequency with which smuggled brandy-kegs were weighted in clusters and sunk for later collection when the excitement of a night run had died down, the place always being carefully marked by an innocent-looking float disguised with feathers or driftwood. When the Coastguard had moved on to somewhere else, the smugglers on recovery-duty would pole along to the floats in ordinary wild-fowling punts.

The Reverend William Gilpin was Vicar of Boldre in the last quarter of the eighteenth century, and during this period he wrote the classic *Remarks on Forest Scenery*, which was published in 1791. He described his poor parishioners thus: 'Exposed to every temptation of pillage and robbery from their proximity to the deer, the game and fuel of the Forest, these poor people were little better than a horde of *Banditti*; and without the opportunity of the humblest education or the benefit of decent example, presented a picture of savage life which perhaps was hardly paralleled in a civilized country.' That was how he found them when he took up his duties, and he did much to improve their lot: what is significant is that he mentioned poaching deer and carrying off firewood, but he left out the smuggling. Perhaps he had not at that point realized how rife it was in his parish, but he soon must have stumbled on the truth: probably someone like Parson Woodforde's *Andrews the Smuggler* called one night when he was just going to bed with a bag of Hysson tea and presented it to the alarmed new incumbent just as he had been in the habit of doing for the previous parson. Did Gilpin accept it or did he send the man away with a stern lecture on the evils of the Free Trade, as Vicar Jackson of Christchurch would have done? And if he did, did he succumb to the smugglers' blandishments later on? We shall never know. What is certain is that smuggling continued in Boldre right up to the end of the age.

A little to the east of Boldre lies the charmingly named village of Sway, a name almost as delightful as that of its neighbour across the Avon Water, Tiptoe. Sway is best known today for its two incredible concrete towers, great and small, but before they were ever started it was notorious as yet another New Forest smuggling village. Four miles from the beaches on either side of the infamous Hurst Castle, Sway was a convenient dumping-place for the staggering tubmen, and the cellars of Sway House were built large to accommodate the goods they brought. It was said that Sway House had a tunnel running down to the sea, probably at Milford, and though, as tunnel-stories always tend to, this may sound difficult to believe, two points may corroborate the claim to a four-mile tunnel: Lymington was riddled with well-made and extensive subterranean passages leading down to the riverside, and that town is very close to Sway; and the tunnel which was said to have run from Isaac Gulliver's house at Kinson was also claimed to be a four-miler. Perhaps this was maximum viable length for such a passage.

The western boundary of the New Forest has two interesting exits: Fordingbridge in the north and Bransgore to the south. Fordingbridge is only ten miles from Salisbury and this made it a convenient place in which to store smuggled goods destined for that great ecclesiastical city, with its long list of customers, from the ordinary innkeepers and tradesmen to the comfort-loving clerics of the cathedral close. The last ten miles into Salisbury would have been a convenient night's journey for a smuggling convoy. Several other smuggling routes, long-distance paths, converged at Fordingbridge, one of the most frequented being that from the east through and go straight on to Fordingbridge, and those which came up from the town of Poole, as well as the landing-places on the coast nearby, would be routed through Ringwood as well as by-passing that town. This must have been one of the great Isaac Gulliver's favourite routes: up from Poole past Wimborne, over Colehill, using the path still known as Smugglers' Lane, and then on either past, or even stopping at, Gulliver's Farm at West Moors, which appears on the Ordnance Survey map, on through Three Legged Cross, Ringwood Forest, Alderholt and so into Fordingbridge.

Today Fordingbridge has a unique quality about it, for it is isolated while yet being the centre for the surrounding country, and its riparian character, which its name expresses, on the west bank of the River Avon only emphasises its function as one of the great gates to the New Forest which dominates the town even though it is almost four miles to the east. Even if this character is not at first apparent to the visitor, the numbers of capacious cellars and the fact that many of the shallows of the wide River Avon here were used for hiding contraband indicates its smuggling character. It cannot compare with such places as Christchurch or Burley as hives of Free Trade industry, but an eighteenth century report claimed that one in three Fordingbridgians was engaged in the business in one way or another. The smuggling fraternity was carefully watched: several Excise men were stationed in the town, and there was the Town Constable, whose ancient Office went back at least as far as the early Middle Ages, when his job was to guard the bridge and keep unlicensed deer-hunters out, or to arrest them if any came out from the other side of the Forest. There were also plenty of soldiers about, for Fordingbridge was a staging-post for the Royal Mail coaches which had military escorts; there were also the irregular patrols of cavalry from such garrisons as those at Christchurch and Wimborne. For this reason, the many footpaths leaving the town and the more recent roads which were built on such paths, were used by smugglers, perhaps the best example being that which leads to Redbrook, through Stuckton, then on up to Frogham and so into the New Forest.

The clearest evidence of the whole-hearted support given to the Gentlemen of the Night by the people of Fordingbridge is found in the account of the terrible Hawkhurst Gang's return across the south of England from their attack on the Custom House in Poole in September, 1747. The smugglers were cheered by the whole population which had turned out to welcome them with the enthusiasm that they would today use to greet a member of the Royal Family.

As smuggling waned dramatically with the coming of the Coastguard and the lowering of duties, the smugglers of Fordingbridge were luckier than most of their brethren, for they found jobs in the gangs of men being recruited for the draining and re-planting of great stretches of the New Forest during the first part of the last century. They also went into sail-making, for the Fordingbridge flax-growing industry (to which 'Flaxfields' at Stuckton still bears witness) was converted to growing the material for sails. There was always poaching to keep the family going as well, which in Fordingbridge meant New Forest deer, for the shooting of which, it is said, many of the cottages on the Forest Edge had small windows specially designed for potting a deer without stirring from home. Quite possibly they were also spy-holes for watching for approaching smugglers' convoys or searching Revenue Men.

The most southerly exit from the New Forest into the Valley of the River Avon is Bransgore. Here once was Beech House, surrounded by thickly-wooded grounds, with its own ice-house, so useful as a delivery-spot for the passing smugglers on their way up to Thorney Hill and Burley. During the days of the Reign of Terror in France, when hundreds of nobles were escaping from their country because they were on the execution-list for the guillotine, this house was a refuge and rallying-centre for them and their families.

These refugees were in their way also contraband goods: there would have been few other ways of getting out of France without the help of English smugglers. A place like Beech House was an ideal receiving-station, being not too far from the coast where they were landed, and, at the same time, in those days still within the sanctuary of the New Forest. As the wars against Napoleon developed, many of these French émigrés joined the volunteer regiments of 'The Royal and Christian Army', which was preparing to invade Napoleon's France and then restore the monarchy.

Not only men came across to find refuge on English soil: the Duke of Orleans' daughter was only a baby when she was smuggled across the Channel, and she was taken into the care of Mrs. Syms of Christchurch, for her mother had not been able to escape with the child. The family was later reunited, and returned to France where the little girl completed her education. The English connection remained strong, for she eventually married Lord Edward Fitzgerald.

Another noble family unable to get away as a single unit contacted the young captain of a fast cutter and engaged him, in return for a large sum in gold, to take their beautiful daughter, Hortense, to England. They promised him that once he delivered the girl and the sealed letter which accompanied her to Beech House in Bransgore, he would be paid the other half of the agreed golden fee by their friends amongst the émigrés already there.

The voyage was long, for the cutter was delayed by contrary winds after leaving France in St. Peter Port, Guernsey, which held it up for almost a week. It was during this time that the young smuggling captain fell deeply in love with his fair contraband charge, and she with him to almost the same degree. By the time they reached Christchurch Harbour they were deeply involved and the whole crew of the cutter knew it. They tied up in the dead of the night, and the young captain sent one of his trusted men ahead to Bransgore on horseback to warn the French community who was coming, so that they could make all preparations necessary to receive a young lady of her rank. Because the Chief Riding Officer was on coast duty on the quay the next day, the young couple was unable to leave the ship until the next night.

That single full day was enough time for mischief to begin its wicked work in Bransgore, for the captain's messenger told not only the French refugees of the lady's arrival at Christchurch, but also his commander's sweetheart, a fiery half-gypsy beauty whose home was just up the road into the Forest from Bransgore, at Thorny Hill. Keeping no detail back from her, the messenger succeeded in rousing the Forest girl's jealousy so successfully that it seems certain he had a personal interest in the matter. Whatever his motives, she swore in her fury that she would never allow her place in the captain's affection to be taken by another, and "a French harlot" at that. She flung herself on to her New Forest pony and galloped off to Number Ten, Bridge Street, in Christchurch and demanded words with the Chief Riding Officer of Customs.

Meanwhile, her former lover was escorting his lovely cargo of contraband to Bransgore, where he safely delivered her to her countrymen at Beech House, receiving not only their sincere thanks, but, as the letter he had brought indicated he should, the rest of the gold which had been promised him. Just as he was about to leave Beech House, one of his escorting sailors rushed in with the news that the Revenue men were coming up the road and that they would be six against four smugglers. The Captain ordered his men into their saddles and dashed down the drive and out into the road, where they saw the posse of King's men approaching at a smart pace. Without hesitation, the smugglers charged into them and broke through towards Christchurch and safety, but not without the young smuggling-leader receiving a bullet in the back from a Revenue pistol. His wound, however, was not discovered until they were all back on board the cutter and it was making all sail down the Harbour in the direction of the Run at Mudeford, and the freedom of the open sea.

That was the last the French refugees of Beech House ever heard of the gallant young captain. The young noblewoman who had fallen so romantically in love with him fell into a distracted fit which lasted many weeks. Whether he died of his wound, or decided that such adventures were just not worthwhile, or whether he swore never to return to a part of England where women were as treacherous as his gypsy sweetheart had been, we do not know. Nor do we know what became of the fair Hortense … .

8
The Bournemouth Smugglers

Thronged with hedonistic holiday-makers in summer, and strikingly sedate in the off-season, Bournemouth seems to be the last place you would connect with smuggling in the eighteenth and early nineteenth centuries. How can this region of villas, avenues, estates and towering blocks of luxury flats have been the smugglers' favourite stretch of coast for miles?

The fact of the matter is that in smuggling days the land from Hengistbury Head to Poole was a deserted wilderness, a vast heath, coming down from the heavily-wooded rides of the New Forest to the east and Cranborne Chase to the west onto the sea-shore itself. It was that shore above everything else which recommended this part of the country to the smugglers, with its uniformly curving and gently-shelving bay of the finest sand, with shingle only at the eastern end, sheltered by Hengistbury Head on one side and to the west by the whole of the isle of Purbeck.

One of the monks of Christchurch penned the first written reference to the place in 1407, calling it 'La Bournemowthe'. Thomas Hardy wrote later: 'This fashionable watering-place … was … like a fairy place suddenly created by the stroke of a wand, and allowed to get a little dusty. An outlying eastern tract of the enormous Egdon Waste was close at hand, yet on the very verge of that tawny piece of antiquity such a glittering novelty as this pleasure city had chosen to spring up. Within the space of a mile from its outskirts every irregularity of the soil was prehistoric, every channel an undisturbed British trackway … It was a city of detached mansions; a Mediterranean lounging-place on the English Channel ….'

Between these two references to Bournemouth are others: in 1535

15. Bournemouth in 1819, an ideal smugglers' landfall.

John Leyland discovered that from Christchurch to Poole stretched only 'black moorish ground, overgrown with heath and moss'; and the Earl of Southampton, surveying the coast for a report to Queen Elizabeth I on possible landing-places for the Spanish Armadas, wrote in 1574: 'We find at Bourne Mouth, within the west bay at Christchurch, a place very easy for the enemy to land, being void of all inhabiting. We find, moreover, a place called Boscombe, within the said bay, which is also an easy place for the enemy to land, containing in length a flight shot.'

These conditions remained the same until the early years of the nineteenth century, making it ideal for the Free Traders. It was then that another enemy, Napoleon, was expected to invade. At that time, the bay was patrolled by such units as the Dorset Yeomanry, under the command of Captain L. D. G. Tregonwell, whose brief also included the watch for smugglers. In 1795, the year which saw the completion of the barracks at Christchurch, the Duke of Rutland toured the south coast and recorded in his diary that, 'From Christchurch we proceeded on horseback to Poole. After going about two miles on the high road, we turned off by the advice of a farmer, who told us we should find a much shorter way by going to the left, which, however, came to the top of a high cliff, where we could not find the least track of road. We were, however, recompensed in some degree by a most delightful view of the sea. After enjoying this noble scene, we turned our horses' heads and rode in the direction of Poole, as we thought, for on this barren and uncultivated heath there was not a human being to direct us.'

In this very interesting passage we have not only a hint of Bournemouth's potential as a seaside resort which enjoys noble views of the sea, but also the evidence that this coast was still as good as ever for smuggling, for the Duke met no one except a farmer. Even as late as 1811 the Ordnance Survey map for that year shows the land on either side of the little stream as 'Bourne Mouth', and it was not until the century had advanced much further that 'Bournemouth' was used as a single name. During the seventeenth and eighteenth centuries the wider region from Christchurch to Poole and for a six miles band inland was always called Bourne Heath.

It is Richard Warner, the invaluable eyewitness of Christchurch, who begins to help in quest of the Bournemouth smugglers. In his description of the smugglers whom he saw from his aerial schoolroom, he wrote of how he saw them 'winding deliberately and with the most picturesque and imposing effect, along the skirts of Hengistbury Head, on their way towards the wild country to the north-west of Christchurch. ...' This was, of course, Bourne Heath, and the smugglers he saw must have landed their cargo on the beach below the great whale-backed promontory, Hengistbury Head, to which he referred. This feature which, together with its low ground, forms the southern side of Christchurch Harbour, once belonged to the town of Christchurch but was sold to the American millionaire and founder of the famous London store, Gordon Selfridge. In 1930 he decided to sell his Christchurch properties and the town, being unable to raise the money for all of it, asked Bournemouth to buy Hengistbury Head while the older town took Stanpit Marshes. So it could be said that the first Bournemouth smugglers were really Christchurch men.

Of all the landing-places along the coast, the undoubted favourite for smugglers must have been at the point where Double Dykes, the great Iron Age fortress-banks at Hengistbury Head, meet the beach. Only nine miles from the Needles, behind which the smuggling luggers could hide and wait their chance if the Revenue Cutters were about in Christchurch Bay, its position was ideal. Hengistbury Head had been an Iron Age promontory fort, and unlike its contemporaries Badbury Rings and massive Maiden Castle, it had required man-made protection only on its landward approach, the sea and Christchurch Harbour defending it on the others. Galloping erosion has, of course, reduced these massive banks to but a shadow of their former majesty, but in the heyday of English smuggling they gave perfect shelter to the convoy of farm-wagons, tub-carriers, pack-horses and horsemen awaiting the luggers coming in to the beach

16. The Smugglers' path from Double Dykes at Hengistbury Head to Wick Village as it crosses Solent Meads Golf Course.

below. There were two buildings on the Head at this time: the barn is still there, but old maps show a Summer House on Warren Hill which would have been ideal, one might almost say purpose-built, as a smugglers' lookout and signal-station. It was probably built by Gustavus Brander, the Swedish timber-merchant and archaeologist of Priory House, Christchurch. The village of Wick has a Brander's Lane, which may have led from the old ford and up on to the Head; perhaps it was used by the enigmatic Swede for visits to the Summer House which were not entirely bent on pleasure.

When a smuggling ship arrived off Hengistbury Head it would show its blue flash, and from either the top of the cliff, or from the Summer House, the answering 'flink' would be shown by means of a spout-lantern. If the lugger or cutter captain decided to come in to the beach, he would have found it ideal in most conditions, though he would need to know the double tides of this part of the coast very thoroughly. With the wagons able to be brought right down to the beach because of the shelter of Double Dykes, their loading would have been very rapid; and with the last keg or packet on board, the Lander would give the order to move off inland between the enormous banks.

The convoy must have turned through the second gap in the landward bank; even today one can follow it in the imagination by walking to what is now the Broadway, following its northern pavement until one meets a gravel path coming in from the right at a shallow angle. This is the ancient smugglers' track to Wick where they could cross the River Stour at its lowest fordable point; it can be followed across the Solent Meads Golf Course. Halfway along it the point is reached where the smuggler convoy could be seen by Richard Warner through his 'tolerable glass' from the schoolroom above the Lady Chapel of Christchurch's Priory Church. Warner stated he saw the smugglers in convoy along this path 'under the meridian sun', which puts a question mark over the need to hide themselves and their wagons behind the Double Dykes. The answer seems to be that they did this almost out of habit, even though they had the Christchurch area so well under their control in Warner's day that they did not need to fear the Revenue men. Before Warner's time, and most certainly after when Christchurch Barracks had been built, they had to resort to night-time work, for the Dragoons were now too close and had to be respected.

From Double Dykes the land was given over to farming in the smugglers' age, which only stopped where the heathland became too sour and hard to be cultivated. The cliffs, though not high, would have made getting the goods away out of the question here. The area just before the beginning of the houses was known as 'The Guns' and was the Coastguard's practice-ground. Exploring Southbourne, the several gravel roads, the Coastguard buildings, the road names, and the proximity of the sea all go to indicate what the place must have looked like long before the name Southbourne was ever given to the area.

Just where the houses begin, old maps give the name of The Cellars, which is preserved on the modern map in the name of Cellars Farm Road, the site of Cellarfield Farm. The 'cellars' referred to may have been caves carved by the sea in the cliffs, although the clay, sand and gravel of which they are composed could not have made them very substantial. Perhaps the smugglers shored up existing and potentially dangerous caves, to provide themselves with the much-needed storage-space which this stretch of the coast so obviously lacked; or possibly the cellars were in the farm itself. In those days, as well as Cellarfield Farm, there was a large house named Stourcliff, surrounded by heath and wild tracks used by fishermen, wild fowlers, for which the area was famed, and, of course, the Gentlemen of the Night. The fact that a Coastguard Station was established here very early in the Service's history, which still functions in Admiralty Road, demonstrates clearly how active the smugglers must have been here, for it was the policy to set up stations in busy running places as deterrents.

Seafield Road was an important lane in the old days and led from the bank of the River Stour itself right down to the sea where St. Catherine's Path (next to the road of the same name) leads in a slope down the cliff to the promenade. This was an area of both oak woods and cornfields, as well as ponds where duck-shooting provided sport for the one or two local gentry. These features must have given ideal cover for smugglers needing to get away from the beaches fast when the King's men were about; if the smugglers suddenly found it necessary to rid themselves of incriminating goods when ambushed, then the ponds and the impenetrable gorse thickets must have been godsends. Cellars Farm Road is in part a gravel track which must be much as all the tracks round here then appeared. It leads almost down to the cliff, debouching into the Southbourne Coast Road.

By the time this area had become known as Southbourne-on-Sea, a resort which was to rival its great parent, Bournemouth, the smuggling age was well and truly over, for it was in 1870 that Dr. Thomas Compton bought three hundred acres of this wild and desolate land with a mile of shore for development. The new little resort's western boundary was, in fact, an old smugglers' track leading up from the sea and existing today as Clifton Road.

Hengistbury Head was not the only fort used by the smugglers round here. The wood named Foxholes rises on the right of Belle Vue Road as it leads up the hill, and must have been a useful lookout post. From here there is a magnificent view of sea and land for miles around; Foxholes was probably a valued early warning station when the King's men were about, for even Dragoons leaving Christchurch could be seen clearly in those days.

Stourcliff, Stourwood and Stourfield were all fairly big houses in which families of quality lived who were high on the smugglers' delivery-lists: Mr. Edward Bott of the last named has already been described. His house had an ice-house, a greenhouse and a dovecote, all of which could have been used as 'letter-boxes' for the smugglers' deliveries. Dense oak woods clothed this hill, as well as a fir plantation, all giving good cover; near Stourfield House, now incorporated into the Douglas House Hospital, were two ponds, the one called the Black Pond encircled by dark and sinister cedars, whose shadowy atmosphere would have been enough to keep the superstitious away in those days.

The old smugglers' track which now comes out on the cliffs as Clifton Road went down to the beach in much the same way as does the present-day zig-zag path; above it towers the jutting headland which in the old days was topped by a sand dune and was known as

Mount Misery. It gained its dramatic name from the incident which occurred here one stormy day during a bitter winter. Although ideal smuggling weather, a contraband-carrying lugger hovered off the shore hesitating to commit itself to coming any closer for fear of the dangerous rocks which at that time jutted up out of the sand, for a very high sea was running that day. The vessel had been eagerly awaited by local folk who had loved-ones on board, as well as the landing-party, amongst them a young girl who was engaged to the captain. Bursting with eagerness to embrace her beloved once again after a long separation, she stood away from the rest and began frantically waving her cloak to show him she was there. Seeing her through the spray, the captain impetuously gave orders for his lugger to edge closer into the land amongst the crashing breakers, apparently intending to attempt to beach his craft below the promontory.

It was a foolhardy impulse: the tempest howled, the waves reared up, and the ship broached to, with all leeway gone. She smashed into the black rocks, capsized, and every man on board was swept away in the angry waves. Horrified, the girl saw it all, knew what had happened, and, determined to reunite herself with her lover in death if she could not be so in life, flung herself with a long-drawn scream from the top of the bluff to a horrible death on the surf-lashed rocks below. For many years after it was said that in the night on the anniversary of the catastrophe her ghost could be seen leaping to her death again, her eerie cry being heard quite clearly by those brave enough to be there to listen.

Along Overcliff Drive, Southbourne becomes Boscombe at Fisherman's Walk. To gain some idea of what 'Boskum', 'Bastome' or 'Baskaw', to use some of its old-fashioned names, looked like in smuggling days, one only has to stand on the cliffs between the path near the edge and the Boscombe Overcliff Drive. Here is the same rolling turf, marram grass, gorse and dwarf oaks which proved useful for escaping smugglers being pursued by their enemies, particularly as this landscape continued for miles and miles inland into tracts of wilderness with its own bogs, ponds, ravines, rides and hills. To gain some idea of what went on here in those days one needs to search no further than that invaluable record, already used, left by Chief Riding Officer Pike in his Journal for the years 1803 and 1804.

He tells how, in the month of April, 1803, he was called on at his house in Christchurch by a boatman named Thomas Lambert, who informed him that he had seen a boat come in to the shore at Boscombe and that goods had been landed from it. Pike immediately set out with a party of his Officers, and on the 'Heath near Baskom', as he wrote, he seized two wagons and a cart carrying 250 casks of spirits, a large amount of tobacco and a case of that strangest of contraband items: playing-cards. He returned to Christchurch Barracks with all speed and called out the Dragoons to help him, his presence being necessary before the military would turn out. He then sent the convoy on to the Customs House at Poole under the soldiers' escort, commanded by his Officers.

17. Bourne Bottom and the beach looking east, about 1840.

It was Bourne Bottom which saw most of the landings along this part of the coast, the location today marked very clearly by Bournemouth Pier and its approach. In the numerous photographs of old Bournemouth, as well as the many paintings and etchings which the place inspired, we can clearly see what a wide, wooded valley the little Bourne Stream had cut down through the low cliffs here to the sea through Bourne Chine. As on the Isle of Wight, the word 'chine' is used on this part of coast to denote ravines cutting through the cliffs, which a little further east are called 'bunnies'. The beautiful gardens which fill the little brook's valley today stretch inland towards Branksome, where the Chine peters out. Down by the pier they are called the Central Gardens, beyond the Square they become the Upper Central Gardens, and further upstream they modulate into Coy Pond Gardens.

A walk up through the Gardens will give a remarkable feeling of continuity with those far-off smuggling days. On reaching Prince of Wales Road, which crosses the Upper Central Gardens, a path leads out to the right where it joins Branksome Wood Road, which, in the contraband-running days, was used for assigning the Stuff by the smugglers after successfully getting it off the beach at Bourne Bottom. In Glenferness Avenue opposite, there is a gate leading into what is left of the wood, which rejoices in the delightful name of Pug's Hole. Pug was, apparently, a smuggler who probably had a hide here, possibly even living in the little woods as a smugglers' storeman. But Pug was only one of several smugglers' agents who settled near their tracks in the Bourne Valley.

By the year 1750 we find mention in documents of a very early Bournemouth building: Bourne House. This was situated near Coy Pond, which can be found in Coy Pond Gardens. No one knows who built it, or even who the regular occupant was, but the few fishermen and shepherds round about knew it as Decoy Cottage. A decoy-pond keeper had the job of looking after the large funnel-shaped nets of the actual duck-decoy, or to give it its more accurate definition, duck-trap, and he may have lived in Bourne House as a servant, looking after the decoy and the gentlemen who came to Bourne Bottom for the wildfowl of all sorts for which this part of the coast was famous. Another house where they stayed was the Tapps Arms, named after Sir George Ivison Tapps, the Lord of the Manor, which was situated on the eastern side of the wide Bourne Valley, on the site of the present Post Office Road. Opposite this inn the Bourne Stream was spanned by a minute bridge known as the Bourne Plank; small but vital, it carried across the stream the traffic on the road from Christchurch to Poole, and so was of considerable importance.

Both these houses were, of course, used by the smugglers: we have already heard from Richard Warner that a gang of them seized Joseph Manuel from his house in Iford in the year 1762 and dragged him across the Heath to 'a lonely house near Decoy Pond, notorious as a house frequented by smugglers', from whence they took him across to the Channel Islands; and the Tapps Arms was almost certainly used by the Gentlemen; a picture of Isaac Gulliver resting with his gang hung in that inn when it had been rebuilt and renamed the Tregonwell Arms. Obviously, the landlord of this hostelry was the first of the smugglers' customers when they came off the beach; and Decoy House must have had outbuildings which were useful as the first dump on the contraband's journey further inland. Even Decoy Pond itself must have played its part: as a watery hide into which to shoot the Stuff when the Revenue men were too close for comfort.

An incident which happened in November 1787 vividly shows how busy Bourne Bottom was. A lugger was coming in for a landing just where the Bournemouth Pier now stands, and was spotted by the sharp-eyed crew of the *Resolution*, the Revenue Cutter then on station in the Bay, commanded by Captain Sarmon of Cowes. *Resolution* had almost reached the lugger when it anchored and smartly sent its tub-boats into the beach carrying kegs of brandy and packets of tea. As this happened, the smuggling vessel slewed round on its warp, clapped on all sail and high-tailed it out of the Bay.

As he saw the tub-boats go down into the water, Captain Sarmon immediately ordered away his jolly-boat with its armed crew, under the command of his appropriately-named Mate, Thomas Quick. The smugglers ran their boats up into the soft sand which made this beach so popular with them for landings, and quickly unloaded the kegs. The King's men also came ashore, yelling, roaring and brandishing their weapons to such good effect that the Free Traders panicked and took to their heels, leaving the contraband kegs behind them. Mr. Quick, laughing grimly, ordered his men to put the Stuff into their boat, a difficult task, as it turned out, for the surf had begun to run high.

Suddenly, as they were working, a mass of thirty mounted smugglers appeared charging down the wild valley, their path being through what are now the Lower Pleasure Gardens, taking them past the spot where the Pavilion stands. The fleeing smugglers had clearly gone for re-inforcements, probably from Decoy House and the Tapps Arms; this force was bent on rescuing what the smugglers regarded as their own property.

As he caught sight of this cavalry charge, Quick commanded his men to face about and present their weapons, which they had laid on the sand as they worked. He then roared to the smugglers to keep their distance or he and his men would open fire, to which the leader replied that they would come on as they were determined to get back their own goods. Faced with such effrontery, Quick had no alternative but to give his men the order to fire, and the volley which followed brought down a good number of the smugglers. Those who survived charged and Quick and one of his seamen named Anderson were felled; the rest of the King's men retreated into the wild surf. Anderson forced himself to his feet, only to find that he was looking down the barrel of a pistol: fortunately, when the smuggler pulled the trigger, it misfired, but the man shoved the weapon into Anderson's mouth, smashing most of his teeth. Mr. Quick was being beaten by two smugglers with cudgels; before he could rescue his senior officer, Anderson was felled to the ground again. While this was happening, the rest of the smugglers were flinging the brandy-kegs into their wagon, making off back up the Bourne Valley when it was fully loaded.

Eventually the leader of this violent gang was arrested and indicted 'for feloniously assembling with others armed with firearms at Bourne Bottom ... in order to be aiding and assisting in the running of uncustomed spiritous liquors, and assaulting Thomas Quick, Mate of the *Resolution*, cutter, in the service of the Excise, and, his boat's crew being then on shore, cutting and wounding the said Thomas Quick, and rescuing and carrying off the said goods.'

Poor Quick was, of course, the principal witness, but when he appeared in court, he was too badly wounded and too deeply in shock to be able to identify the accused with any certainty; one of his arms was in splints and a sling, and he walked with such difficulty that he had to have a chair in court. There is the possibility, of course, that he had lost his nerve, or even been threatened with reprisals by the smugglers still at liberty if he contributed to their chief's conviction. However, Anderson was in better condition than his superior officer, and together with another sailor named Cross, he named the gang's leader, a John Butler, alias Bishop, as the one who had led the bloodthirsty attack in Bourne Bottom. Bishop, a young smuggling chief apparently of good parentage, paid the penalty when he was hanged in Newgate Prison on 23rd April, 1788.

Although Abraham Pike's Journal only covers the years 1803 and 1804, he gives several accounts of incidents which took place in Bourne Bottom. For instance, in October 1803, his Officers called at his residence to tell him smugglers were making a run at Bourne. Mr. Pike does not record whether he asked them why they had not sent just one man to summon him while the others kept watch: one gets the feeling his Riding Officers liked to keep together as a group, especially in Christchurch.

The posse left the town and called at Christchurch Barracks to collect a party of the Twentieth Regiment of Light Dragoons, and then galloped on, much re-inforced, to Bourne Mouth. Pike's Journal continues. 'At Bourne and in the Heath I found and seized sixty-three casks of foreign spirits and one cask of tobacco, in company with [my] officers and party. At Bourne, met Mr. Buck, Landwaiter, and his boat's crew, and corresponded. From thence with Mr. Wise, Mr. Bacon and Mr. Newman to Poole with the seizure [and] secured it in His Majesty's Warehouse, and corresponded with the Comptroller. On our return, called on Mr. Wise and examined his Book, and surveyed the coast home with Mr. Bacon and Mr. Newman. In the Heath near Kinson found and seized two cases of cordials, one of spirits, and one small parcel of tobacco. In company with my officers secured it at my residence.'

It had been quite a successful day for Abraham Pike and his men, but the Journal's terse account tells us no details of how they seized the goods, or from whom, and in what circumstances. It also does not explain why they called on Mr. Wise when he was riding towards his home at Parkstone with them. One gets the impression that these Officers were blessed with a good deal of serendipity, for they seem to have stumbled on contraband which careless smugglers had just left lying about the heath behind Bourne Mouth.

Another entry in Abraham Pike's journal about Bourne Bottom is rather charming: 'Surveyed the west coast to Bourne, and found a small boat on the shore: the *Invisible* of Poole. From thence to Flagstaff and Parkstone: examined Mr. Wise, who informed me there had been a run of some prohibited goods. On my return surveyed Wallisdown, Kinson and Redhill: nothing more occurred. Returned, and went to Christchurch Quay on coast duty. ...'

If ever there was a time to worry about Mr. Wise, this must have been it: why had he not been keeping watch on the *Invisible*? It had obviously been the vessel in which the run goods had been landed. Only a smugglers' boat could have been called *Invisible*, for the Poole smugglers clearly had a sense of humour. Perhaps Mr. Wise made a lame joke on its wonderful name to his chief in trying to laugh off such an awkward question.

One of the most interesting questions with regard to the Bournemouth smugglers is whether Captain Lewis Dymoke Grosvenor Tregonwell was one of their number. Born in 1758 at Anderson in Dorset, the man to whom the founding of modern Bournemouth is universally attributed lived at Cranborne Lodge, which lies on the opposite side of the Wimborne Road from Cranborne Manor, the ancestral home of the famous Cecil family. The Tregonwells originally came from Cornwall, and Lewis married well, twice, in fact, and both ladies were considerable heiresses.

While Abraham Pike was toiling back and forth along the coast on the lookout for smugglers, he may well have met Tregonwell, for by 1796 the Squire of Cranborne Lodge was a Captain of the Dorset Volunteer Rangers, otherwise known as the Dorset Rangers, with his son St. Barbe as his Lieutenant. He must have been busy, for as well as being on the watch for smugglers and French invaders, he was also Justice of the Peace and Deputy Lieutenant for the County of Dorset. The boundary of the Rangers' patrol-area was the Bourne Stream itself, and no doubt they 'corresponded', as the official term used by Pike in his Journal had it; this means they exchanged notes and observations for the good of the services they both worked for, and with their opposite numbers in the Army on the other side of the brook, the Hampshire Fencibles.

In 1810, after the Battle of Trafalgar had reduced the threat of invasion by Napoleonic forces, Tregonwell was able to leave the Dorset Rangers, and in that year he and his wife Henrietta took a well-earned holiday. Unable to go abroad to Italy or France, he took her to that up-and-coming holiday resort within easy distance of Cranborne Lodge: Mudeford. The resort had become famous on 29th June, 1789, when King George III and the Royal Family, on their way to the monarch's favourite resort of Weymouth, had called in from the royal yacht to see William Rose, the Christchurch Member of Parliament, at his unique villa, Gundimore.

Tregonwell's wife was recovering from illness brought on by the death of her infant son, Grosvenor, who had died on his christening-day, and on a sunny July afternoon her husband took her along the coast to show her where he used to patrol with the Dorset Rangers. At Bourne Bottom she fell in love with the place, and a short time later she suggested, it is said, that it would be a lovely spot for the building of a marine villa of the sort which were then growing in popularity at such places as Weymouth in the west and Brighton in the east. They could then indulge in their new-found passion for sea-bathing, the taste for which the Tregonwells had just acquired at Mudeford.

Tregonwell purchased eight and a half acres of land between Bourne House (or Decoy Cottage) and the sea's edge, from Sir George Ivison Tapps, paying him the sum of £180. Soon the residence was under construction, named by the few people who lived in the area The Mansion, but eventually given the name Exeter House. It still stands, but as part of the larger building to which it gave its name: The Royal Exeter Hotel. Tregonwell bought more and more land round his fine new summer residence, and even purchased the Tapps Arms, that undoubted haunt of smugglers and the only public-house between the New Inn at Iford in the east and Poole in the west. He re-built the inn and re-named it the Tregonwell Arms.

Tregonwell had a highly-valued butler named Symes, whom he installed in a delightful thatched cottage specially built for him. This was at first known simply as Symes' Cottage; but as Tregonwell's estate grew into Bourne Tregonwell, and he became known more and more as The Governor, the big house had to have a lodge, as on all proper estates further inland. Symes' cottage became Portman Lodge, named after Mrs. Tregonwell's maiden name, and presumably the butler doubled as lodge-keeper.

It could be that the excellent manservant was required to be so versatile that he could take on another role: smugglers' storekeeper.

Portman Lodge, at all events, became his widow's residence when Tregonwell died in 1832; the cottage remained until it was severely damaged by fire almost a hundred years later. It was restored, but its days were numbered: in 1930 Portman Lodge was razed to the ground and the site cleared. Probably no one, least of all the local Bournemouth building-workers who did it, were surprised at the discovery amongst the foundations three feet below ground-level of a chamber ten feet long and seven feet wide, and with a height from floor to arched ceiling of six clear feet. Like other secret chambers, the only entrance had been through a trapdoor. The walls were unsafe, collapsing as the workmen tried to empty the room of rubble, so orders were given for yet another secret room to be filled in, a scenario often repeated many times in this area. A further interesting fact concerning Butler Symes is that it is pretty certain that he did not accompany the Tregonwell family when they returned to Cranborne Lodge, nor when they went up to London for the season: everything indicates that he stayed at Portman Lodge the whole year round, looking after Tregonwell's house and his interests.

One can legitimately ask whether Captain Tregonwell knew about the secret store-room. If so, then he was technically a receiver of smuggled goods, and if he was that, then he was a smuggler. One only has to stand outside the Royal Exeter Hotel today to see what an ideal location this would have been for a contraband dump: better than any Southbourne Cellars or Purbeck quarry-cave, and far better than any Poole storm-drain with its linked cellar. The location would have been worth every penny of the £180 price paid for this parcel of land.

Tregonwell's real home, Cranborne Lodge, lay on the main smuggling-route north from Bourne Mouth: one only has to trace the line very slightly west of north on the Ordnance Survey map to see that there was a direct run up through West Moors where Gulliver's Farm is clearly marked and on through Edmonsham to Cranborne. What would have been more convenient than for contraband to be landed at Bourne Bottom, lodged for the night, or day, in Symes' cellar, and then taken on by convoy, leisurely and quietly, or perhaps by the ordinary, regular carriers' carts which were such a feature of this area in those days? That would certainly avoid such unsavoury incidents as that involving Mr. Quick and his man Anderson.

Symes was probably the most efficient and well-equipped clerk in the whole history of English smuggling, as would have befitted someone working for a man known all along the coast as the Governor. It must be remembered that the famous Dorset smuggler Gulliver made his last run about 1800, so he and Tregonwell or Symes could have met. There is some speculation as to why the Dorset Yeomanry or any other military unit or Revenue men never took

Gulliver, or indeed, encountered him for any length of time. Could it have been that Tregonwell, having learnt all there was to know about preventing smuggling from his Dorset Rangers days, actually met Gulliver and fell under the spell of his apparent charm, his persuasive tongue, his courtesy and correctitude, and, most potent of all, his golden guineas and his endless supplies of that which makes the life of a gentleman worth living? Could Gulliver not have offered Tregonwell a gift which only a man of his stature and position was fitted to accept: the governorship of Gulliver's smuggling organization after the great man had retired or passed away, whichever came first? Certainly, if this had been the case there would have been plenty of both time and opportunity to instruct the heir to the crown in everything there was to be known. The fact that Tregonwell had married into money does not make indulgence in smuggling unlikely: like Temple Simon Luttrell he may simply have done it for the excitement.

From all accounts, Tregonwell appears to be everything that a respectable Dorsetshire squire should have been when lording it at Cranborne Lodge, which he always gave as his address; what else would one expect of the founder of England's most decorous watering-place: Bournemouth? However, one reads very little of the Governor's youth, and no wonder, for there is a family tradition that in the seventeen-eighties and nineties he was a member of the Prince of Wales' (later the Prince Regent) select circle of drinking companions, and was admired by them as a rather reckless and sensation-seeking young man. In addition to this, an amusing pencil sketch exists of Tregonwell, his wife and child, drawn in 1814 by Mrs. Drax Grosvenor of Charborough Park, near Sturminster Marshall. This lady and her husband had, by 1814, a holiday cottage on the western slope of Bourne Bottom, and became close friends of the Tregonwells. Mrs. Grosvenor also sketched a friendly satire describing life at Bourne Tregonwell. It is an idyllic vision centred on the sea, but it does include references to smuggling, for Bourne Bottom was being used by the Free Traders just as frequently then as in the past.

For example, in 1820 the local Lander had five hundred men in a party, which was attacked by Revenue men and dragoons just as the convoy was making its way up the valley. The King's men must have been there in large numbers too, for in the very fierce battle which ensued, the smugglers managed to hold on to only nine brandy-kegs that night. In March of the following year, 1821, the sea-smugglers must have come in too early, for, finding no Lander and party awaiting them, they stacked their 130 kegs of gin and brandy on the beach and got out to sea again, having completed their part of the contract. Before the tardy Lander could arrive, the Preventers had whisked the lot off to Poole.

18. The Grosvenor Drawing.

In the following October, a smaller haul of forty-two tubs of spirits fell into Revenue hands, though the details of this triumph are not known. To cap all these examples of the constant smuggling going on here, the Governor himself one day tripped over a small clutch of kegs half hidden in the sand while taking his constitutional along the beach.

Mrs. Grosvenor obviously knew about the smuggling; and she believed that everyone else at Bourne Tregonwell knew about it, for they could not have thought that the drink of which they are so merrily partaking in her drawing had just been washed up on the golden sands. Brandy kegs are very much in evidence, Tregonwell himself holds high a brimming glass, while behind him a boatload of suspicious barrels heaves-to offshore. And at the bottom of the hilarious drawing we are told that 'the Bournist's motto is: "Spirits from the Deep, Arise! Oh, arise!"' The lady descending a little unsteadily from the cottage is said to be 'flying to catch a breaker, well-armed in case of bandits', 'breaker' meaning both a large wave and a container of liquid; and her need to be prepared for 'banditti' shows Mrs. Grosvenor well knew the sort of Gentlemen who frequented Bourne Bottom in those years.

It may be far-fetched to suggest that Tregonwell actually took over from Gulliver as the smuggling chief at Bourne; but one can hardly doubt that he was, at least, an agent for some smuggling enterprise or other.

The rest of the Great Heath, the tawny, barren land on which Bournemouth now stands, had many more smuggling associations. Westward along the coast from Bourne Bottom, lies Branksome Chine. This was Gulliver's favourite landing-spot; one of the reasons may have been the fact that near Seaward Path are the remains of a well that was known for years as the Smugglers' Well. It was probably used not just for refreshment but also as a dump when the 'Gobloos' got too close behind them.

On 25th October, 1982, a front-page story about the garden of a house in Cromer Road appeared in the Bournemouth *Evening Echo*. At the foot of an old plum-tree a deep hole had suddenly been revealed, and was said to be a well with a depth of thirty feet. When I examined the shaft the next day I saw that it had a fine brick lining and was perfectly dry; and on being told by the householder that the plum tree's roots had been surrounded by a square of timber, the rotting of which had, apparently, revealed the hole, I was reminded of the Smugglers' Well and the method used by smugglers to the west in Dorset to conceal subterranean hides in which they dumped their contraband when the Revenue men were hunting for it after a run. This method is clearly described by Thomas Hardy in his smuggling short story *The Distracted Preacher*, and entailed the planting of an apple tree in a wooden tray filled with earth, which could be removed by the smugglers when they needed to open their cavern or well-like shaft. I was convinced that this Cromer Road well was such a hide when I consulted my map of Poole and saw that the house and its garden was actually a few feet to the east of the well-known smugglers' path coming up from Flaghead and Branksome Chines.

Branksome Chine has another smuggling connection: it was not only a favourite place for Isaac Gulliver, but also to his father, who was also called Isaac, and was also a smuggler. In the year 1758 young Isaac was only thirteen, so it is doubtful whether he took part in this escapade; but whether he did or not, what is certain is that Isaac the Elder led his gang of some fifty men in an attack on four Revenue men who had seized a sizeable packet of tea, which had probably been left on the beach in the traditional Bournemouth smugglers' fashion. Old Isaac's view was also traditional: that he was only taking back from the Gobloos what was rightfully the smugglers'. Needless to say they beat the King's men soundly for their impertinence. One wonders whether when he heard his father's account of this incident the younger Gulliver resolved never to stoop to beating King's Officers because he knew it would be bad not only for business but also bad for an Englishman to do.

Flaghead Chine marks the end of the Bournemouth cliffs, and was the westernmost limit of Abraham Pike's endless patrols. It is not clear, now, where the flag came in, but possibly it was a sea-mark for vessels entering Poole Harbour; or perhaps it was kept by a smuggler for signalling whether the coast was clear and the King's officers never realized its true purpose. After all, if it was the Union flag, one could hardly ask an apparently harmless private citizen to refrain from flying it when he chose. Flaghead Chine was on Pike's list of places to visit simply because it was a splendid way up from the end of the vast beach of Poole Bay when the others were not useable, or when Poole was out of commission as far as the smugglers were concerned. It will come as no surprise to learn that Pike never tells us of any encounter with smugglers in the Chine, even though smugglers emerged from it into the path which today is Canford Cliffs Road, but which in those days and for many years afterwards was called Smugglers' Way. The modern road goes north like an arrow, crosses Poole Road, and then continues as Alder Road, running very close to the end of the Upper Pleasure Gardens, the highest reaches of the Bourne Valley itself. The two smugglers' highways joined here to continue through the Heath, onwards and northwards to the great smuggling capital of Kinson, from where the wagons rolled northeastwards, northwards and particularly northwestwards to Salisbury, Blandford, Bristol and all points between.

Along all the smugglers' routes lay the great houses, the homes of the gentry, their biggest and best customers. The supply of gin, brandy, port and sherry was not only to satisfy normal consumption, along with table wines like claret, but also to accommodate what, after all, was a national sport: getting very drunk. One of the ways, perhaps the best way, that the young Englishman of the eighteenth and nineteenth centuries proved his manhood was by drinking deeper than the next. It was the method by which you showed your 'bottom', that is: how much bottom, or guts, you had, and it is still true today, though, of course, beer is the more usual drink. One only has to look at the wine-bills for dinners in the colleges of Oxford and Cambridge in this period to appreciate what a demand there was on the part of the gentlemen of England for the most intoxicating wines and spirits that the smugglers could supply. If it had not been for the smugglers, the upper classes would have often had to make do for their revels with plain beer and cider.

There are three large country houses on the Great Heath, in what is now the Bournemouth area. They were all on the smugglers' route, which usually started as they came up off the beach at Portman Ravine, Boscombe. Following this path today, one has to leave the Cliffs, that strip of parkland running along the coast of Boscombe and Bournemouth, and cross the Boscombe Overcliff Drive to enter Ravine Road. Following this, one reaches Wentworth Avenue which forms a T-junction with it. From here one has to resort to the Ordnance Survey map because the old smugglers' track cuts across the modern Woodside, Darracott, Granville and Harcourt Roads, and then possibly takes the same route as Queensland Road, after which it joins what is now Christchurch Road.

The track from Christchurch Road probably cut through King's Park and entered Littledown Common, or Great Dean Common as it was also called. Across the east-to-west drive which bisects this open heathland lies Littledown House, with its complementary Littledown Farm.

This good-sized house is a real Georgian mansion, which comes as something of a shock in the middle of one of Bournemouth's open spaces. It was, in fact, built by John Dean, some time before his death in 1794. He was a member of the Dean family who, with the Meyricks and Malmesburys, formed the triumvirate of great original Bournemouth families. It was the first house of quality for smugglers as they came off the beach and began their inland haul. After leaving their order at Littledown House, they would have made their way to Hurn Court by way of one of the River Stour fords, of which there were several to choose from.

Hurn Court lies immediately to the north of Littledown House, and in smuggling days it was still called Heron Court, the home for most of the eighteenth century of the Hooper family. Again, this stately home so near the upstart Bournemouth is another surprise, for its main part is Elizabethan in origin. At the end of the eighteenth century the main road from Christchurch to the north actually passed very close to the front of this house before joining Parley Lane. The following story was recounted by the Earl of Malmesbury in a book entitled, *Memoirs of an Ex-Minister*. One evening in the year 1780, Edward Hooper, the master of Heron Court, Justice of the Peace and a Commissioner in His Majesty's Customs, was entertaining to dinner his kinsman, Lord Shaftesbury, who was at that time the local Chairman of Customs and Excise. Their dinner was barely halfway through when their talk was interrupted by the rumble and clatter of a convoy of hard-driven wagons coming along the road right in front of the house. His Lordship leapt from his place and dashed to the dining-room window, from which he was amazed to see six farmcarts trundling past, loaded high with keg upon keg of spirits. Lord Shaftesbury called his host to witness the sight, but the eighty-year-old Squire, sitting with his back to the window, would not stop eating, nor would he raise his head from his plate. Nothing Lord Shaftesbury could say would interest Mr. Hooper in the events outside, and the convoy passed on its noisy way.

The meal was continued, Mr. Hooper talking of a host of subjects, none of which featured carts and convoys, until a second commotion in the road disturbed their digestions. This time it was a full squadron of Dragoons, whose Officer was shown into the dining-room where he asked the two gentlemen if they had seen a convoy of wagons go past Heron Court. Lord Shaftesbury politely took his cue from his host, who gravely informed the King's Officer that he had seen nothing untoward outside his house that evening, least of all the smugglers whom the Dragoons had been chasing.

With high Customs officials acting in this way, is it any wonder that smugglers, on the few occasions when they were caught, were never tried by magistrates or higher courts in their own parts of the country? One wonders whether the noble Lord mildly remonstrated with his host when the officer of Dragoons had departed, or whether they agreed to forget the whole incident over glasses of the best smuggled cognac Mr. Hooper's cellars could provide.

One more incident shows how popular Heron Court was with the Gentlemen of the Night. The Third Earl of Malmesbury lived there from 1807 until 1899, and when he was a boy he went birds' nesting in the park. He was just putting out his hand to lift an egg, when his wrist was grabbed by a hairy hand, and a hoarse voice demanded his identity and his reason for being where he was at that time. On learning who the boy was, and that he was so scared he would be unlikely to tell anyone that he had seen them hiding their contraband in the woods, (probably in the ice-house which still lies in the park) the smugglers told him they would let him go when they had finished their little act of camouflage. They even offered the little lord a nip from one of their brandy-kegs. When they finally released him, they made him swear to remain silent about his terrifying experience, though his family in the big house would have had to have been very different from the previous residents for them to have felt alarmed at the smugglers' presence on their land.

Continuing due north, like the convoy Mr. Hooper refused to look at, the smugglers' next dropping-point would have been the house, still known as Matcham's. At the turn of the last century this was actually the home of Lord Nelson's sister; and the great Admiral visited this branch of his family several times, on one occasion planting several trees in the grounds. With family and guests of that calibre at Matcham's, the smugglers' regular services would always have been necessary, supplying gin, fine wines and, of course, the drink which was closest to the great sailor's heart, in more ways than one: brandy. After his death on board H.M.S. *Victory*, his body was placed in a barrel of brandy to preserve it on the long voyage home to England. When the body had been taken out of the barrel by the undertakers, the liquor left was sold off to the general public at prices even the smugglers would have envied.

In the Free Trade days, the Great Heath was divided into named districts, even though they supported no actual village or other settlement. For instance, Muckleheath, which actually means Great Heath, lay on either side of Castle Lane, the ancient route into Christchurch from the west of England, and extended as far as the swampy valley then known as Great Dean Bottom, through which Queen's Park Avenue now runs. The valley which forms such a challenging feature of the famous Queen's Park Golf Course, was, in those days, called Longman's Bottom and was a vital routeway for the smugglers, as were Littledown Common and Puck's Down, now called by its modern name of Pokesdown. All three places were covered by gorse so high that it grew in trees rather than bushes, so that wagons could lose themselves completely there and journey on invisible to the eyes of any pursuing Revenue Officers, even though they were mounted on horseback. Surprising though it may seem, local tradition says that these heathy hills were punctuated by springs which conveniently cut small caverns of varying size for the smugglers. The mouths were screened with welcome gorse-fronds and clumps of the coarse grass which is still a feature of the Heath, especially along the cliffs.

Holdenhurst is the oldest village close to which the smugglers must have passed on their way from Littledown House to Hurn Court. Holdenhurst was the mother-parish of Bournemouth, and has a very long history. It could be called a smugglers' village, though not on the same scale as Burley, but certainly with a high proportion of its population taking part in the Trade at some time or other in their lives. Even before the Free Trade was set up along the Bournemouth coast, men were in the habit of walking down to the sea from inland villages and hamlets such as Holdenhurst, Throop and Sopley to fish for mackerel, helping the local fishermen to haul in the nets. During the night, these same men would have hauled in tub-lines from smuggling luggers. It is more than likely that the offer of something more than a few mackerel enticed men from Holdenhurst to stay on the beach until night fell in order to assist the smugglers; or even to help them during the day in the time when daylight smuggling was flourishing.

Both by helping with landings and living on the smugglers' route inland, Holdenhurst men could be involved in the trade; it is fairly certain that several full-time smugglers had their homes there. One such Trader was said to have hidden around 1000 golden guineas in his garden. It can only be assumed that he was either the agent of one of the local Venturers, or that he was a guinea-smuggler. Whichever he was, the fate of the man and his guineas has not been handed down: perhaps he was robbed of them or even killed when they were taken from him. Another smuggling-resident of the village was said to be connected with gold, in a far more incredible and bizarre fashion: he was apparently so rich from contraband traffic that he buried his wife in a gold coffin on one of the local hills — Hadden, Red, or perhaps Bury Hill. This fantastic story has to be dismissed as a case of smuggling-mythology run riot.

What can be said with certainty is that the village's inn must have been one of the best-supplied in the whole of the south of England. The Three Elms, as it was named, would have been well worth visiting for the riches of its cellar and the smuggling yarns its clients could spin. A market-day always saw furious contraband activity, for even women going to sell their countrywares used to hide raisins, brandy-kegs, tobacco and lace in their capacious baskets under the cheese, butter and eggs which they took to sell at such places as Ringwood and Wimborne. Holdenhurst was not only a smugglers' dormitory but also a large-scale dump, a vital halfway house only two and a half miles from some of the finest landing-beaches in the whole of the British Isles.

One smuggler links present-day Bournemouth with those far-off times in a striking manner, for many of his descendants are still living. In the *Bournemouth Times and Directory* there appeared during the year 1905 the following report: 'Mr. William Butler is a veteran of ninety-four years, still hale and hearty, who has lived all his life in the neighbourhood of Kinson, and who at present resides with his son George at Ebenezer Cottage, Newton.

'Butler. ... has had seven children, fifty-five grandchildren, sixty great grandchildren, and at present, one great great grandchild ... He is still able to "potter about", as he says, and do a little work ... He eats heartily and has hardly ever known what it is to be ill, and, judging from present appearances, seems likely to become a centenarian. ... [He] was one of the fraternity under John Eason of the Rose and Crown ... who troubled the countryside in the early part of the last century from Chapman's Pool to Chewton Bunny; and many a cargo of lace, tobacco and brandy has he assisted in smuggling into the country under the noses of the Preventive Officers themselves.

'He tells with glee a yarn about landing a cargo at Christchurch Old Quay on a Sunday morning, and conveying the goods through the Priory Churchyard to the appointed rendezvous just as the people were coming out of church, to the great amazement of the congregation who met them.

'In his early days, labourers were happy on ten shillings a week. Bournemouth was a shooting-station with about three or four fishermen's hovels, and Poole was the port of the south. What a difference now!'

9
Isaac Gulliver: King of the Dorset Smugglers

Although the zealous Riding Officer Abraham Pike had a beat which stretched from Hurst Castle to Poole, several smugglers probably held sway over their personal patches within his area. It seems likely that during smuggling's heyday, Christchurch smugglers regarded the little Bourne stream as the furthest western limit of their activities, for beyond it was the province of a powerful smugglers' leader.

His name was Isaac Gulliver, and he extended his province from the Bourne in the east to the border between Devon and Cornwall throughout the course of an amazingly long and successful career. Isaac was a real Wiltshire Moonraker, born in the year 1745 in the little village of Semington, which lies between Melksham and Trowbridge. By the time he had reached manhood he was noted for his great stature, his commanding presence, and a natural flair for leadership and organization. As the years passed he was seen also to possess a keen financial sense and great bravery. The first portrait of Isaac was probably painted to celebrate his coming of age for it is dated 1766. Two years later he married Elizabeth Beale in the Church of St. Mary at Sixpenny Handley on Cranborne Chase. His bride happened to be the daughter of the landlord of the Blacksmith's Arms at Thorney Down on the busy Salisbury to Blandford Forum road, and soon after their marriage Isaac took over from his father-in-law as landlord. He changed the inn's name to the King's Arms to underline its new management, as well as his loyalty to the Crown, which was later to be royally acknowledged.

Like many another smuggler of the time, Isaac was the son of a smuggler, and had probably married into a smuggling family, for his new inn was only six miles from Tidpit Down where smugglers regularly sold their contraband in an open market. But in 1778 the Philistines swooped and near Thorney Down they seized a quantity of tea and nine casks of brandy, which were taken to the house of the

19. The King's Head at Thorney Down, on the road from Blandford Forum to Salisbury. Isaac Gulliver married the landlord's daughter and eventually took over the inn, changing its name from The Blacksmith's Arms.

Supervisor of Customs in Blandford and locked up. At about seven that evening, having re-grouped, a large party of well-armed smugglers came to reclaim their 'Stuff'. They burst open the door of the house, fought their way in, grabbed what they regarded as their property and carried it off through the town, letting off their pistols into the air; their shouts of delight, no doubt assisted by a swift sampling of that which they had recovered, were echoed by the good folk of Blandford whom the Gentlemen rewarded by presenting them with two of the re-captured casks. This incident is just one of many which illustrates that the area in which Gulliver started his famous career as a smuggler was full of smuggling activity, even though it was not on the coast.

In the same year Isaac himself moved to Longham, taking over the White Hart, closer to the perfect, gently-sloping, sandy beaches of Poole Bay, and only five miles each way from those busy centres of the Free Trade, Poole and Christchurch. Isaac had probably been smuggling successfully for some years by now, for it was clearly a strategic move. It is more than probable that the raiders of the Blandford Customs headquarters were his men, although their behaviour after the raid would seem to indicate that he had not licked them into the shape he later imposed upon his gang with a discipline which became the hallmark of his leadership. He later became known as 'the gentle smuggler', who could boast at the end of his life that he had never killed anyone. Longham was the obvious headquarters and command-post for a smuggling chief who had chosen as his field of operations the triangular Great Heath between Bournemouth and Poole.

With his smuggling operations in full swing, Isaac had fifteen luggers bringing in from France, the Channel Islands and Holland, brandy, gin, silk, lace, tea and all the other items on the standard smugglers' shopping list. These vessels dropped their anchors off Bourne Mouth, off Alum Chine, Branksome Chine and Flag Chine, those invaluable valleys cutting up through the cliffs and leading into the Great Heath where his convoys of pack-horses and wagons could easily lose any Revenue men quick enough to surprise them. Branksome Chine he found the most useful, for it led up through Pug's Hole, a clearing which can still be visited in Talbot Woods, and on up to Kinson. Close study of the Ordnance Survey map for Bournemouth and Purbeck will show how today's roads follow the smugglers' track up to Kinson, as do so many of the roads in Bournemouth, for very few others used the Heath besides the Gentlemen of the Night.

Kinson was known as Kingston in smuggling's heyday, and was on Abraham Pike's regular patrol-route, as this entry in his Journal for January, 1803, shows: 'Surveyed the west to Flagstaff; from thence to Parkstone. Examined Mr. Wise and signed his book. On my return surveyed Wallisdown, Kingston [Kinson], and Redhill. Nothing occurred.'

In actual fact, by 1803 Gulliver had moved further to the west, but Kinson had been the inland centre of the Free Trade for many years. It was here that run goods were stored until a market had been arranged for them and their destinations fixed. The village was crammed full with hiding-places, and these were crammed full with goods.

It was in 1780 that Isaac himself moved to Kinson, having had Howe Lodge built for his residence, a custom-built palace for a King of Smugglers. Its crenellations clearly indicate its fortress-like quality, and inside had been lavished all the ingenuity of its hiding-place architect. The house's largest secret room had its door ten feet up the chimney and was impossible to detect. In the floor of the dining-room a trapdoor, covered by the carpet, provided the

20. West Howe Lodge, Kinson, Gulliver's purpose-built stronghold.

entrance to the vast cellar from which, in turn, a neatly-bricked tunnel led away south. It was a good six feet high, for a later tenant stated that he was able to walk along it upright for about forty feet before meeting the brick wall which had been put in to seal it off. Strong local legend said that this tunnel ran all the way to Parkstone Bay in Poole Harbour, a distance of about three and a third miles. Another story says that another tunnel led from Gulliver's house northward, meeting the smugglers' paths leading to both Poole in one direction and Christchurch in the other. Certainly, before it was demolished in 1958, secret doors, passages, cupboards and recesses were found in plenty all over this odd building. Gulliver lived here, as his smuggling business trips allowed him, periodically from 1780 to 1816, staying at his other residences as necessary: a house at Crichel, near Blandford, another at Corfe Mullen, and at his farm at West Moors on the edge of Holt Heath, which to this day is called Gulliver's Farm.

The whole of Kinson was, according to a local historian, riddled with tunnels. A few years ago a resident described how, as a lad, he was taken by an old inhabitant along a complete system of them which seemed to link every house of any size or antiquity, each of which had a subterranean store-place into which the connecting tunnels led. The centre of this labyrinth was the Parish Church of St. Andrew, to the north of which the land drops away into the flood-plain of the River Stour, a convenient exit for a tunnel from the church if the smugglers working in it were surprised by the King's Officers.

For the contrabandists the church was a look-out tower, storehouse and head-office, and the Parish Clerk probably kept their accounts. Up on the parapet of the tower can still be seen the grooves worn by the smugglers' ropes as they hauled brandy casks up to the hiding-place on the leads. The tops of towers like these were the best places not only to stow 'the crop' and guard it, but from which to keep 'the Gaugers', another name for the Revenue men, under constant surveillance. In Thomas Hardy's short story *The Distracted Preacher* there is a vivid picture of smugglers doing just this, as well as many other little tricks of their trade in their efforts to fool their old enemies. Hardy was a keen student of smuggling ways, one of his father's servants at Bockhampton having been a tub-carrier over Lulworth way at the turn of the last century.

At the foot of Kinson's church-tower is a table tomb which was used for leaving small amounts of smuggled goods for specific customers who only placed small orders. They only needed the knack of moving the lid of the tomb to remove the goods. The tomb was, like so many things used by the smugglers, custom-built, and was dedicated to a series of fictitious tenants.

It is on the north side of St. Andrew's Church that the most striking survival from smuggling days is to be found, outclassing any other record or relic. By the very nature of the game, smugglers left few written records. Much was written in the early years of Victoria's reign, when the Trade was on the decline, to romanticize the craft: ballads such as *The Smuggler*, *The Smuggler's Boy* and *The Smuggler's Bride*; the local play, *Billy Coombes' Last Fight*; and countless novels. But this record is one chiselled out of stone, and it reads:

'To the Memory of
ROBERT TROTMAN
Late of Rond in the County of Wilts
who was barbarously Murder'd on the Shore near
Poole the 24 March 1765

A little Tea one leaf I did not steal
For Guiltless Blood shed I to GOD appeal
Put Tea in one scale human Blood in t'other
And think what 'tis to slay thy harmless Brother.'

Wiltshiremen will know that there is no such place as Rond in their county: apparently, when the stone was cleaned and restored some years ago, the name 'Rowd', which should, of course, have had a final 'e', was misspelt 'Rond'.

Unless Gulliver was already smuggling at the age of twenty, it is unlikely that Robert was one of his men, for he died long before Isaac moved here. But what the stone *does* show is that his smuggling mates felt that Kinson was where he belonged; and that, far more significantly, the local sympathy with the Trade was very deep, the pure folk poetry of the verses bringing this out.

It was not only the church and Howe Lodge which were, literally, connected with the Trade. Kinson House was always considered a smuggling house. It was for many years the home of the Russells, great aunt and uncle of Russell and Sybil Thorndike, and although he set them in Romney Marsh, it is certain that Russell gained his inspiration for his tales of Dr. Syn, the smuggling vicar, from his rides over the Heath round Kinson. Woodlands, which stood near Howe Lodge, was another smugglers' house, and said to be haunted. One day the cause of this was discovered: a woman's skull was dug up in the grounds and was found to have a marlin-spike firmly embedded in it. What desperate sea-smuggler did that?

Kinson's Manor House, formerly called Ensbury Manor, was 700 years old when it was demolished in 1936. Set well back from the road behind a screen of trees, it contained a maze of corridors and some strangely-shaped rooms, as well as two staircases. But strangest of all were the windows: they had shutters on the inside, and some had iron bars on the outside. This ancient building, as was only proper, had more than one ghost: a sea-man who appeared in dripping oilskins, and another, more 'capricious', who had the habit of snatching the caps of the maids' heads as they scuttled terrified along the interminable corridors.

Even Ensbury Vicarage in Kinson, built in 1785, had its tunnel leading from a cellar under the kitchen, a fact which was recently revealed by land subsidence. This building is still standing, and its smuggling connection emphasises the link between Cloth and Contraband.

Lastly, the Dower House, once called Ensbury Cottage, and still standing, had three brick-lined hides in the garden, which had lids to them: large stone slabs which made the cavities rather like the table tomb just down the road at the foot of the Church's tower.

Gulliver must have made a great deal of money while he was at Kinson. But the essence of his method at this stage in his very methodical career was to buy land with houses and farms on it, build cellars, hides and tunnels, establish his collection and distribution network, and then move on, usually westwards, extending the boundaries of his kingdom as he did so. By 1776 he was aged thirty-one and had beneath him a team of smugglers second to none along the whole British coast. Usually said to be a steady fifty in number, he decked out his men in a uniform: a smock of the type worn by the Dorset shepherds, and a particular way of wearing their hair: long, dressed with white powder, and tied in a neat, seaman-like cue. He obviously wanted everyone to know whose smugglers they were, just as he wanted to be able to recognize them from a distance or when the action became particularly sharp. Bearing in mind also the probability that he was given a certain amount of leeway by the authorities, such a uniform would have been a protection for them if captured. The hair powder was also a boast: powder carried a high Customs duty, so it added to his prestige along the coast; it also gave his gang their famous name of the White Wigs, although it was their own hair.

21. 'Halt: Smugglers by Henry Perlee Parker, whose fondness for smuggling subjects led to his being dubbed 'Smuggler' Parker. Doubt about the central figure being Isaac Gulliver should be resolved by studying both it and the miniature on page 152.

A remarkable painting tersely entitled 'Halt: Smugglers' was produced by Henry Perlee Parker. His pictures of smuggling scenes became so popular in this country during the 1850s that he was known affectionately as 'Smuggler' Parker. This particular example of his work hung for many years in the Tregonwell Arms, the first public house to be built in Bournemouth, and a notorious haunt of the Free Traders of the Great Heath. While it hung there, the scene was always assumed to be of Gulliver and his gang having a break after getting yet another crop of contraband successfully up the cliffs from the beach at Bourne Bottom, the spot where Bournemouth Pier now stands. It is full of interest, for the central bald figure certainly resembles the miniature of Isaac which was painted when he was in old age; and, in addition to the technical smuggling details it depicts, particularly the horses' pack saddles and the size of the spirit-kegs, it clearly shows that there was no colour prejudice in Gulliver's gang, a very cheerful-looking group of contrabandists.

By 1776 Isaac had extended his realm as far as West Dorset, for it was in that year that he bought North Eggardon Farm, ten miles west of Dorchester and five miles from the sea. Eggardon Hill with its Iron Age fort adjoined the farm, and here Isaac planted a circle of fir-trees to serve his incoming ships as a sea-mark. This was smuggling on the truly grand scale. Today Gulliver's Lane still leads down from the hill through the beautifully picturesque Shipston Gorge; but the sea-mark is gone, felled by officious Customs men, although the octagonal bank he added to the ancient ramparts to protect his trees can still be seen.

At this time, Burton Bradstock, Swyre, Bexington and West Bay were his choicest landing-places, the goods being taken off these splendidly straight though gravelly beaches through Puncknowle, Powerstock, over Toller Down, and on through Corscombe and Hallstock, and so to the eager customers in thriving, fashionable Bath and the great City of Bristol beyond. Gulliver's White Wigs were to be seen operating at Lyme Regis, landing goods in broad daylight within plain view of the Customs House, and then packhorsing them off through Whitchurch Canonicorum to Crewkerne on the Dorset-Somerset border, and thence to Bristol. Not only did they work where they could be easily seen from the Customs House, but they took their ease after a hard day's smuggling at an inn which was also close to the Revenue retreat. Clearly, Gulliver had this part of the coast as firmly under control as he had had that stretch further east where he began his remarkable career.

It is more probable that he achieved his supremacy not through violence and the threat of violence, but through bribery, for it became his boast that he had never killed a King's man. His pistol, preserved in the Russell-Cotes Art Gallery and Museum in Bournemouth, shows that he put little trust in weapons, for it is little more than a lady's reticule-gun. While his men brought the goods ashore, Gulliver went about the country in the guise of a respectable wine, spirit, and tea merchant, and employed representatives to ride the countryside calling on the gentry and rich merchants and inviting them to place orders for his cut-price, but highest quality, luxuries and necessities.

There are many stories of his exploits. On one occasion his lugger, the *Dolphin*, dropped anchor at night off Branksome Chine where he was awaiting it, mounted on his famous, favourite white horse, for he was acting as Lander. When everything was loaded into the wagons, Isaac took one cask of brandy for himself and trotted off at the head of his convoy through Branksome Woods, now called Branksome Park, and out on to the Great Heath. Through the gorse, heather and low oaks went the caravan, until Isaac decided to gallop ahead of the ponderous wagons and leave their conduct to his lieutenant.

As he reached the crossroads he suddenly caught the sound of hooves and heard a challenge ring out, coupled with a demand for him to halt in the King's name. Tradition has it that the challenger was none other than Abraham Pike from Christchurch; but whoever it was rash enough to challenge the great Gulliver, the smuggler-chief merely laughed and dug his spurs into his horse's flanks. He gave his pursuers a very good run for their money, reaching Kinson only minutes ahead of them. Ordering his stable-boy to unsaddle his horse and turn it loose in the paddock, he dashed indoors with his keg and told his wife what was happening. She whipped open the trap-door under the parlour carpet and Gulliver was soon hidden in the cellar, the carpet replaced and Mrs. Gulliver's chair firmly positioned on it.

Suddenly she saw the tell-tale brandy-keg. She flung a cushion on it, rested her feet on the cushion, and arranged her skirts decorously over it. She was only just in time, for the Customs Officer was hammering on the door. Calmly, when she was quite ready, she told her maid to let the visitor in, and although he blustered his suspicions to her, she blandly told him that her husband was not at home, and that he was wasting his time demanding to see him, for if he intended searching the house, he would, of course, need a magistrate's warrant. Thwarted, Pike, if it was he, dashed out to the stables determined to find Gulliver's horse still sweating from his swift ride home. But he found all the horses in the stables had obviously been there for some time. Only the single empty stall seemed suspicious, but, as the stable-boy pointed out: as his master was not at home, neither was his horse. So the King's Officer had to ride off, but not without promising malevolently to return with a search-warrant.

Sure enough, the next day he was back with the document, but only to be told that Isaac Gulliver had died and was lying in state in his coffin upstairs. The Officer asked to see the corpse, and was convinced that the great Gulliver had passed on, particularly from the pallor of the body's white face, no doubt the result of applying hair-powder from Gulliver's own store. The Revenue Officer apologised for intruding on the family's mourning and rode back to Christchurch, no doubt examining the crossroads as he went. For him it was yet another case of 'No success'. Of course, the news soon spread and the Gullivers went through with the mock-funeral, even the Vicar being fooled by the coffin filled with stones which they asked him to bury. Isaac left Kinson and spent some months in another part of his realm.

Another story tells how he was very nearly captured on a business-trip to Poole, not the best place for a well-known smuggler to visit, for, being a large port, it was watched over by a Collector of Customs and his large staff. He was spotted, and the Philistines gave chase. Isaac dodged into an inn and the landlord, eager to help his distinguished supplier, whisked him into a large empty cask, set it on his wagon, and the great man was driven through Poole High Street under the Customs men's noses, out of the town into the safety of the country beyond.

On yet another occasion, Gulliver was spotted near Wimborne, where in due course he bought several properties on the outskirts, and one in the town itself. Borrowing a Dorset shepherd's smock from a farmer friend, he decided the best place to hide was in a crowd, and spent the whole of the day in the middle of busy Wimborne Market pretending to be a rustic herdsman. Then, as the sun went down, he escaped once again.

It was in 1782 that the Government offered a free pardon to any smuggler who would enter the Royal Navy, or, if that was unattractive, who could provide a substitute to serve the Lords of the Admiralty in his place. There was considerable surprise in smuggling circles when Gulliver himself applied for the King's clemency and announced that he had found a substitute. He also let it be known to the Brotherhood that he was moving away from the county of Dorset where he had been active for so long, and that his new base of operations would be Teignmouth, and that Devon would be his new 'patch'. He finally astounded all who knew him either personally or by repute, by announcing that from that day forward, for the rest of his career, he would be concentrating solely on the selling of fine wines and the best spirits to the gentry, hoping, as he put it, 'for continued favours of friends and customers'. The readers of the *Gentleman's Magazine* in a hundred stately homes must have been delighted at this news.

Those of the smuggling fraternity who had thought he had been overtaken by premature senility need not have worried: asking Gulliver to stop smuggling would have been like requesting the lion to lay off the zebra. Clearly, he did do more wine-selling, taking orders personally as he travelled about the region; but, just as clearly, he did not cease to smuggle. The Commissioners of the Board of Customs in London were not fooled, for in 1788 they asked the Collector of Poole for a confidential report on Isaac's status as a smuggler. They had either heard something or else it was a routine check on a former notorious contrabandist who had just taken the King's Pardon. Whatever it was, the Collector told his masters that a few years before, Isaac had been one of the most active and successful smugglers in the whole of the west country, but that, after availing himself of His Majesty's Clemency, he had ceased his wicked ways and had turned honest wine-merchant, opening legitimate vaults all along the coast to the west of Poole. It stated that these vaults were in 'remote places', and that Gulliver sold wines and spirits well below other merchants' prices. Presumably, he was able to do this because he was selling smuggled goods from smugglers' stores, with the advantage that these goods were much better for being kept in cool, sea-washed caves.

The Collector of Customs at Poole then concluded his report rather strangely: 'He is a person of great speculating genius, and besides this he has carried on a variety of other businesses, but we find he is not known at present to be concerned in any sort of merchandise, and lives retired at a farm in the neighbourhood, having acquired, as it is reported, a very considerable property.' (This farm was very probably Lilliput House on the shore of Poole Harbour.)

It sounds an ambiguous, even contradictory, report: certainly the Poole Customs men seem to have been very keen to assure London that there was no need to worry about Gulliver any more. Perhaps he had them in his pocket; it would have been odd if he had not. Perhaps that trip to the town mentioned above had been made in confidence that the Collector would ignore his presence, and he had been spotted and pursued by some new, keen young Revenue Officer whom the Customs chief had omitted to brief on the official attitude to the smuggling chief. It may be of considerable significance that shortly after this report was made, Mr. Weston, the Customs Deputy of Poole, was dismissed from the Service because he was suspected of passing information useful to the other side to a notorious smuggler of the area named John Early, who may have been one of Isaac's men.

Whatever the truth of the matter, Gulliver was described in 1791 as 'a Dorset merchant', and not as 'Isaac Gulliver, the notorious smuggler'. He always spoke of himself at this time as 'Isaac Gulliver, of Kinson, Wine Merchant'. It would seem that he had not very far to go to complete respectability. Then, as so often happens in the story of this man's remarkable career, the contrabandist thread comes uppermost once again. Around 1800 he made his last run. Three of his luggers came into the beach at Bourne Bottom, loaded with brandy, silk, tobacco and other unspecified goods. When loaded, tradition boasts, the convoy of his wagons and screens of horsemen stretched for two miles as it wound its way inland, 'at the head of which rode the Old Chief, mounted on a spirited charger', as the rather sentimental report in *The Gentleman's Magazine* puts it. The writer expressed an affectionate admiration that struck a chord in his many readers.

By this time Christchurch Barracks had been built, and Dragoons were being used not only to guard the coast against the threat of a French invasion, but also to hunt smugglers. There were other garrisons further west, the one at Wimborne having as its Commanding Officer Captain Tregonwell with his Dorset Rangers who only ten years later was to start building the first house of Bourn Tregonwell, or Bournemouth.

Many people believe that Gulliver enjoyed immunity, if not from pursuit, then from capture and prosecution, and that this useful state of affairs came about during the French wars. In his commercial intercourse with France and the French, he was what we should today call not a spy, but an 'information-gatherer'; while keeping his ears open he heard details of a French plot to assassinate the King, who, when told of the source of the warning cried, 'Then let Gulliver smuggle as much as he likes!' This was supposed to have been treated as a Royal Command, especially by the Board of Customs, though whether it went so far as to send orders down to the south coast advising its Officers to turn a blind eye to Isaac's doings is rather doubtful. Another version tells that, when at sea, one of Gulliver's captains spotted Napoleon's invasion fleet heading towards England and reported the matter to his master, who promptly informed no less a person than Admiral Nelson himself, who straightaway dealt firmly with the fiendish French threat. Whatever the truth of the matter, it seems clear that Isaac Gulliver did not merely bear a charmed life: accepting his great ingenuity and courage, as well as his other qualities which fitted so eminently for his calling, there is little doubt the Customs authorities were extremely lenient to him. They may not have been capable of completely stopping the Trade, but they *were* capable of taking Gulliver himself had they really made up their minds so to do.

To this official blind eye, one must add the fact that the whole population of the coast, let alone of the rest of the country which benefited directly from the smugglers' activities, was sympathetic towards smuggling for a whole variety of reasons. Isaac Gulliver could well boast that he had never harmed, much less killed, anyone during his long career: he never had to. One has only to read Abraham Pike's Journal to feel that something other than incompetence made him write over and over again at the end of countless fruitless days spent looking for hidden contraband: 'No success....No success....No success.'

22. Isaac Gulliver at the age of 76, a year before his death in 1822. The miniature, together with its companion piece of his wife, is preserved in Chettle House, near Blandford Forum, by his descendants.

By the time he eventually retired, Isaac Gulliver had made a fortune: one of his descendants reckons it would have run into several millions of pounds in today's money. His will was itself 12,000 words long, and reveals that he owned land and property in Dorset, Hampshire, Wiltshire and Somerset. His family still treasures his diamond ring, a striking piece of evidence of his wealth; and the many charities he endowed show he was a philanthropist as well.

In 1815 he moved back to Howe Lodge, his Kinson home; and two years later he made his final move when he bought the large, T-shaped house in Wimborne Minster's West Borough, which today is called Gulliver's House. Having comfortably settled down to enjoy the closing years of an amazingly active life, he commissioned the travelling portrait-painter Thomas Gosse to paint, according to *The Gentleman's Magazine*, 'Mr. Gulliver, who was formerly a smuggler of disreputable notoriety'. He regularly attended the Minster Church of Wimborne, no doubt weighing the plate down considerably every

Sunday, and soon was elected Church Warden. As age caught up with him, he took to a bath-chair and so became one of the interesting sights of the little town as he was wheeled along its streets by his doting daughter, greeted cheerfully by everyone who recognized that striking face which still exhibited 'great determination .....with those Herculean proportions apparent yet'.

23. Gulliver's House, West Borough, Wimborne Minster, his final home, where he died in 1822.It had access to the house next door through the attics.

His daughter Elizabeth had already married William Fryer of Lytchett Minster near Wimborne, a banker with his own bank: Fryer, Andrews, Woolfrey and Company. This was later known as the Wimborne and Blandford Bank, then the Wimborne, Poole and Blandford Bank, and later still it was absorbed into the National Provincial Bank. Gulliver's grand-daughter, Ann Fryer, also married a local banker, whose building is the Lloyd's Bank in the Square of Wimborne Minster today. In fact, all his descendants did remarkably well, becoming solicitors, soldiers and colonial administrators: two grandsons were knighted, and one became the first Lieutenant-Governor of Burma; not a bad record for the family of a man who had once been habitually described as 'that notorious smuggler'.

On Friday 13th September, 1822, Gulliver died: he was seventy-seven years old. His death was reported not only in the local paper, the *Salisbury and Winchester Journal*, but also in the *Gentleman's Magazine*.

Here was national fame indeed. Many a local squire, from Hampshire right along the coast to Cornwall, must have genuinely mourned his passing, remembering the service Isaac Gulliver had rendered to both peer and ploughman for so many years with his high-class contraband at such reasonably low prices.

With great sorrow, and no doubt escorted to the grave by those of his beloved White Wigs who could make it, he was buried in the vault of the lovely Minster Church he had served so well. Town, gown and hunting-pink must have been represented in the church that day. His tombstone was placed in the north transept, but with restoration-work, it was moved to the centre aisle under the Minster's Tower. Now well worn and very plain, it can be found there today under the western tower bearing the words: 'Isaac Gulliver, Esquire'.

That may sound too brief an inscription, but that 'Esquire' would have been enough for Isaac, who was, essentially, a modest man. But he wanted more for his descendants, for in his will he asked that his daughter Elizabeth's male descendants, 'who derived benefit from his will, should apply for, and endeavour to obtain, an Act of Parliament, or proper Licence from the Crown, to enable him to take, use and bear the Surname and Arms of Gulliver'. Isaac could not have applied for Heraldic Arms for himself, but he wanted to think that his descendants might, their claim resting soundly on the vast fortune he had amassed by smuggling.

10
Poole: the Devil's Pool

'If Poole was a fish-pool, and the men of Poole fish,
There'd be a pool for the Devil and fish for his dish!'

So ran a local eighteenth century tag in the countryside surrounding the ancient Dorset port of Poole; it is often assumed 'the men of Poole' referred to were the smugglers for which the town was famous. However, Poole had its pirates before it had its smugglers. Harry Paye flourished in the reign of King Henry IV, and this privateer became so famous that one eminent scholar called him 'the Drake of the first part of the fifteenth century'. His heyday was in the middle of the long wars with France, during which the periods of official peace were grand opportunities for privateers, that useful euphemism for pirates.

Smuggling, however, started in Poole much earlier than it did in most other parts of the British Isles, for a royal charter of 1433 established it as a staple port which had to collect customs dues on behalf of the king. In 1486 a smuggling ship called the *Rose* was seized after being rummaged by the Poole Customs Officers who found on board 1,200 pounds of best paper, considerable amounts of ginger and cloves, bales of silk and even a quantity of diamonds. The smuggler on this occasion was actually a Spanish merchant.

In the reign of Elizabeth I the town's Controller of Customs was examined by the Queen's agents and found to be thoroughly corrupt. As time went on successive governments were asked by the few towns along these coasts who were against smuggling to provide garrisons of troops, in particular Dragoons. They were needed, said the petitioners, to assist the inadequate and overworked Customs men, especially the Riding Officers. Christchurch did not get her barracks and soldiers until the very end of the eighteenth century, and then only when Napoleon's invasion was believed to be imminent; but so

24. The Quay and Inner Harbour, Poole, in the 1830s.

acute was the problem of the proper combating of smuggling at Poole that a squadron of Dragoons was quartered there as early as 1723.

Why was Poole such a paradise for the contrabandists? The answer is so simple that it is often obscured: its natural harbour was the second largest in the world. One of Poole's present-day captains, who plies regularly to Wareham, claims that it is now the largest in the world, because Sydney Harbour's shoreline is shrinking as land is reclaimed from its waters. The vast sheet of water is fringed with countless inlets and is dotted with islands; a look at the Ordnance Survey map will show that once a ship or boat is past Brownsea Island and the Town Quay with its Customs House, it is, in fact invisible to watchers on that shore wherever it chooses to go in the Harbour. Another reason for Poole's popularity with smugglers was its proximity to the Isle of Purbeck, another great smuggling area. Again, the map shows how contraband goods would have been brought down from the heights of the Isle to the shores of Poole Harbour, from where they would have been conveyed across the calm waters, either into the town itself or to the remote northern shores with their inlets and creeks which complement those on the southern.

An eighteenth century link between Kent and Poole was forged in 1747 in an episode which turned out to be one of most outrageous escapades in the history of English smuggling. The fact that the pivotal act took place in the town of Poole may be the reason why some people thought badly enough of the place to compose the damning couplet at the beginning of this chapter; if so, then the full story must be told, as far as space permits, in order to clear the names of the majority of 'the men of Poole'.

The chief villain was a Kent smuggler named Thomas Kingsmill, who led a lawless band which had its headquarters at his home village of Hawkhurst. About twelve miles from the infamous smuggling port of Rye, this village was close to the edge of Romney Marsh, perhaps the most notorious smuggling land on the entire south coast. The Hawkhurst Gang traced its origins to the change-over from the 'Owling' period to the age of spirit and tea smuggling; and it was in the year 1747 that Kingsmill took over the leadership of the gang from Arthur Gray, under whose command it had dominated the whole of the Rye area for many years. Even though about 100 Dragoons and seventy infantrymen were deployed to oppose them, they respected neither soldier, sailor nor Customs man, and their word was law throughout both Kent and Sussex.

In 1744 the Hawkhurst Gang, which could assemble itself to the extent of 600 men within an hour when the need arose, such as a large incoming cargo, attacked the Riding Officers of Shoreham, who had come upon them and caught them red-handed during a landing. The King's men were beaten up and severely wounded, their horses and weapons taken from them, and they were then marched off like prisoners-of-war to the Gang's headquarters in Hawkhurst. The smugglers then interrogated the soldiers, as a result of which it was discovered that two of the Officers had once been gang-members in the distant past. Highly incensed, the smugglers took them to a wood outside the village, tied them to trees, and then flogged them to within an inch of their lives. The smugglers then took the half-dead Officers back to the coast and shipped them across to France in their lugger, turning them loose in a foreign land where their British uniforms would have made them liable to instant death, or at the best, imprisonment. This bizarre version of transportation was a favourite smugglers' way with Revenue men all along the coast.

During this particular incident the Gang must have been in one of its more charitable moods: when really angry, they frequently murdered King's Officers outright on far slimmer pretexts. Informers, of course, they always killed: farmers who refused or failed through negligence to lend them horses, carts or storage-space they ruined by burning their farms and crops; while any wretched tub-carrier daring to take a surreptitious swig from the keg he was carrying would certainly be beaten to death.

Eventually the people of the nearby village of Goudhurst, decided that things had got out of hand, and that a determined effort had to be made to put an end to the Hawkhurst Gang's reign of terror. The villagers of Goudhurst realized only too well that they were going to get no help from either King George's government, his army, or his Customs Service, so they decided to form the 'Goudhurst Militia', the command of which they unanimously gave to a young ex-sergeant of a Foot Regiment, John Sturt, and every able-bodied man in the village signed their names to a written declaration of what they were about. It was completely illegal, of course, but the village and its neighbourhood had had enough and had decided that the only way to survive was to take the law into their own hands. They were, in fact, turning outlaws in order to protect themselves and all they held dear against the outrageous threat posed by other outlaws.

The Goudhurst Militia set up anti-smuggler patrols, and it was soon in action, for directly the Hawkhurst Gang learned of its existence, it attacked, sending the amateur soldiers reeling back to Goudhurst. In the mêlée the smugglers snatched a militiaman, and he was soon in the notorious Hawkhurst torture-chamber telling them all they wanted to know about the Militia. The broken wretch was then released and took a message back to Goudhurst from the Hawkhurst Gang. This was a formal declaration of total war, in which the smugglers informed the villagers that they would attack their miserable village at a certain time on a definite day, put every man, woman and child to the sword, and then raze every building to the ground.

'Captain' Sturt accelerated his defence-building, and sent the women and children away to safety. The village's citadel and redoubt was to be the church and its yard. On the appointed day of battle, the Hawkhurst Gang surrounded the village of Goudhurst, asked Captain Sturt if he was ready to be sensible and surrender, and when they received a negative reply, fired into the defences and defenders. But the fire that was then returned was far fiercer than they had anticipated: one smuggler dropped dead on the spot, and two more were shot to pieces before the Gang drew back bearing many wounded. The retreat then became a rout as the Militia emerged from its defences and pursued the cursing smugglers.

It was the Hawkhurst Gang's next outrage which brought it to Poole. Severely shaken by their recent defeat at Goudhurst and very worried by the effect of the recent cut in tea-duty on their profits, at the end of September, 1747, the Gang was awaiting the landing on the shore of Sussex a huge consignment of contraband tea, which, they hoped, would do much restore their flagging fortunes. The vessel expected from Guernsey was a cutter named the *Three Brothers*, and she would be carrying £500 worth of the finest leaf.

Unfortunately for the Gang , the cutter was intercepted off the Dorset coast by the Poole Revenue cutter *Swift*, commanded by Captain William Johnson, who had acted on a tipoff from someone else who was obviously eager to damage the Hawkhurst Gang. After a hard stern chase lasting seven hours, Captain Johnson was able to get close enough to loose off his guns into the smuggler to such good effect that its captain hove-to and surrendered. Johnson put a prize-crew aboard, and when the Poole Customs Officers examined the *Three Brothers* they found that, as well as the vast amount of tea, they had forty barrels of the finest brandy and rum, as well as a big bag of coffee. This impressive seizure was quickly lodged in the King's Warehouse in the vast cellars of the Customs House of Poole on the Town Quay.

As one might expect, when the Hawkhurst Gang heard what had happened, they became mad with fury. After their humiliating defeat at Goudhurst, they knew that if they did not recover what they fiercely regarded as their property, they would be the laughing-stock of the smuggling world. Kingsmill immediately assembled a raiding-party of some sixty of the Gang, who armed themselves to the teeth with swords, hangers, pistols, carbines, muskets, blunderbusses, axes and crow-bars. Mounted, and leading pack-horses carrying the weapons, this horrifying cavalcade made its way across country to Poole, passing through Lyndhurst, Minstead, Fritham, (where they dined at the *Royal Oak* and were entertained by John Parnell, the landlord, who was a great friend of all smugglers), Amberwood Inclosure, and Fordingbridge, before reaching Constitution Hill, from which they surveyed their target, Poole.

Thomas Kingsmill, the force commander, sent down two scouts to spy out the lie of the land in the evening twilight. One scout returned and told him a King's ship was moored immediately alongside the quay and would be quite capable of firing her broadside into the Gang as it was attacking the Customs House. On hearing this, many of the smugglers declared their intention of returning to Kent. But then the second scout arrived, a man who was obviously a seaman where his mate was not, for he had studied the state of the tide and assured Kingsmill and the rest that it was ebbing and would take the ship below the top of the quay and so out of range. Vastly cheered by this, the leader urged his band of cut-throats down into the sleeping town of Poole, and if anyone saw them threading through the narrow alleys they must have shrunk away and gone indoors. The Gang apparently encountered not a living soul: no Constable, no Dragoon, and certainly not a single Customs man. They dismounted and got to work on the Customs House door, with the aid of their axes and crow-bars, soon had it open, and burst in the inside doors until they found the vault housing their tea, brandy, rum and coffee. The building was completely deserted; they found no one on duty. They took nothing more than the cargo which had been removed from the *Three Brothers*, and soon they had loaded up their pack-horses and were trotting back up Constitution Hill out of Poole, still without a single person having been encountered.

They reached Fordingbridge just as dawn was breaking, having ridden all night, and at the George Inn they breakfasted and had their horses' needs attended to. The smugglers then borrowed two steelyards, weighed out the tea and shared it amongst themselves. This done, they set off once more, and as they passed through the streets of Fordingbridge they were loudly cheered by the crowd that had gathered to watch their departure from the inn. Smuggling Fordingbridge, which had never lived under the Gang's reign of terror, sent off the Hawkhurst Gang with loud huzzas because it knew its members, if not individually, then by reputation; and it wanted to show its appreciation as a smuggling town of what the Gang had just done at the Poole Customs House.

One of the Gang rejoiced in the professional name of 'Jack of Diamonds' for no better reason than that his surname was Diamond, and this character spotted a friend in the crowd of townspeople lining the route, a cobbler named Chater. As they greeted each other across the heads of the crowd, the smuggler tossed the cobbler one of the bags of tea he had just received in his share, a gift for old times' sake. It was a gift which was to cost the Fordingbridge man very dear indeed.

Some weeks later Chater read of the reward for information leading to the arrest of the raiders of the Poole Customs House which was being offered by the Board of Customs in London, and the £200 persuaded him to turn King's evidence, in spite of the retribution which would undoubtedly catch up with him once the Hawkhurst Gang heard of his public spiritedness. It had happened that Jack Diamond had been arrested on suspicion of being involved in the raid of the Poole Customs House, and the Collector of Customs for Southampton had heard all about the gift of tea made by the smuggler to the shoemaker, Chater. The Collector sent one of his Officers, an elderly Tide-waiter named William Galley, to escort Chater to Sussex and the home of the magistrate who was to hear the case against Diamond.

Witness and escort broke their journey at the White Hart in Rowland's Castle, Sussex. They were in smuggling country: the landlady had two stalwart sons in the Trade. She divined just who the two travellers were, and, knowing all about the Poole raid, she immediately sent for her boys, put them in the picture, and then suggested that they had a smugglers' reunion that same night with

Chater and Galley at her own expense. In an excess of bonhomie and smuggled spirits, the two men told their new friends their mission.

They were eventually put to bed, quite incapable, but the next morning the smugglers tied the two wretches on to the same horse, intending to take them to Hawkhurst, where they would be kept close until the hue and cry was over. But the smugglers' females proved more deadly than the males: pointing out that as Chater and Galley had come into their part of the country to get their menfolk hanged, the womenfolk demanded that they should be hanged instead. Argument ensued and tempers flared, the prisoners receiving lashes from the smugglers' whips as the horse they shared trotted on towards the Hawkhurst headquarters. Then, whilst tied together, the saddle-girth snapped and they slipped under the animal's belly, their bonds holding them still, and the Gentlemen of the Night, by now much enjoying their cruel sport, drove the terrified animal onwards with their whips so that it struck the men's heads with every step it took. Eventually this sport palled on the smugglers, and the victims were remounted on individual horses. But the torture continued, growing even more barbarous, especially for the old Customs Officer: he received the brunt of his tormentors' attentions, among these being the lashing of his private parts as his horse carried him along the rough roads.

The gruesome calvacade at last arrived at the little village of Rake, near Liss in Hampshire, where Galley, the Customs Officer, at last fell unconscious from his horse, more dead than alive. The smugglers decided to bury him in a shallow grave scraped out of the sandy heath, in which they buried him, even though he was not actually dead.

Chater, the shoemaker-informer of Fordingbridge, was taken a further four miles on to Trotton, where he was imprisoned for two days in the outhouse of a farm while his tormentors decided what to do with him. They were particularly keen to make his end so horrible that it would be told throughout the whole of the south of England, in order to deter anyone else from informing. After mutilating him vilely with a clasp-knife, they took him to a well and attempted to hang him from its windlass, but the rope was too short. They cut him down, he plummeted down the well-shaft, and they finally finished him off by hurling stones down on top of him until the shaft was choked, and his mangled remains were covered.

The murderers, who had all involved themselves in the grisly deaths of Galley and Chater so that they would all be held equally guilty as members of the Hawkhurst Gang, then took to their horses and made themselves scarce, satisfied that the fate of the informer would be spread throughout the maritime counties of England. The law took six months to catch up with them; the vital lead came from one of the murderers himself while he was in prison on another charge, who thought he could do himself a bit of good by turning King's Evidence. This led to a Royal Proclamation which listed the names of the murderers and then demanded that they surrender by a given date on pain of being declared outlaws. In addition, a reward of £500 was offered to anyone lodging information which would lead to the arrest of any one smuggler. This extreme measure eventually resulted in getting seven of the murderers behind bars, and a special Assize was set up at Chichester, at which all seven were convicted and then executed. One corpse was hung in chains near the spot where Galley had been buried alive, another on Rooks Hill near Chichester, and a further two on the seashore near Selsey Bill where, in life, they had frequently run ashore their contraband cargoes.

Soon after the murder trial, five of the Hawkhurst Gang including the leader, Kingsmill, were arrested and put on trial at the Old Bailey in London on the charge of breaking into the Poole Customs House. The Prosecuting Counsel described their crime as 'the most unheard-of act of villainy and impudence ever known'. Kingsmill and his lieutenant, William Fairall, were found guilty and condemned to death. They stoutly protested in court that they had committed no crime because the tea was, as far as they were concerned, the property of those who had sent their money over to Guernsey in order to purchase it. The two displayed complete contempt for the court and the whole proceedings, including their sentences, and remained defiant right up to the point of death. Afterwards, their corpses were hung in chains in their respective villages. The Hawkhurst Gang was finished.

The outrages of the Hawkhurst Gang did not involve the smuggling men of Poole themselves. No special names have come down to us, for there are no characters like 'Slippery' Rogers, and no one like Abe Coakes, the Swimming Smuggler of Mudeford. However, in the stories which still circulate round the Harbour, one thing emerges: the smugglers of Poole always showed themselves to be brave, resourceful and, above all to have had a sense of humour. A study of these men and their deeds shows there must have been a strict code of conduct which prevented names being bandied about, and certainly nothing was ever written down in smuggling days. In any account of Poole's smuggling, it is the character of the whole town that emerges most strongly, and not that of individual men and women. Even her motto proclaims the supremacy of the town over its people: 'According to the custom of the Town of Poole'.

A glance at any eighteenth century map will show how well served by roads the town has always been. To it came the road from Christchurch in the east over the Great Heath; from Longham came what ultimately became the Winchester and London road; from the north came the Salisbury road down through Wimborne; and to the north-west, both from Poole itself and from the ancient Roman port of Hamworthy, went the road to Blandford Forum, from where smuggled goods were taken on to Bristol and beyond. Due west went the highways to Wareham and Dorchester. Poole was like Christchurch for the smuggling Venturers, their agents and landers: neither town would have been smuggling centres had it not been for the roads linking them to markets far inland.

Poole is similar to Christchurch in another way: it is at the west end of the bay to which it gives its name, and a map will show Poole Bay and Christchurch Bay forming two huge welcoming arms for the incoming sea-smugglers.

While in the New Forest it was the hardy ponies which carried the brandy-kegs and the other goods from the coast, in Poole it was the wagons of farmers from Longfleet, Parkstone and Hamworthy which were used by the smugglers to get the contraband quickly away from the waterside, and into the barns, farmhouses, cottages, ponds and hayricks round the outside of the old town.

In the old town itself little remains of the authentic smugglers' haunts, so much has been swept away. But every house, shop, and inn of the period almost certainly had its cellar with a trapdoor under the carpet, its secret cupboard behind the false wall, its real cupboard with false back, its recess in the fireplace protected by the fire itself, and the door connecting the house with the next in the row, as in Christchurch.

Like Lymington, Poole had its tunnels running down to the waterside, in her case the long expanse of the great, ancient Town Quay. Many of these were ordinary drains, but others were special storm-drains, or overflow channels. At low-water one could row along the quay edge and see the mouths of these tunnels quite clearly. The Poole drains must have been very like those in Kinson, for there are several stories of Poole smugglers crawling along them from cellar to cellar under the many inns, and under the many merchants' town-houses which would also require the smugglers' regular deliveries. Like the miners' children further north, smugglers would push and drag their kegs throughout the labyrinth which still exists to a large extent under the town of Poole. During recent extensions to the quay several more tunnels have been revealed.

Rain was welcomed with satisfaction by the crawling smugglers of Poole. One of their methods was to introduce a heavy float with a line attached to it through one of the manhole-covers, into the torrent of escaping rainwater surging down to the harbour under the quay. A boat would be waiting at the outfall, and willing hands would catch the float, loose the line, and tie it to the tub-line. A tugged signal would signify the goods were ready to be hauled up, and the potboys of the inn would pull away with a will, even though the Customs men were at that very moment on the watch up in the tap-room. It was not an easy haul if the rainwater was still flowing out of the pipe.

It is said that on one occasion Customs Officers seized a boat hovering under one of the outlets in the harbour and waited patiently until a float appeared. This they grabbed, undid the line, and fixed to it a single keg on which they had chalked the text 'The end is nigh!' The inn-based smugglers got quite a shock when they hauled this into the cellar, and an even greater one when, at that very moment, the Poole Customs men burst into the vaults from above and arrested them!

If Lymington and Christchurch are anything to go by, there were almost certainly larger tunnels dug on the orders of the smuggling chiefs of the town, for several of the great warehouses which can still be seen on the quay, and which were used for the Newfoundland timber trade as well as other ventures, have traces of such subterranean passages, though many of them have been blocked up. It must have been very easy for a Baltic timber merchant to have smuggling as the other side of his business, so that his legal goods.....timber, furs, fat and fish....would be landed openly on the quayside and taken into his warehouse, while his illegal goods would be bundled into the mouth of his own private tunnel, destined for the cellars of the same store. No doubt the Customs Officer was standing over the tunnel the whole time, thanking Providence for honest merchants who brought wholesome goods to Poole, unlike those rascally smugglers who brought such dishonour on the good name of their town.

Poole was very different from Christchurch for it was a deepwater port, able to take ocean-going ships which crossed the Atlantic to Newfoundland as a matter of course, while Christchurch, with its shallow harbour which the townspeople refused to have dredged, even when eminent experts like Smeaton recommended it, could only cope with little coasters carrying such commodities as bricks, beer, and rushes. Abraham Pike's Journal does not report one successful rummage which uncovered contraband hidden under such cargoes. The Poole ships from Newfoundland and the Baltic must have had enough room for a vast store of contraband in their capacious holds.

Ships coming into Poole Harbour between Sandbanks and South Haven Point had two Customs lookouts to pass. First there was the

Water Guard of the Revenue Service on Brownsea Island, which made a visual check, nine times out of ten without stopping the vessel; but when a known smuggling-ship was spotted, it was usually stopped and rummaged. The Brownsea station also managed sometimes to prevent smugglers getting out to sea when they had been challenged further up the harbour, or at the quay, and were making a break for the open sea.

The second Customs post was in the Customs House on the quay itself. Directly a ship rounded Brownsea Island telescopes trained from there would have her under full surveillance. The House was built strategically at the mid-point of the long Town Quay so that the Collector for the Port of Poole and his Officers had every ship under their eyes directly they had passed the Water Guard on Brownsea. The King's Beam still stands before the building, the device used from medieval times for the purpose of weighing goods landed on the hard, so that the duties due to the government could be assessed and demanded, an impressive reminder of Poole's long history as a busy port of great importance. The original House was completed in 1730, but burnt to the ground in 1813 and was replaced by the present building.

As we have seen, local merchants had their own well-tried and highly efficient way of getting their contraband across the Quay, but casual smuggling vessels had to be far more crafty. One such was the *Vigilant*, a swift sloop, which came into Poole Harbour one quiet Saturday afternoon in 1796, possibly hoping that the Revenue men were taking it a little easy after a busy week on duty. If so, the *Vigilant's* captain was disappointed, for when he was still several hundred yards off the quay the Customs Officer standing there challenged him with a loud cry and asked him what he was carrying. On hearing that the cargo consisted entirely of timber offcuts, he waved the *Vigilant* to tie up, and then watched as one of the most boring cargoes in the world was unloaded. Perhaps it was this mercantile dullness which made him forget to rummage the sloop. At last it was over, and he waved the crew a cheery goodnight as he went off duty, and left them in peace.

The *Vigilant's* crew went ashore and sampled the delights of Poole night-life which centred on the numerous pubs along the quay, several of them actually next door to each other. Then they returned and, leaving a watch, retired to well-earned rest after a hard day. It was not until around three o'clock in the morning that the watch perceived a flotilla of Poole Harbour punts of the type used for wild-fowling, and unofficially for bringing contraband across the harbour from the back of Purbeck. Soon the *Vigilant's* crew was roused and at work loading brandy barrels into the punts, which, when full, were poled away under the old bridge connecting the town

25. *A Smuggler* and *The Preventive Service*, two prints of the 1830s, when the modern Coastguard Service, which brought about the end of smuggling, was formed.

with Lower Hamworthy and through to Holes Bay, where the power-station now towers. Here a lander was awaiting them, and soon the kegs were being loaded aboard his wagons.

For some reason the Customs Officers grew suspicious of the little sloop over the Sunday, perhaps because some officious citizen had heard about the punts gliding stealthily up the harbour, and on Monday morning, they boarded the *Vigilant* in force. She was deserted, but they saw several smashed brandy-kegs on the deck. Where was the rest of the brandy?

Much of it had been stashed in hides around Corfe Mullen, the location of one of Isaac Gulliver's many houses. Soon the Revenue men were making a cottage to cottage search. One door they knocked

at was opened by a little girl, and as they invited themselves in, her mother sat down on something in the middle of the floor and managed from that position to convince the Philistines that there was no point in searching the place. Her daughter saw them off at the door. The woman had seated herself on a brandy keg which the smugglers had left that morning. Her skirts had been invaluable in disguising and hiding the incriminating contraband.

The Poole smugglers used a method of floating barrels into the harbour with the tide similar to that employed at Mudeford. However, no guide of the calibre of Abraham Coakes seems to have existed, or at least no single name has come down to us. The fact that we do not know of any name in this connection may indicate that Poole smugglers took great pains to remain anonymous.

One reason may have been the long-standing Customs establishment in the town. Directly a newly-posted Preventer looked out of the

Customs House windows for the first time on to the bustling quay and harbour he must have smiled with satisfaction. Collectors of Customs at Poole rarely requested transfer. One, named Lander, stayed for thirty years in service and then enjoyed a long retirement.

The Commissioners of Customs in London frequently asked for reports on the amount of smuggling going on in the Poole area. In 1764 the Collector told his masters that he believed the Trade had 'greatly increased within the limits of this Port since 1759 till the Admiralty cutters were appointed; but by vigilance of their commanders we are certain it has of late greatly decreased, and apprehend that the goods usually run are tea and other India goods, raw coffee, tobacco, brandy, rum, gin and other spirits, tobacco-stalks and currants.'

By 1783, the situation had certainly deteriorated again, even though the Collector of that day skilfully implied otherwise at first: 'We do not apprehend smuggling has much increased on this coast within the last three years, but that this pernicious trade, in that period, has been and still is, carried on in the most daring manner imaginable, inasmuch that no kind of secret practices or strategems are used, some of the smuggling vessels being of such force that they undauntedly come to the shore between this port and Christchurch and run their cargoes openly, and frequently in the daytime, when there have been no soldiers on the coast, in defiance of the Revenue cruisers and the joint efforts of the Land Officers, and the goods are carried off by such large and desperate gangs that the Officers have found it impracticable to oppose them without the assistance of the military.....No addition to the number of Officers would be of any material assistance at present, as nothing but a proper force by sea, and of the military on land, can possibly answer to the purpose of Government to suppress the smuggling trade carried on along this coast.' The plea for more troops and complaints about daylight smuggling which the Officers were powerless to prevent has been heard before from Customs men operating elsewhere on the south coast throughout the period; but the most interesting point made by the Poole Chief Officer was his assertion that there would be no point in the Customs Commissioners sending him any more Officers at that time: could it have been he was afraid that more Officers would have meant smaller shares for him and his men in the all-important seizure-money, which most Customs Officers regarded as the most worthwhile aspect of their thankless and dangerous tasks?

Twenty years later still the situation was even worse, because of the wars with Napoleon. In 1804 the Collector of Poole's report was exceptionally detailed, telling the Commissioners in London that spirits, wine and tobacco were the main items smuggled, as well as small amounts of salt, which came from the Channel Islands in specially adapted tub-boats.

Some strange things went on in Poole, there can be no doubt of that. One Collector wrote to his masters asking if he could take into the Customs Service a John Stoddard, at that time languishing in Winchester Gaol for the crime of smuggling. The Collector asked if this man could be freed, once the costs of the prosecution had been paid, continuing: 'We humbly report that, notwithstanding he has been a most notorious and daring offender, yet Captain Lisle, [the Commander of the Poole Revenue cruisers at that time] apprehends that from his knowledge of the English and French coasts, by being on board one of his luggers, he will be of great service to the Revenue....'

Exactly ten years later the same Captain Lisle just mentioned had retired from his post at Lyme Regis, and decided to tell all he knew about corruption in the Revenue Service along the coast of Dorset. He wrote to the Home Secretary of the time and in one of his letters is the passage: 'The smuggling trade between the Isle of Wight and St. Alban's Point is now carried on in large armed cutters and luggers, well manned with English, Dutch, French and American sailors from Dunkirk or Ostend, with French commission, and large cargoes of tea, gin and brandy, few less than £3,000 value. [Of the two Revenue cutters guarding] this station, that one from Southampton makes some good seizures; the other, from Poole, very few, and, I am well informed, owing to the Master, Mate and Crews being corrupted; and on certain signals, now in my possession, the latter withdraws to another part of the coast to give opportunities to the smugglers to land and carry off their cargoes without interruption though sometimes they are bribed with a few casks, to save appearances, and very often no less than twenty wagons to carry off their cargoes, and frequently whole cargoes of Portugal, Spanish and French wines.'

These irregularities were still going on in Poole in 1804, the year before the Battle of Trafalgar, when the French wars were at their height, for in that year the Collector told London that he had for some time suspected that several of his Officers were under the influence of the smugglers, sometimes actually being frightened of doing their duty. However, as he had no positive proof he had taken no steps against them. Then in 1807, this letter was sent by the Controller to the Commissioners of Customs:

'Honourable Sirs,

Referring to our accounts of seizures brought to this Port, we observe that Mr. John Wise, Riding Officer, has been concerned in one seizure only, viz. 16 pounds of tobacco, since December, 1804, notwithstanding large quantities of smuggled goods are very frequently landed in his district, and sometimes within two miles of his house, and from thence conveyed past his door into the interior of the country.

'A short time since, a cartload of smuggled goods remained on the shore in district upwards of 36 hours.

'As we have strong reason to suspect that he is either extremely inattentive to his duty, or that too good an understanding subsists between him and the smugglers, we most respectfully beg leave to propose that he may be removed to Wareham for a short time and one of the Officers stationed there substituted in his room.

'We trust this proposal will meet with Your Honour's approbation, as we humbly conceive it will materially tend to benefit the Revenue, and to ascertain if our suspicions are as well founded as we expect they are.'

We do not know if this was the same Mr. Wise whom Abraham Pike habitually visited at Parkstone; and if so what did Pike think of moving him to Wareham? Should the Collector of Poole have dealt with Wise through Pike? Was Wise acting on the Collector's instructions in neglecting his duty? Abraham Pike's Journal stops at the year 1804 so no further details are given.

Perhaps the most sensational revelation about the Revenue Officers of Poole was made in the year 1789, when a Captain of the Royal Navy was looking through the ship's papers of a contraband suspect. He found a letter which had been written by the Comptroller of Poole, the Collector's deputy, whose job it was to keep an eye on his superior for the Commissioners, and particularly on the accounts of duties paid. It was addressed to John Early, a Christchurch man and a great friend of the notorious John Streeter, a leading smuggler in the Battle of Mudeford of 1784, and owner of the illegal tobacco and snuff factory at Stanpit. The letter gave the smugglers full details of the patrol-routes of the Dragoons stationed at Wimborne and Poole, and the names of the Revenue Officers of the area, where they lived and where they rode their patrols. When the letter's contents were made known the Customs Service was rocked to its foundations, and the age-old rivalry between the Service and the Royal Navy must have reached a new height.

Regretfully, it must be said that the Customs Officers of Poole do seem to have been of a coarser grain than those of Christchurch; but, there again, they were in charge of the Revenue Service in a busy, ancient port. The unfortunate Robert Trotman, who lies buried in Kinson Churchyard, was, as his tombstone tells us, 'Murdered on the shore near Poole, the 24th March, 1765', by the Officers from Poole. On the other hand, the Officers may only have been doing their duty according to the tenets of the time.

In common with the rest of the kingdom, it took the foundation of the Coastguard Service to bring anything like satisfactory control over smuggling in Poole, its vast harbour and its surrounding country. By 1824 the local paper, the *Salisbury and Winchester Journal*, was printing reports of seizures by the Riding Officer of Bourne, of casks of spirits being raised, or 'creeped up', from Studland Bay by the Brownsea Island Coastguard, and even of brandy kegs found floating off Boscombe by the Coastguard. All were brought into the Poole Customs House. Perhaps by this time Poole was no longer regarded as 'the Devil's Pool' by the God-fearing country people roundabout; at least by then their traditional couplet about the place could no longer refer to corruption in the high places of the Customs Service in their town.

In one of Poole's many inns of smuggling days, the landlord combined his first calling with that of undertaker, and hired out a magnificent funereal vehicle for conveying the departed to their final resting-places. Today we might call this equipage a hearse; but in fact its name was far more splendid: it was a Shillibier. This was a glorious, tasteless pun on the name of the inventor, George Augustus Shillibeer. Of enormous size, it was a mobile catafalque on the lines of the funeral-car of the great Duke of Wellington himself, and it delighted the morbid taste of the Georgians and Victorians with the huge team of black horses required to haul it, their nodding heads with inky ostrich-plumes, its yards of black crêpe, and the mournful majesty of its motion.

Those who could afford it hired not only the glorious Shillibier but also the fine sable coaches which fitted its train when a really impressively solemn cortege was required. However, it was not only the genuinely bereaved who were on the landlord's list of clients: smugglers with a macabre sense of the fitness of things would also call, usually in the dead of night, and deliver contraband. The goods would then be stowed within the huge body of the Shillibier, the coaches, and even the coffin itself. The usual routes for this unusual smugglers' convoy were the roads out of Poole towards Wimborne and Ringwood, and villages along the way would welcome the prompt arrival of the vehicles of bereavement.

The local Revenue men could never summon up the pluck to stop and rummage the flying Shillibier of Poole; indeed, local tradition tells us that they never even suspected it of carrying contraband.

11
The Isle of Purbeck

As every schoolboy and girl will probably know, the Isle of Purbeck is not an island but a peninsula; and some would say it is not even that. But most people, even schoolchildren, would agree that it is an area of outstanding natural beauty, as Parliament has decreed it so. Its flora, fauna, geology and scenery make it a huge attraction for people from all over the world. It has been inhabited from the earliest times, and was seen by the English kings as yet another ideal hunting-ground over which they could chase deer to their hearts' content. They ruled that no Purbeckian could build a wall or grow a hedge higher than a deer could leap; and there were other, harsher royal rules and regulations. One of the most intriguing was that no Purbeck lad could marry a girl from outside, which must have suited smugglers very well, for they like a close community which could keep its secrets and traditions.

The Isle of Purbeck is fringed by some of the most beautiful beaches in the country, with smooth sand, a gentle sea slope, and with the great advantage of being superbly sheltered by being either in shallow coves and bays, or lying on the eastern side of the Isle and therefore sheltered by its own high land-mass from the prevailing south-westerly winds. The smugglers of Purbeck could work in any weather and at almost any state of the tide. The high cliffs made approach by Revenue men and their soldier-assistants very hazardous indeed. The tight sense of community, which to this day knits the people of the Isle together, ensured the smugglers a co-operation, sympathy and protection higher than in any other part of these coasts. Stone-quarrying was the main occupation in Purbeck, and the fact that it was, and still is, organized and directed by the Ancient Order of Purbeck Marblers and Stone-cutters should have made the wide use of the quarries as smuggling dumps a very simple matter.

Another factor which aided smugglers enormously must have been the exits from the beaches, for the steep-sided valleys running up from the bays and coves to the south were densely wooded and their sides precipitous, discouraging sudden swoops by keen Customs men and, later, zealous Coastguards. Once up the cliffs the smugglers were threading along tracks which, for the most part, ran between stone walls, an unusual feature here in the south. Stone walls made welcome shelters; and when the pursuit was too hot and close, it would have been easy for the smugglers to pull a wall down across the path behind them to block the Preventers' way, especially those on horseback. Again, these stone-lined mazes were meshed in with tracks through woods and thickets, as well as suddenly-revealed farmyard-entrances into which laden pack-horses could dodge and be hidden in stone barns before the King's men knew what was happening.

The stone of Purbeck also gave its smuggling sons natural caves and those chiselled out with their hands when they were engaged in their lawful occupation as quarrymen, both inland and on the coast. Many of those at the sea's edge had their own quays, built, or at least trimmed, from the natural rock, for the dispatch of the coveted Purbeck stone in coasters to the great cities of the kingdom, principally London. Many of these hards had their own cranes, which were very useful for any smuggler who used the quays. Tilly Whim Caves are the best example. Tilly was the owner of the caverns, the 'whim' was the local name for a crane. Even the slant of the shore on which these delightfully-named caves lie fitted the smugglers' purpose, for between Durlston Head and Anvil Point the coast has a south-west to north-west slant which means it faces the Continent from which the contraband would arrive. The open-cast quarries in the fields above these world-famous caves were linked to them by tunnels, a most convenient labyrinth for the smugglers.

Another example of incredibly convenient caves is Seacombe Quarry at Seacombe Cliff, with Seacombe Bottom leading up to the smuggling village of Worth Matravers. Seacombe is one of the earliest quarries in Purbeck. Its galleries are twelve feet in height, and the roof is held up by great pillars over vast storage spaces for the old-time smugglers.

Having seen Seacombe and Tilly Whim, it is difficult to imagine a more profitable use of land than this: digging out the finest building stone in the world, and then using the spaces left for the storing of goods upon which huge financial returns were absolutely certain.

As for the stone houses and cottages of the Isle, their hiding-places were in their thick stone walls; and beneath were cellars large anough to have served whole churches. Purbeck cellars were in fact designed like church crypts, for they were vaulted and buttressed to provide wonderfully cool and dry conditions for storage, probably of the finest spirits, and the choicest teas.

Purbeck is a wild, high land, surrounded by sea, forest, harbour, heath and marsh, all of which separate it effectively from the outside world, and to all of which elements the smugglers owed a great debt of gratitude. Its valleys are deep and secluded, running up for great distances inland, ideal smugglers' ways, and on the high ground there are very often still tracks linking the Purbeck beaches with that other great smuggling paradise Poole Harbour. From those perfect beaches, by way of the high tracks protected by the stone walls of the local masons, the contraband was taken down to the quays and creeks of the harbour's southern shore, where it would be re-loaded into punts and taken across to the town. Thus one smuggling area, with its clearly-defined boundaries and individual character, served and complemented another.

The Isle of Purbeck's austere character in its higher reaches must have made it unpopular with the Preventive men stationed within its confines; and as for the military units, principally cavalry in the form of Dragoons, it must have been positively hated, for its country was the worst possible for horses and their riders. This is borne out by the very few references to cavalry being used in the Isle; and it is also significant that it was in Purbeck that the Coastguard was most active, for its innovative character was ideal for the area. Only Coastguards with their high degree of organization and their heavy armament were able to make any impression on the smugglers who enjoyed the most perfect conditions for plying their Free Trade here.

In such smuggling places as Christchurch, Kinson and Wimborne further east, there is little recorded of a common smugglers' practice which was very much used in Sussex and Kent: that is, playing up local tales of ghosts and macabre sights in order to keep the inquisitive away from churches and their precincts used by the Gentlemen of the Night. But in the Isle of Purbeck the dread of approaching churchyards was so strong that Revenue men, and their successors, the Coastguards, would take almost any detour to avoid going near a graveyard at night. Quite clearly, the men of Purbeck used their white sheets, rattling chains and sepulchral groans to such good effect that they could use tower, tomb and crypt as stores for their goods with complete confidence. On more than one occasion an over-zealous Customs Officer was warned off permanently by having the eerie experience of having his 'bugalug', or effigy, burnt in front of his house while he watched. Spectral coaches with their headless horses and drivers, ghastly giant dogs and phantom hearses are all part of Dorset's uniquely rich ghostly heritage, and Purbeck had a great share of this, thanks to the imaginative smugglers.

The first place on the smugglers' trail in Purbeck is Studland, with its wonderfully curving bay which might have been designed for landing contraband, so gradually does it shelve, so fine is its sand, and so well sheltered is its position, with a southern arm which actually curves round so that it runs with an east-north-east axis. Studland Bay still attracts the smuggler today: not long ago a huge haul of drugs was found here, buried shallowly in the sand in a plastic bag. In earlier days tubs of brandy, waterproof packets of tea, and other luxuries, were left in the finest sand anywhere round the British coast, and the plentiful seaweed crowned the smugglers' work, just as the bracken did in the heathland behind the beach, where contraband was also left in the full knowledge that it would be secure both from the Preventive forces and local Purbeckians, for no brother would steal contraband from another. This low heath was another reason for Studland Bay's popularity: there are no cliffs, just a gradually rising wild land to no very great height, and then Poole Harbour behind: perfect smuggling country.

In the eighteenth century, seaweed was the main Studland crop: it was burned on the beach and the resulting kelp carted up to the fields. It was a simple matter to take the temporarily hidden 'stuff' out of the sand and load it into the seaweed-carts, covering it with kelp, to see it on the first stage of its journey inland. Once in the kelp-hungry fields, the goods would be again hidden, and then under cover of darkness on they would be taken down to the indented shore of Poole Harbour, rich in creeks, bays and inlets. Most of these had a stout wooden quay or jetty ready; such places as Brandy Bay, which probably took only that smugglers' staple, Newton Bay, Redhorn Quay, Goathorn Pier and Brand's Point. Over the harbour went the smuggled goods, perhaps being stored on an island in some cases, but in the main reaching land at Poole or Hamworthy, where the Roman road and the green tracks of even older times were used by the Gentlemen as they fanned out into England and Wales.

The village of Studland itself must have provided ideal watch-houses for the smugglers, and one of the cottages is still called Smugglers' Watch. The loft over the chancel of the church of St. Nicholas, which the guide-books tell us was a priest's room, may also have been a smugglers' store, and also a lighthouse, for there is a high slit window facing the sea. The entrance to this upper room was, apparently, through the hatchway high up on its northern side, extremely convenient for the smuggler who wanted to dump stuff without disturbing the congregation and priest at their prayers. The stonework seems to indicate that this loft was actually built later than the chancel.

Apart from the carvings under the roof above the porch, which have nothing to do with smuggling, Studland Church is also of

26. Studland Church, showing the loft over the east end with its only entrance, the high hatchway under the eaves.

interest because in the graveyard lies the body of a Preventer, surrounded, of course, by those of many smugglers. The tombstone in question bears the following inscription: 'In memory of William Bennett, Chief Officer of the Poole Preventive Station, who departed this life July 26th, 1833, aged 45 years.' It is interesting to note that the title 'Coastguard' is not used here, the reason presumably being that as it had only come into being two years before, it had not become current in popular use. Another interesting point is that this highly-placed official of the Coastguard appeared to live in Studland. He may have sailed in to work in Poole every day, or else he may have actually been stationed at the Coastguard lookout-post on the bay from which he commanded not only a perfect view of the approaches to the shore before him but also the outer approaches to the port of Poole.

South from Studland is the Foreland or Handfast Point, with those amazing chalk stacks paddling in the sea like an ancient Dorset family: Old Harry and his Wife, collectively known by their family name of Old Harry Rocks. Between this famous family and the Pinnacles is Parson's Barn, once a huge sea-cave used by the smugglers, the name of which was actually a joke against the clergy, for parsons' tithe-barns were said to be the biggest in any area. Unfortunately, it is no longer a cave: the severe winter gales of 1963 brought down the mighty roof; but in the Free Trading days it must have been a wonderfully convenient sail-in store for the smugglers of Purbeck.

There are many smuggling stories about this stretch of coast from Old Harry Rocks to Ballard Point. One tells of a little boat carrying shoppers and market-bound produce from Swanage to Poole, somewhere about the middle of the eighteenth century. The regular passengers on this route knew better, of course, than to remark on any odd objects they saw floating on the sea off this coast, or lying visible in the depths; or on men, signals or movements on the cliffs. But on this particular voyage two visitors to the area, who had chosen to make the passage to Poole, spotted a line of corks bobbing on the sea as they came abreast of Parson's Barn. Asking the boatman what they might be, they were told that they were lobster-pot markers, and then, delighted with this news, they asked the mariner to pull up a pot so that they could see what one was like. The old salt agreed and brought up, as he must have known he would, not only a lobster-pot, but several other pots containing brandy. Imagine his feelings when, with a cry of satisfaction, one of the strangers grabbed the line from his hands and hauled it in vigorously with the help of his colleague, so that in a few minutes the deck of the little boat was full of brandy-kegs. Ordering the boatman and his mate to stand back, in an authoritative voice, the first stranger took out a very seaman-like clasp knife, and proceeded to mark every float and every tub with the dreaded broad arrow, the symbol of His Majesty's Government. The horrified boatmen were then ordered to return floats, pots and kegs to the sea, and the interrupted voyage continued to Poole.

A couple of days later the local smugglers came out in their boat when they thought the coast was clear, and hauled up their 'crop'. Imagine their horror when they saw the King's sign on float and tub. Before they could weigh anchor, the Revenue cutter was upon them, and in command of it was the very man who had made the marks which had so unnerved the boatman. He was the new Chief Customs Officer, just appointed to the post at Swanage. What a promising start to his career!

Just north of Ballard Point the smugglers must have made use of the caves which are still marked on the Ordnance Survey map, but up

Ballard Cliff, with Ballard Down rising behind it to a height of 382 feet, they sailed their luggers right in under and had the kegs swayed up all the way on long ropes. This end of Ballard Down was the principal signal-station for the smugglers, where they used spout lanterns by night and bracken fires by day to warn the luggers to stay off or come in, according to the disposition of the opposition.

Once kegs and packets were safely up on the Down they were given to the tubmen, and loaded on farm-wagons and pack-ponies, for the descent to Studland, or the passage along the top of Ballard Down. From there they would go down to what was, perhaps, the most important collecting-centre and store in the whole of this part of Purbeck: Jenny Gould's Cottage, which stood on the Studland to Swanage road near the site of the present Waterworks at Ullwell. This redoubtable lady, Jenny Gould, must have been very similar to Hannah Siller of Mudeford and Lovey Warne of Burley, an outstanding smuggling woman of great character; but she had one attribute they did not: she was supposed by many to be a witch. Certainly, her house was near Godlingston Hill where tumuli, the Giant's Grave and the Giant's Trencher may have had some supernatural and eerie significance for the local people. The Customs Officers of the area were probably uneasy about them too, for as we have seen in connection with their dislike of graveyards in Purbeck, they were a superstitious group of men. It may well have been that Jenny played up the weird connections of her dwelling-place to great advantage.

Without doubt Jenny Gould was the 'smugglers' guardian angel' in these parts, and her supernatural connections must have served her well in this rôle; but she must also have had some very real ability in accounting, checking, and storing the goods her comrades in the Trade brought to her all-important house.

From Ballard Point to Peveril Point sweeps Swanage Bay, ideal for smugglers in its small way for it has a gently-sloping beach and a pleasant little chine leading up to Whitecliff with its useful farm. Near Battlemead Gate the spirit-kegs were often run ashore and then taken along the field-path to the barn at Calton, the owner of which was always helpful when storing was necessary. With hardly any tides to speak of, Swanage was such a good place for the old smugglers, so sheltered and well protected at each end of its bay, and so full of inns to which the contraband could be sold, that when the Coastguard was formed in 1822, no fewer than sixteen Officers were assigned to the town. As in the rest of the Isle of Purbeck, stone was lord, and the stone-boats had always used Swanage as a port. It was impossible to compute the amount of smuggled goods which went out in them after coming in on the luggers, so extensive was the trade in this unique town. Their beat stretched from Swanage itself right round to St. Adhelm's, or St. Alban's Head. So closely were these Coastguards and the smugglers mixed together in the town's daily life that one night a Coastguard tripped over the smugglers' rope as they were hauling in a crop virtually in the middle of the town. This Officer immediately fired his pistol in the air and lit his blue firework, the agreed alarm-signals, and the Gentlemen ran off to their homes which were all close by, rather like a lifeboat-crew on hearing their maroon, but in reverse. The rest of the Swanage Guards were soon on the scene and they hauled with a will on the abandoned rope and had a fine collection of seized contraband to their credit.

However, one of the smugglers must have been a fairly prominent citizen, for he was very anxious not to be mixed up in the inquiry which he knew would follow. So when he reached home he had swiftly changed out of his smuggling suit into faultless evening-dress, lit an expensive-looking cigar, and then left his house and strolled down the street towards the sea-front. On his stroll he met an old friend who asked him if he had heard about the big seizure made that very night by the Coastguard. He professed complete ignorance and begged for full details. 'What a good job I wasn't there,' mused the smoking smuggler, 'for had I been, they might have caught me.'

Swanage must have shared a problem with other smuggling places like Mudeford and Christchurch: did one stick with the trade, or did one encourage the new craze for marine holidays and sea-bathing? This must have been debated in the council-chamber of many a seaside township along this southern coast, the stout burghers finding that the nub of the matter was the fact that, while the seaside holiday was growing in popularity, aided by the spread of the railways, a wet spring or a cold summer might spell seasonal ruin, whereas contraband was always moveable, the worse the weather the better, and a successful run brought 300 per cent profit every time.

A final anecdote about smuggling Swanage concerns two houses standing side by side, both with a similar porch over the front-door. In one house lived an old smuggler, and in the other an Officer of the Customs Service. The ancient contrabandist was in the habit of loading his solitary horse up with as many kegs as it could carry and then sending it off into the night to smell its own way home. Inevitably came the night when the old nag homed in on the wrong porch, for they were so similar, and stood inside it, conscious of another journey well done.

The Customs man must have heard a hoof scrape outside his front door, for he discovered the load of kegs, unloaded them, marked them with the government's broad arrow, and sent the horse back for some more. This was too much to ask, and the beast went next door to his

27. *Smugglers Alarmed*, a popular print of the early nineteenth century.

own porch, where he was at length found by his amazed master, who decided that particular means of nocturnal transport could not be used again. It is an unlikely story, but epitomizes up the smuggling character of Swanage.

From Swanage the next port of call is Durlston Bay, in the great cliffs of which all three forms of Purbeck stone outcrop. Consequently, the cliff-face is a positive warren of quarries which provided the smugglers with marvellous receiving-depots, the quarrymen themselves while on duty becoming regular porters for small amounts of contraband, as they used their empty luncheon-baskets to take home tea, brandy and the occasional length of lace either for their own use or to sell when the chance offered.

In the Scientific Age of the Trade Coastguards were always haunting the quarries, trying to catch the workers-in-stone moving small or large quantities of illicit goods, but, once again, they seemed to have had little success. The members of the Durlston Branch of the Ancient Order of Purbeck Marblers and Stone-cutters always managed to see them coming, and since they came to know the King's men and their patrol times pretty well as they lived amongst them, were able to hold them in friendly conversation while their mates removed any incriminating kegs from the threatened gallery or stone-hole. These were ideal stores, with their square recesses in the ground from which the great blocks of stone had been extracted, leaving big, dry, spaces between the stout columns and pillars.

In one of the surface quarries the Coastguards once became obsessed by a huge pile of ragged stone offcuts which had been waiting for a purchaser for years. The quarrymen always assured the Officers that one day someone would come along, but it was a question of patiently waiting for a customer who needed such poor stone as rubble. If no one came along soon, the Coastguards were told at one point, then the quarry-master would give orders for the petrified rubbish-dump to be removed, but not just at that particular moment, as he was rather busy.

If the Coastguards could only have got close enough to examine the rock pile as they would have liked, they would have discovered that it was actually constructed far more cleverly and carefully than any church from which the more perfect stone-blocks were made. Inside was a stout room, with four thick walls and roof-timbers which had come from ships wrecked on the Purbeck coasts. It was roofed with Purbeck stone slabs on the inside, but on the outside the ragged offcuts were scattered and piled in artistically-abandoned profusion. The entrance to this unique smugglers' cellar was a small hole, rather like that in an eskimo's igloo, but it did not have the usual entrance tunnel. The actual door consisted of a huge boulder which was rolled aside when entrance was needed. This hide served the smugglers excellently for many years, but at last its record became too much for some smuggling rodent, who decided to squeal to no less a personage than the Collector of Poole. One day the dump was surrounded by the King's men, the horrified quarrymen were moved out of the way, and it was broken open, ransacked, and then razed to the ground.

As they stood powerlessly by and watched, the local Gentlemen vowed to find the informer, and, directly the Preventers had left the quarry, they held a meeting at which they decided to hang the traitor high when they found him. But it was not to be. They limited their vengeance to merely telling the man of their awful intention, and then burning his effigy before his very eyes as they held him pinioned, another example of the use of a 'bugalug'. (The word comes from Cornwall, where the word 'bucca' meant scarecrow.) The incident had its effect: the informer, treated unusually mercifully by the Purbeck smugglers, became a recluse for the rest of his days, never daring to venture beyond his front door.

From Anvil Point to Dancing Ledge the coast is exactly on an east to west line, which must have made it easy to find, if not easy to land contraband on. Dancing Ledge has a lovely name, but the local quarrymen and seamen were not particularly fond of it. It was trimmed out of a natural quay for the loading of stone into coasters, and gained its name from the remark made by some wag when it was completed who claimed it was big enough for a dancing-floor, rather than a platform for putting legal or illicit cargoes onto vessels. But it turned out to be a grim joke, for there is no beach here, only about an acre of flat rock which in fact slopes into the sea and is difficult to walk across, especially when a sea of any height is running. To reach it one has to descend the cliff by means of an iron ladder stapled to the rock.

One day in the 1790s a large cargo of brandy was brought in here, swayed up the cliff by ropes, and then taken on by the smugglers to Spyway Farm to be lodged in the barn for the night. The next day, a Saturday, the kegs were taken in pairs to be loaded into the space between the ceiling and the roof of Langton Matravers Church, entrance to which was made through a door in the tower. This was done without the permission of either vicar or verger.

All went well until the next day, the choir was singing that phrase in the psalm which runs: 'And Thy paths drop fatness'; then, as if at a signal, the ceiling of the nave gave way with the most horrible rending noise, and the congregation was bombed with 200 kegs of French brandy. One parishioner was killed outright and many were injured, several crippled for life. The lander who had arranged the stowing had not checked on the floor of the roof-space on which his barrels were to be laid; if he had done so, he would have realized that the lath and plaster of which it was made would not have been sufficient to hold his brandy in place for long.

Needless to say, the rescuers were evenly divided between those who succoured the injured and those who saw that the brandy-casks still intact were immediately taken off to securer hiding-places.

It is said that St. Aldhelm's Head is called St. Alban's Head because the local people could not get their tongues round the saint's real name. It is from this Head that the western boundary of the Isle of Purbeck runs, in a straight line to Wareham. Imagining this line running across the map, one is struck by the central position of Corfe Castle in the Isle of Purbeck, and the question naturally arises: how could such a strangely splendid place avoid being a strategically-placed store for contraband, just as it was a strategically-placed castle? The castle was apparently not lived in by anyone after Cromwell's troops caused it permanent damage, but there is a story about the Rector of Corfe living in the west tower where he was visited by John Wesley. Perhaps the founder of Methodism had heard the rector was the contraband controller for the Isle of Purbeck, and had come to persuade him to give up his hobby and return to his pastoral duties.

St. Aldhelm's Head must have been used as a signal station for smuggling ships out at sea, for the Norman chapel dedicated to the saint would have been hard to resist; but the smugglers had to be careful, for the Coastguard Station which is still there was set up early, and must have had a deterrent effect, even though it is set well back from the coast, nearly in the village of Worth Matravers. Even so St. Aldhelm's Head must have been a busy place for the station to be put there. There is a wide beach below the Head and on it, in 1827, just a few years before the Coastguard actually came into being, two smuggling luggers came in and beached their bows. They were met by a gang of eighty land-smugglers, under the command of a lander named John Lucas, the landlord of the Ship Inn at Woolbridge. As they were peacefully unloading the cargo of tea and Valenciennes lace, they were surprised by a party of ten Preventers under the command of a Captain Jackson. Seeing how heavily outnumbered he was, he gave the order to his men to fix bayonets and cover the smugglers; he then called on them to surrender in the king's name.

It seems clear that smugglers did not like the word 'Surrender'. Captain Jackson's call caused the eighty smugglers under Mr. Lucas to drop what they were carrying and go for their weapons. Seeing this, the Captain immediately gave the order to open fire, and two smugglers dropped dead in the surf, while many others were badly wounded. They rallied, and then came for the Preventers, firing and cursing horribly as they advanced. Fortunately for the King's men reinforcements soon arrived, attracted by the rattle of the musketry, and in the end the two luggers were seized, and the smugglers themselves fled back along the beach towards the west. John Lucas escaped, which annoyed Captain Jackson who would have liked to have captured this well-known smuggling-leader.

Next morning the Captain, accompanied by a much larger party, was knocking on the door of the Ship Inn at Woolbridge. Among his other qualities of bravery, persistence, and determination, Captain Jackson numbered the invaluable gift of mimicry. When he heard the landlord's voice enquiring who was knocking at that hour, he replied in the voice of a sweet little girl that a drop of brandy was needed for her mama because she was feeling poorly, and had not a drop in her house.

Landlord Lucas' natural kindness made him hasten to draw back his bolts and open the door, whereupon he was immediately grabbed, hauled outside, and held fast while Jackson's Preventers poured into the inn, where they seized not only many of the gang but also a good part of the cargo which had been landed from the two luggers on the beach below St. Aldhelm's Head the previous night. Captain Jackson and his men were highly commended, and Lucas and his gang ended up doing hard labour in Dorchester Jail, or as it was popularly known, 'St. Peter's Palace'.

Round the corner from St. Aldhelm's Head is Chapman's Pool, a perfect round cove, wonderfully sheltered from the east wind by the Head itself, and from which an ideal combe or bunny leads up and inland, making unerringly for Corfe. Chapman's Pool was the scene of the initiation of a very young Coastguard into his duties of smuggling prevention, for one evening as he was coming down the combe, he saw a rowing-boat coming in to the beach loaded down with what were quite obviously contraband kegs of brandy. Seeing the chance and the challenge, he stepped importantly on to the sand and shouted 'Hi! You can't land those barrels here, you know! I've been ordered to stop anything like that along this coast. So kindly get away with you, or else you'll get me into trouble, if you please!'

'Oh,' said the smuggler holding the painter in the bow of the tub-boat, 'Sorry, sir. I didn't know. Thanks very much for the warning. Turn around, lads: it seems we've come in to the wrong beach!' And, under the approving gaze of the satisfied Preventer, the smuggling vessel turned itself around and rowed quietly out of Chapman's Pool, its crew struck dumb with amazement, completely unable to believe what they had just heard. It is said that this young Coastguard eventually made a very good Officer, perhaps because his approach was radically different from the other members of his corps.

Along the rocky shore known as Kimmeridge Ledges, the tides are very dangerous indeed; but to the local smugglers, who knew their every rise and fall, their minute variations of time, their ebb and their flow, they were steadfast companions and vital allies. This was a stretch where wreckers were active. The Kimmeridge Ledges were the last call for many a ship which fell prey to them.

Kimmeridge Bay itself was placed on a par with those of Studland and Swanage by the smugglers of Purbeck, because it had the gently sloping, fine sandy bottom which was, for the most part, completely free from treacherous rocks. The gradient was, for sea-smugglers, known and predictable. Because of their classic shape, these three bays could be used in all weathers, no matter where the wind was coming from, and at all states of the tide. At the eastern corner of Kimmeridge Bay is a strange-looking tower right on the cliff edge, Clavel's Tower, erected in 1800 by the Reverend John Clavel, who was not only a Clerk in Holy Orders but also the local squire. Smedmore House, above and behind Kimmeridge Ledges, was his country seat. Books on the area give the Tower three descriptions: observatory, folly, and lookout-post. The last was probably the most accurate, for it could have been used as a lookout for smuggling ships, rather than an observatory for stars. That the Reverend Mr. Clavel was the local squire made a smuggling intention very much more likely than if he had been merely the local vicar; and the fact that in the middle of Kimmeridge Ledges the Ordnance Survey map shows that there was a Clavel's Hard, obviously built by him, or at the least, used by him and his servants, would seem to clinch the matter. Clavel's Tower would have been every bit as efficient as both signalling-tower and clearly-seen sea-mark as its counterpart, Luttrell's Tower, further east in Hampshire, its white masonry and its lantern-floor being designed specially for its purpose. Certainly, any ship coming in and making for Kimmeridge Bay would have needed a clear indication as to where the deadly Ledges ended and where the safe haven of the bay began. If anyone had suggested that Clavel had built his folly just for the smugglers, he only had to point out that the bay was a small port, much used by fishermen, miners of the alum deposits, glass-makers, and even the Frenchmen who had been allowed to set up a business shipping the famous Kimmeridge shale home to France where it was to be used in the manufacture of grease, lamp-oil and even gas. All these ship-users needed a lighthouse, a sea-mark, and even a lookout-post. Smuggling could fit in very neatly beside other local industries at Kimmeridge just as it did up and down this long contraband coast. It was one enterprise amongst many, dangerous, illegal, but by far the most profitable.

12
Weymouth, the West Dorset Coast, and Lyme Regis

From Kimmeridge westwards the rocky heights, the precipitous cliffs, the deep ravines, and the quarries give way to an amazingly varied coastline which is dominated by the Isle of Portland and Chesil Bank.

Immediately after Kimmeridge Bay are two more: Hobarrow and Brandy Bays, the name of the latter needing no further explanation. In September 1840, well after the establishment of the Coastguard, a local smuggling gang was manhandling a cargo of kegs up Gad Cliff, above Brandy Bay, probably with the use of long hauling ropes in the Purbeck manner, after which they hid the goods in the bracken, for it was time for the Coastguard to pass the spot, on its way to the station at Worbarrow.

Sure enough, the patrol came along, and sure enough, even as the smugglers watched from their hiding-places, the Coastguards found the contraband kegs, after which they moved off, to summon more help for removing them. One smuggler, old and very experienced, told his mates that he knew for a fact that the commander of the Coastguards was in the habit of giving his men their orders at a spot near the bridge spanning the stream which cut into the cliff near the flagstaff outside his house. The veteran smuggler said he would follow the patrol and crawl under the bridge to overhear the Officer's orders. When he returned he was able to inform his gang which way the entire Coastguard force would be returning. The smugglers grabbed a pair of tubs each and raced off in the opposite direction from the enemy's approach, and so escaped.

Immediately to the west of busy Brandy Bay towers Waggon Rock, possibly named after a smugglers' wagon which went a little too near the edge of the steep cliffs. The headland at Worbarrow, however, is called the Tout; this word means the 'Lookout' in Old English, again an example of what was good enough for coastal defenders being even better for the smugglers of the eighteenth century. Worbarrow Tout must have been a wonderful vantage-point for those watching for luggers coming in to either Brandy or Worbarrow Bay. Here again the Coastguard built a station to dominate a heavily-used smuggling point, for they were worried about one of the features of this coast: the plentiful supply of seamarks, on which the approaching smuggling ships took their bearings by day or night. From the sea, every rise and fall of the cliff can be easily 'read' by the skilled local sailor.

Worbarrow Bay is held by some to be the most beautiful bay in Dorset, if not the whole of England. Certainly it was a favourite for the smugglers, especially the gap in the cliffs and the minute beach of the curiously-named Arish Mell in its middle, which would have been a very useful landing-place. Tyneham Church may have been used for contraband-storage as often as was Kinson; and the 560-feet high Ring's Hill is in fact the end of a high ancient ridgeway which leads east to Corfe Castle.

Mupe Rocks at the west end of this fascinating bay are as dangerous as Arish Mell is serene in stormy weather, and they protect a smugglers' cave of ancient provenance, much used by the men of Lulworth, who cleared a channel for their tub-boats to enter through the rocks scattered at the base of the cliffs before the cave. It was a classic smugglers' cave, such as one can see in many romantic pictures of smugglers at work which flooded the market in the nineteenth century as the smuggler passed into English folklore. It is marked on the larger Ordnance Survey map, one of the few to be so around our coasts.

Just past the famous Fossil Forest lies Lulworth Cove, perhaps the most famous cove in the world; but the name of Lulworth first catches the attention just north of the Arish Mell gap at Lulworth Castle. It is said that maidservants of the Weld family, which still lives there, would warn smugglers' boats coming in to Arish Mell beach when they knew the Preventers were about, by signalling with candles from their windows high up in the castle. They would also undoubtedly show their lights to act as a bearing for those same boats when it was safe for them to come in. The castle's smuggling connection spanned practically the whole of the eighteenth century, the earliest mention of it being in 1719 when Revenue Officers from Weymouth mounted a large-scale raid on the whole of the Lulworth area, the two villages of East and West and, of course, the castle itself. It seems more than probable that it was a combined operation, coming in from both the sea and the land. Certainly, it was a very thorough search, for the

Collector of Weymouth was a very keen officer who had been horrified by the extent of the Trade in his area, especially the large numbers in the local gangs, often as many as a hundred in a single group, who landed their goods heavily disguised and heavily armed with blunderbusses, pistols, carbines, swords and even quarter-staffs, a favourite weapon round those parts. In common with many other concerned people of the time, the Collector told the authorities that only troops could enable his Officers to combat smuggling properly here. However, his raid on Lulworth yielded little, some brandy, a quantity of pepper, a little red wine and a large amount of vinegar.

It would seem that the smugglers of Lulworth were a fairly rough lot, including those round the famous Cove, for the Coastguard built a station there very early in its history, and a lookout is still marked on the map. Two Preventers were once caught by the local gang watching out for them in a clump of bushes. The Officers were disarmed, bound and taken to the edge of the precipitous cliff, over which they were hung on the end of ropes. The smugglers carried on with their business which had been so rudely interrupted, landing a huge cargo of brandy kegs, the Officers presumably watching every move from a precariously upside-down position. When the lander was satisfied that the contraband was on its way inland, he had the King's men hauled up to the top of the cliff and dumped in a field still bound, to await collection by their colleagues the next morning.

Another Lulworth Customs Officer was not so lucky: he was so zealous in the pursuit of the smugglers, that one night they attacked him and threw him straight over the cliff and into the cove.

Perhaps the greatest authority on smuggling in this part of Dorset was Thomas Hardy, the great novelist and poet. He was not a smuggler, of course, being born in 1840 when the Trade was well and truly on the decline, even in these parts; but his father employed a servant for over thirty years who had carried many a tub in his time, and his grandfather told young Thomas that he had enough room at Higher Bockhampton, the family home, to conceal up to eighty kegs of smuggled spirit. From his earliest years, Hardy was enthralled by the tales the ancient family retainer was able to tell him, so that he knew that the now-famous cottage he lived in just outside Dorchester happened to stand on an important smuggling route from the coast at Osmington Mills to distant Sherborne and the Somerset town of Yeovil. All of these towns, and even the county town of Dorchester, were prime markets for the contraband goods. Higher Bockhampton itself was the point where tired tubmen who had carried their kegs from the coast on the first leg of their journey into the interior would hand over to the convoys of carts supplied by local farmers, for it lies just under eight miles from the sea, the usual first leg distance for tub-carriers. Here they slipped out of the sling-ropes of their harness; but if the King's men were about the tubs had to be dumped swiftly in a known spot — outhouse, brush-wood pile, log-stack, potato-clamp or some subterranean cellar specially dug out for the purpose. Once the stuff was safe, a watch had to be kept both for the Preventers and Revenue as well as for the lander returning to load the goods for the next stage of their travels.

Hardy's cottage has a projecting porch, with a window cut in one wall, which, the boy was told, had always been used by the family to keep watch for Revenue Officers approaching the cottage through the woods which surround it still. This could only mean that there was a place at the back where the contraband was stored when the need arose.

Not surprisingly there are many references in Thomas Hardy's short stories and novels to Revenue officials. It is in his *Wessex Tales* that Hardy presents us with actual smugglers and realistic Revenue men. In the short story *A Tradition of Eighteen Hundred and Four*, the narrator, the old shepherd Solomon Shelby, says that he lived near Lulworth Cove, and that in 1804 the local people were expecting Napoleon's invasion at many places on this convenient coast 'and for choice the three-quarter round Cove, screened from every mortal eye, that seemed made o' purpose, out by where we lived, and which I've climmed up with two tubs of brandy across my shoulders on scores o' dark nights in my younger days...' What was good enough for Napoleon crossing with his heavy galleys on a dark night, was even better for smuggling luggers coming in on ghostly sails. A little later Solomon describes how his Uncle Job, an infantry sergeant, then in camp on the Downs above Weymouth, came home and 'had a drop to drink from the tub of sperrits that the smugglers kept us in for housing their liquor when they'd made a run, and for burning 'em off when there was danger...' No doubt the Hardy family had enjoyed the same fee from the Gentlemen of the Night. But they did not live near enough to the coast to have as their duty warning the luggers when King's men were about by the standard method of firing the dry bracken and gorse by day, and lighting beacons or flashing lamps by night.

As Hardy's story is set in the time when Dorset was expecting the imminent arrival of Napoleon, this is an appropriate place to mention a very interesting building which stands on the Knoll between West Bexington and Puncknowle. This is known locally as the Lookout, and was built as such and as a signal-tower for the Fencibles, the Home Guard of that age, which were raised round here to repel the French. This company was drawn from Bridport, Burton Bradstock, Swyre and Puncknowle. The lookout is a two-room, two-storey structure, with large, shuttered windows looking out on three sides, and the view it commands stretches beyond Portland and Weymouth to the east, and over Bridport to Lyme Regis and Lyme Bay to the west. Its beacon-fire must have been just outside, and there can be little doubt that it was lit as a signal that ships were coming into the coast. The coast here runs very straight and even, for the shore is in actual fact the western start of Chesil Bank.

28. The Lookout, the Knoll, Puncknowle, between Abbotsbury and Burton Bradstock.

Was the lookout used by smugglers? What seems to clinch the answer to this question is the fact that East and West Bexington, West Bay, Swyre and Burton Bradstock, were all used in the years after 1776 as landing-places by Isaac Gulliver, for it was in that year that he bought Eggardon Farm and then planted his grove of pines in their octagonal bed to act as the vital seamark for his incoming luggers. Gulliver's Lane is still the name of the road down through Shipston Gorge, and Puncknowle itself was one of the villages through which his men were traditionally said to have taken their contraband. Of course, the Lookout was built long after Gulliver's time, but it is on one of his main routes, which went on being used after he had moved on to pastures new; and one only has to go up the building to appreciate what a wonderful place this was for both invasion-watcher and lugger-spotter, the two rôles undoubtedly being combined by one and the same sentinel. Evidence for its military importance is seen by the siting of a Second World War 'pillbox' just below the summit, for the Knoll was used in that war's invasion-defences as well as the earlier.

Weymouth was not only very popular with King George III, who liked it as a holiday resort, but also with smugglers, who found there and in the adjoining countryside a rich market for their goods, as well as splendid landing-places for contraband going further inland. By the climax of the smuggling period around 1830 ships from Cherbourg were using nearby beaches, and the most daring came in to the beach of Weymouth itself. Several ships had only just been launched in that year, showing that both French and English smugglers were unaware of any threat of decline in their industry, for they had put their faith in such vessels as the *Eliza* and the *Betsy*, but far more in the *Louise*, *L'Amité*, *L'Espoir*, the *Bien Aimé* and *L'Aimable Vertu*.

One of the great strengths of the English smuggling was the fact that it could be carried on all the year round; but for the French and English contrabandists bringing in their goods to Weymouth, their traffic was strangely seasonal. This was probably because of the King's periodic visits. When the King was in Weymouth he brought literally thousands of people with him, practically all of them there to enjoy themselves with the things which made comfortable life worth living for the courtiers, court officials, officers and men of both army and navy, and, of course, the visitors who came to the town to see the King. Not only was there a great market for the smugglers' basic items of tea, tobacco, brandy, and wine, but also the more courtly commodities such as playing-cards, lace, silk, satin, dried fruits, coffee, cocoa, and other exotic articles. However, when the influx of visitors left, there would be few people who required these luxuries.

A vivid illustration of this 'Weymouth Trade' was found in a crevice of the wall of the George Inn of Weymouth when it was being dismantled in 1885. It was a piece of paper on which had been written:

'W. Matthew, Esq., bought of Peter le Coq:

April the 24th, 1776.

To eight casks of brandy at 16/6:	£6:12:0.
To seven casks of rum at 15/6:	£5:12:6.
To one flagon of brandy and one flagon of rum:	11 shillings.
To one cask put in for storage:	1/6d.
To 24 pounds of Bohea tea in paper:	1:12:0.
	£14:5:0.

17th September, 1776. Of W. Matthew, Esq., the sum of fourteen pounds, five shillings, for Mr. Peter le Coq. Received by Thomas Martin.'

Did the King know about this smuggling which catered especially for his court? He must have known, for 'Farmer George' was no fool, even though he was subject to bouts of madness. A monarch who could, on being told that Isaac Gulliver had brought news of a plot against his life, say 'Let Gulliver smuggle as he will!' would surely not have been too distressed by the contraband trade, even though the Revenue which was being defrauded was his Revenue, and the Officers who strove to destroy the Trade were his Officers. And we have mentioned already in this book at least one smuggler who specialized in bringing in dutiable goods illegally for the Royal Family.

As one would expect, Weymouth was said to be riddled with tunnels, though at some stage they must have been superfluous if the smugglers could actually land their goods on the beach itself without fear of interference from the King's men. At the end of the last century rumours of tunnels were strenuously denied by the respectable burgesses of Weymouth, just as they were, no doubt, in Kinson, Christchurch and Lymington. There is evidence, however, that not just one but several tunnels ran from Gloucester Lodge, (the King's residence which had been built by the Duke of Gloucester and lent by him to the King,) under the Esplanade on which it stood, and on to the cellars of a building in St. Thomas's Street, which was situated close by the brine baths which the King used when the sea itself was a little too cold or choppy for a dip from the royal bathing machine.

As one would expect, Weymouth has several old smuggling inns. The Black Dog, with its overtones of Stevenson's *Treasure Island*, dates from the sixteenth century, and has a violent history. When the Civil War was raging in Dorset, the landlord killed one of the guests who had sought shelter under his roof, but the reason for this has not come down to us. When smuggling came along, there was another murder here, for a Revenue Officer was cut down while attempting to arrest a smuggler on the premises. A literary connection is that Daniel Defoe worked on his most famous book, *Robinson Crusoe*, while staying at the inn.

It is in Thomas Hardy's short story *The Distracted Preacher* that we get the most accurate account of smuggling not only in Dorset but possibly in any part of the country. The story takes place in the 1830s which puts it in the scientific age of smuggling, after the formation of the Coastguards, but the King's Officers are called Customs men by Hardy. He calls the village involved Nether Moynton, which was Owermoigne, six miles south-east of Dorchester, and about two and a quarter miles from Ringstead Bay, above which is Burning Cliff. This may have gained its name from the smugglers' habit of firing the gorse and bracken on its top to warn their mates at sea to keep away when the King's men were near.

Although there was a direct smuggling route from Ringstead Bay to Owermoigne, the contraband which is the cause of all the trouble in *The Distracted Preacher* was brought in to Lulworth Cove. Rather than give a summary of this splendid smuggling yarn, the reader cannot do better than to get hold of Thomas Hardy's *Wessex Tales* and read the story right through: the author's usual narrative skill and grasp of local colour combine with his deep knowledge of smuggling to make a memorable account of those Free Trade days in this part of Dorset.

Osmington Mills is the next Dorset smuggling location, with its wooded combe coming up from the beach and its ancient inn, once called the Crown, then the Picnic Inn, and now the Smugglers' Inn. It started its long life in the thirteenth century, and for many years brewed its own ale in the brewery which still stands at the back of the premises. It was in the 1790s that it earned its present title, though it was not officially taken until 1973, for it was in the last decade of the eighteenth century that it became the headquarters of one of the several foreign smuggler-chiefs who used this part of the Dorset coast for landing their fine goods. His name was Pierre Latour or la Tour, known to the local folk as French Peter.

His favourite vessel was a speedy cutter named *L'Hirondelle*, meaning 'swallow'. Its speed and light armament enabled Latour to make very swift passages across the Channel and allowed him to carve out for himself one of the most successful careers in the history of Dorset smuggling. His agent and main accomplice was the then landlord of the Smugglers' Inn, Emmanuel Carless, whose extensive network of distribution and delivery must have rivalled that of Isaac Gulliver himself.

Latour had plenty of opposition to face, no doubt made all the keener because its prey was not of English blood. At one point the Board of Customs had as many as five cutters based on Weymouth for the sole purpose of catching him red-handed. The Commissioners put a price on the Frenchman's head, a measure often employed in campaigns to catch highwaymen but not often used in the war against smugglers.

There is a story that one day French Peter anchored just off Osmington Mills and made his way up to the inn. Here he was surprised to find that his friend the landlord was behaving with none of his customary amiability. When Latour asked him how he fared, the host merely placed his finger to his lips and rolled his eyes towards the great fireplace, visible today in the house's Old World Bar, which was then the kitchen.

The landlord then asked Latour whether he would like his usual drink, Geneva, or gin; at this Latour, knew for certain that something was wrong, for everyone knew that he never drank anything other than cognac. Pierre declined the gin and asked for the brandy, saying that he felt a chill in his bones, unusual for summertime; and then he suggested that they might have a fire in the hearth so that he could warm himself after his Channel crossing.

The truth was that the local Revenue Officer, named John Tallman, was hidden up the chimney. He had come to the inn an hour or so earlier, and, new to the area, had started asking questions about Pierre Latour, for the reward of £100 had just been posted in Weymouth Customs House for information which would lead to the arrest of the Frenchman. The landlord had poured the young Preventer a large tot of brandy on the house, and proceeded to tell him several tall stories in which the doughty smuggling deeds of French Pierre were so impressive that the Officer, green to the game as he was, grew rather nervous of the man he had come to ask about. After several more stories and a good few further brandies, the host glanced out of the window and was able to inform the uncomfortable Mr. Tallman that he was in luck that day for Captain Latour had just at that moment dropped anchor below the inn.

With an oath, Tallman sprang to the window and stared out, and then turned to the landlord and asked if there was anywhere where he could hide until he could escape and call up further assistance from Weymouth to arrest the smuggler-chief. The host promptly suggested that without doubt the capacious chimney was by far the best place for such concealment, and that he was welcome to use it if he felt that way inclined. So the Officer scrambled up the flue, the landlord promising to let him know the moment the coast was clear.

When the wretched Tallman heard Latour's call for a bright fire in the hearth he realized that he had been well and truly fooled. Horrified, he hung in the black filth of the ancient chimney while wood was brought and kindled, gorse, heather and damp bracken being added to make a dense stream of choking smoke soar upwards. Of course, it soon grew too much for him, and the coughing, blackened figure of the Revenue man fell down the flue, rolled through the fire, and out on to the flag floor, tears of pain and rage mingling on his grimy face. To the hearty guffaws of the delighted smugglers, captain, host and tubmen customers in the Inn, he was hauled to his feet and given another large tot, before being sent on his way.

It is said that Latour eventually married the landlord's daughter, Arabella Carless, took her back to live in France, and retired from smuggling to live happily ever after on the fortune he had salted away during his smuggling days on the Dorset coast.

Just outside Weymouth, lying on its hill behind the end of Chesil Bank, its tall church-tower a welcome seamark for mariners, is Wyke Regis. The church's yard is crowded with victims of the fierce seas which pound the great Bank, and amongst the tombs of both soldiers and sailors, is a smuggler's last resting-place. At the top of the headstone is a beautifully carved scene, in which His Majesty's Revenue Schooner *Pigmy* is shown attacking a smuggling cutter, and blowing away its sails with its gunfire. The epitaph reads:

'Sacred to the memory of William Lewis, who was killed by a shot from the Pigmy *Schooner, 21st April, 1822, aged 33 years.*

Of life bereft, by fell design,
I mingle with my fellow clay.
On God's Protection I recline
To save me on the Judgement Day:
There shall each blood-stained soul appear:
Repent, all, ere it be too late,
Or else a dreadful doom you'll hear,
For God will soon avenge my fate…

This stone is erected by his Wife as the last mark of respect to an Affectionate Husband'.

There is no doubt where the stone-mason's sympathies lay, as well as those of William's family and the vicar of Wyke Regis.

The great expanse of Chesil Bank, stretching eighteen miles from the Isle of Portland to Burton Bradstock, was one vast landing-beach for contraband to the smugglers of the eighteenth century. Its unpleasant pebbly construction was discounted, to a large extent, by the smugglers' ability to tell, even on the darkest night, exactly where they were along its great length by simply feeling the pebbles, for those at its western end are smaller than those at its east, the change being a gradual increase in size.

Chesil Bank was, and always has been, a place of danger. In the Channel gales, especially when the wind is from the south-west, the waves crashing on the stones can be heard miles inland; as recently as 1979 the sea cleared the Bank and devastated Portland for the second time that winter, and in Chiswell caused almost a million pounds-worth of damage. In 1824 it not only came over the top at many places, but actually breached the bank, flooding Abbotsbury to a depth of twenty-three feet, and sweeping away most of the village of Fleet, not even sparing the church, only the chancel of which remained standing.

In the same storm the sloop *Ebenezer* of ninety-five tons, carrying munitions and ordnance stores for the Army, was blown towards Chesil Bank, seized by a gigantic freak wave, dumped on the summit of the Bank, and left there very high but not dry. The crew, amazed at their narrow escape, for only two were drowned, stepped out on to the pebbles and walked into Portland. Their ship was eventually dragged down the landward side of the great bank and launched for the second time in her life into the Fleet lagoon, as though her owner felt she had earned a long and peaceful still-water retirement.

The Dorset coast bettered even this story fifteen years later, for in a storm in the year 1839 no less than ten ships were driven ashore on the Bank: nine were swiftly reduced to matchwood by the fury of the elements, while the tenth, which weighed over 500 tons, was hurled clean over the Bank and made a safe splashdown in the Fleet.

In the calmer months of the year the great, elongated lagoon behind Chesil Bank is a place of peace. At its mid-point lie the villages of East Fleet, Fleet Common, West Fleet, and the bulge of open land projecting into the lagoon which is also called Fleet. The lagoon itself is known as the Fleet, and for smugglers it was like a huge duckpond, for as well as providing fowl for the table, as it still does, it was an amazingly useful dumping-place for goods brought ashore over Chesil Bank with the Revenue men too close for comfort. The creeping and dredging up of the 'crops' when the king's men had gone away must have been a very easy matter.

The actual hamlet of Fleet itself, and the mansion which is now the Moonfleet Manor Hotel was the setting for J. Meade Falkner's famous smuggling novel *Moonfleet*. This author was born in 1858, and was an antiquarian who wrote the occasional book. Many think that *Moonfleet* deserves to be ranked alongside such classics as *Westward Ho!*, *Lorna Doone*, and even *Treasure Island*. In the church is a plaque to

Falkner, and another commemorating the Fleet squires, the Mohuns, who lived at the Manor. Their vault beneath the old church figures in *Moonfleet*, and this actual name was obviously an amalgam of Mohun and Fleet. In the book a tunnel is described as leading from this vault to the Fleet itself; and, indeed, in the 1920s a tunnel *was* found by a gravedigger, and it seemed to lead from the direction of the Mohun vault.

Abbotsbury, at the western end of the Fleet, was as well-known for its smugglers and wreckers, according to local gossip, as its ancient Swannery. Even the vicar was involved in smuggling which went on all along Chesil Bank, so it was said. It is easy to imagine the huge Benedictine barn of the old Abbey being used for the storage of contraband, for under the products of several grain harvests from the local fields, one would have been able to hide many lugger-loads of smuggled goods. St. Catherine's Chapel, on its striking hill, must have been a boon as a watch-house and signal-station for the Abbotsbury Gentlemen of the Night, and when that could not be used then the hill-fort of Abbotsbury Castle, on its 626-feet high eminence, would have served instead; both must have been invaluable seamarks to sailors coming in on errands both legal and illegal. The village headquarters of the smugglers was the Ship Inn, now the Ilchester Arms.

The many ancient barrows just inland from Abbotsbury remind us of an old smuggling custom in this part of Dorset: local farmers on whose land they stood obliged the smugglers by clearing them of any old bones and funerary relics, particularly if the latter had some little value, and then allowed the burial-mounds to be used as storage-dumps. Any local legends surrounding them with ghostly tales of being haunted by the spirits of departed Bronze Age warriors would have been kept in currency and no doubt embroidered by both smuggler and farmer in order to keep the inquisitive away from the graves. One can sympathise with the farmers in their usual uneasy alliance with the smugglers: the more contraband the latter put into the barrows, the less they would demand should go, more incriminatingly, into the farmers' barns.

Mention has already been made earlier of Isaac Gulliver's connection with the Bexingtons and Burton Bradstock, from where his route ran inland through Shipston Gorge and on to his farm under the protection of massive Eggardon Hill. Mention must be made here, though, of the ghosts of Burton Bradstock, a remarkably strong contingent for such a small place, even in the much-haunted county of Dorset. A dog without a head is said to have been seen crossing the road at Catholes, not an unexpected place for such a sight, though the lack of a head would have been a disadvantage when dealing with the cats there. And a procession consisting of a coach, its horses, and four horsemen escorting it, without the slightest trace of a head on any of them, is seen at midnight on a road from Shipston Gorge to Burton Bradstock at the very place where funeral cortèges were in the habit of pausing to breathe before ascending the hill. These are the sort of stories which smugglers delighted to keep alive, embroider and spread, so that as few people as possible would be out on those routes during the hours of darkness. If volume of ghostly traffic is anything to go by, then Burton Bradstock, with its known smuggling connections, must have been busy in the days of the Free Trade. Certainly, the old Dove Inn is still pointed out as the depot where contraband was shared out and sold to the country-folk who made up the bulk of immediate customers along this part of the coast, where there were few big houses on the smugglers' delivery-list.

A number of great coaching-inns made up for this deficiency, however, a fine example being the large Bull in the main street of Bridport. Originating in the sixteenth century, it was greatly extended to take the coaches thundering down this way into Devon, and became so famous that George IV was a guest here. With such a clientele, the smugglers probably did a good trade with the Bull at Bridport.

There are few smuggling connections in the town itself apart from seeing Isaac Gulliver walk its streets. One reason is likely to have been the great prosperity it enjoyed in the days of sailing ships, for rope-making was Bridport's staple. In those days its people must have enjoyed full employment and high wages, so the need to eke out a living by smuggling would have figured little in their economics.

Bridport's harbour, West Bay, is a mile and a half away and as early as 1395 its first full-time Customs Officer was appointed. His successors of the eighteenth and nineteenth centuries were kept busy, for rope, timber and gravel were the port's main exports. Into it must have come smuggled goods picked up further along the coast by legitimately-trading ships, out at sea where the smuggling luggers met them, or stowed into their holds in the French and Channel Islands ports from which they brought their legal cargoes. No wonder West Bay has always needed efficient and experienced Customs men to rummage the thousands of ships which have come in through the narrow harbour-entrance over the centuries.

Between Eype Mouth and Seatown is a promontory on the cliffs called Doghouse Hill, with a little inland its complementary Doghouse Farm. Like the chicken and the egg, we do not know for sure which came first, but if the hill gave its name to the farm, then it is possible that it was the site of a dog-kennel, the inhabitant of which would play a vital part in the smuggling of contraband on to this coast. It is a known fact that further west on the coast of Devon, homecoming sailors were used to identifying the farms and villages onshore by the characteristic sounds made by the different dogs when they barked; and there is a suggestion that some dogs were kept specifically for their penetrating bark which carried well out to sea, and were even irritated on purpose to encourage them to keep up their noise when fog was about. Is it not therefore only logical to assume that at some points along the coast such 'dog-horns' would have been activated by the local landers when smuggling-luggers were expected at night?

Chideock and its seaside Seatown, nestling in the shadow of great and glorious Golden Cap, comprised a smuggling community of no mean extent, and with a signal-station 617 feet high. The Chideock Gang of smugglers had a leader known simply was 'the Colonel', a title refreshingly different from the usual 'Captain' which adorned the leaders of other groups of Gentlemen. He must have been a true Gentleman for he was certainly an officer, yet exactly who he was, or how an apparent landlubber of an army officer came to be leading a set of smugglers has never come to light. It may be that he was a local landowner, who had been invalided out of the Army and had returned home to find life as a small squire very tame after soldiering at a high rank. It is certain that the Chideock smugglers specialized in using pack-horses, not all that common along this part of the coast. Organizing the logistics of the Trade, transport, storing and distribution must have come easily to the Colonel; and when the time came to beat off the Revenue men and their military assistants in action, he was probably the ideal leader for the men of Chideock.

The Colonel limited his followers' activities to a relatively short stretch of the coast, following the military dictum that short lines of communication are best. The Chideock Gang worked only from Seatown to Charmouth, their main landing-beaches being the significantly-named Cain's Folly at Stanton, just east of Charmouth, and St. Gabriel's Mouth, just under the western flank of Golden Cap itself. St. Gabriel's House must have been a customer; perhaps it was the cunning Colonel's own home. The nearby church, the thick wood, and Filcombe Farm would all have been useful stores for contraband just brought up the combe from the beach, but the Colonel was more interested in taking the Stuff well inland, rather than to local customers. His main route passed through the lovely Marshwood Vale and along the valley of the charming little River Char, and the goods were dropped off at market towns such as Beaminster and Broadwindsor, and at the small manor houses along the way, like Pilsdown Manor and Bettiscombe Manor House. Then on the Colonel's packhorses would go into Somerset, calling at Crewkerne, Chard and Yeovil itself.

Approaching Yeovil they would have gone through Corscombe, a name deriving from 'Corfwedges Cumb', which meant 'the valley of the pass roads', indicating the antiquity of this route. Near Court Farm House in Corscombe is a cottage called Woodwalls, which was once a school. The master of this tiny grammar school was a smugglers' ally, for he actually used his pupils to dig a number of subterranean store-houses for his contraband-carrying colleagues.

Lyme Regis is the last town on the Dorset coast, for the Devon border is just on the outskirts of this ancient, famous town. Though very far west, it was here that Isaac Gulliver came in 1776, his White Wigs, in their smocks and powdered hair, landing their goods in full view of the Customs men, then awaiting their next summons in a cave where they could also be seen clearly by those same King's men. Clearly, Isaac must have had Lyme Regis as tightly sewn up as all the other places where he had operated. Like Poole and Weymouth, Lyme had its 'Smugglers' Quarter', said to be composed of the old houses crowding the banks of the River Buddle, much like the overhanging, back-to-back dwellings lining the banks of the old Fleet River in the teeming City of London. Any smugglers or their families caught with obvious contraband in these houses would not have needed to have an escape-hatch through to the next, but would only have had to step out of their back-window into that of the house across the river. In those days, it was little better than a common sewer taking all rubbish and human effluent down to the beach and the sea. All in all, it was not a part of fashionable Lyme Regis in which the resident or visitor chose to wander in search of the picturesque, especially after dark!

Lyme Regis was possibly the birthplace of Warren Lisle, a Customs Officer of the same heroic stature as William Arnold of Cowes; and it is fitting that we should meet him at the end of this book where he will balance the other half of a matched pair of outstanding Revenue men who were a credit to a profession which was not without its black sheep, and in which they shone as burning examples of zeal, ingenuity and incorruptibility. Lisle was born in 1699, the son of a Revenue Officer. At the age of seventeen he was appointed Patent Searcher in the Port of Poole, and was soon asking for a bigger salary to support himself and his horse, which he needed for his duties. He worked in Poole, Weymouth and Lyme Regis, where his father had been appointed Collector.

In 1724 he made his first seizure: a small smuggling vessel at Small Mouth in Portland Harbour, and went on from strength to strength. In 1730 he was being referred to as 'Captain' Lisle, and although there is no clear picture of how he actually won this title, which was unusual in the Customs Service, he must in those seven years have gained an enormous amount of sea-experience, and this stood him in excellent stead in his subsequent career. His next promotion was to Supervisor of Riding Officers for the Weymouth Collection, and this, of course, brought him into direct contact with smugglers all along the West Dorset coast. His Riding Officers were stationed at Dorchester, Abbotsbury, Portland, Osmington, Langton and Wyke; and he and his men could call on the assistance of Dragoons at Corfe Castle, Wareham, Dorchester and Weymouth.

Warren Lisle's zeal and attention to duty made him a very active and efficient Supervisor, getting the best out of what turned out to be a rather poor lot of subordinates, many of whom were too old for their duties, while others were too addicted to the bottle to be of any use to him. One incredible incident involved the Riding Officer of Abbotsbury who rode hell for leather into the sea swearing loudly that he intended to ride all the way to Bridport that way. He was brought ashore with difficulty, and, not surprisingly, died two days later.

By 1732 Lisle was settled in Weymouth Customs House on the corner of St. Edmund Street near the Quay, a residence usually assigned to the Collector of the Port, a clear sign of the high esteem in which the Service held him at this time. Although Weymouth was declining as a port while Poole was increasing in importance, it was still a vital centre for the Preventive Service because of its strategic position. It was Warren Lisle's expertise and skill as a smuggler-catcher that made him a vital man to have in Weymouth, and the only office and residence for him was obviously the Customs House itself, particularly as there were frequent changes of Collector during this period.

It was in 1734 that Lisle took over as commander of the Customs sloop *Walker*. He had done his fair share of service against the smugglers on land: now it was time to begin his longest and most notable period of success, on the water. He would be able to receive not only part of the value of all smuggled goods seized, as he had been doing on land, but would also be awarded a share of all smuggling vessels seized and sold.

He found the *Walker* had been disgracefully neglected by her previous commander, the ship and her weapons being almost unfit for service, so he actually bought her from the Crown. Then he immediately spent a huge sum on a complete refitting and overhaul, afterwards hiring her back to the Collector of Weymouth at the rate of two shillings and sixpence per ton per month.

In 1737 he seized the cutter *Guernsey Packet*, which had been regularly smuggling contraband from the Channel Islands under the pretence of her legitimate trade. When he received his half share of the seizure money he immediately paid it to the Crown, refitted the cutter, re-named it the *Beehive*, and hired it out to his superior, the Collector of Weymouth. With these two ships, virtually his own little squadron, Lisle began operating against the smugglers from Christchurch (or, as we could call it, Hengistbury Head) in the east to Start Point in the west. Success came the very next year: in 1738 the *Beehive* gave chase to a smuggling sloop off Portland, following it for over five hours and at last came abreast, but the smuggler would not heave-to when challenged. A Royal Navy cutter happened to be in the vicinity, so *Beehive* signalled to her for assistance. The captain of the senior service ship, the *Diamond*, and the *Beehive's* mate, boarded the smuggler with their men, took control of her, and started to bring her into Weymouth. But the captured smugglers, desperate as they always were when in a tight corner, broke free and, superior in number, overpowered the King's men. The two Officers and three Revenue men were actually nailed up in the ship's main cabin, and the sloop escaped. Lisle had to sail across to France and arrange his men's release, as well as that of Lieutenant Forbes, R.N., Captain of the *Diamond*.

It was in 1740 that Warren Lisle was made Surveyor of the Sloops along the south coast by the Commissioners of Customs, clear recognition of his quality as one of the best sea-commanders the Service had ever had. His area of command stretched from Portsmouth to Land's End, and he was consulted by and deferred to by his masters, the Commissioners, on all matters relating to the prevention of smuggling and the hardware with which it was commissioned.

It was around 1745 that Lisle moved to Lyme Regis, for it was more convenient for the Surveyor of Sloops to run his command from there. It was also a very fashionable place to live. As he prospered he became a leading burgess of Lyme, and then in 1751 he was elected Mayor, his first term being followed by a second, to which he added a third in the early 1760s.

Captain Lisle replaced the *Beehive* when she became too worn out for the Service. In 1756 he bought a new cutter, the *Shaftesbury*, and stationed her at Penzance. He followed this by buying yet another, named the *Sherborne*, basing her at Lyme Regis. Not only did he keep up the war against the smugglers of the south coast, but he was also used by the Commissioners to examine charges of bad administration of Customs matters in both Plymouth and Penzance, as a result of which the Collectors of both ports were fired for being in collusion with the smugglers of those areas.

It was some time in the early 1770s that Warren Lisle returned to Weymouth from Lyme Regis, which was very convenient, for his wife had inherited the Minterne and Clapcott estates; by 1780 they were living on a fine estate at Upwey near Weymouth. In 1773 he resigned a post he had held for fifty-seven years in favour of his son William, that of Searcher for Poole and Weymouth; and then six years later he resigned from his position of Surveyor of Sloops. He was seventy-nine, but his age was not the reason for his resignation: he wanted to be free from the constraints of the Customs Service so that he could speak out against abuses. So began a series of reports made directly to Lord Shelburne, the Home Secretary, in which he outlined the state of smuggling, which was, of course, increasing in intensity, and of corruption in the Customs Service in his area.

He kept up his keen interest in his beloved Customs ships, for in 1782 we hear of his making a report on the *Orestes*, which took such a prominent part in the Battle of Mudeford in 1784. He wrote that she was a most suitable vessel for the Service, and went on to obtain a crew for this seized prize.

Warren Lisle died at his home in 1788 and was buried in the Church of St. Lawrence at Upwey, one of the finest Customs officers ever to grace the service, as great a credit to Dorset as William Arnold of Cowes is to Hampshire.

Epilogue

The Coastguard was formed in 1831, and as it tightened its grip and Customs Duties declined in number, so smuggling gradually lost its attraction for the men and women who had practised it on such a gigantic scale. But the British public seemed reluctant to let the smuggler go: to all sections of the community, both high and low, he was a raffish supplier of essential goods which made life worth living; but to the common people from which he sprang, he was much more. He was the chap next door who brought in the contraband just as Robin Hood had taken the Abbot's fat purses, he was the 'good lad', he was themselves.

To hundreds of contemporary artists who made their livings by producing works which caught the public's fancy by giving it what it wanted to see and hear, he was the honest rogue who, particularly since his day was drawing to a close and the roseate aura of romance was gathering round his persona, should take his place in popular art alongside Robin of Sherwood, Rob Roy, Hereward the Wake, Tam O'Shanter and Falstaff.

English and Scottish painters had latched on to the Smugglers as a subject while they were still in their heyday. George Morland, who lived from 1763 to 1804, made countless sketches of them chatting, lifting boxes and lolling on the shore in attitudes which made it clear he had never hidden behind a rock and observed them at first hand. But his drawings went into thousands of homes as etchings, coloured by the hands of women and girls whose sweated labour was carried on in the conditions bewailed by Thomas Hood's heroine in *The Song of the Shirt*. Morland's smugglers look like removal men who have had their wagon taken away by bolting horses, for their boxes and barrels are far too large and cumbersome to be transported by real contrabandists; and they are certainly blissfully remote from any possibility of being surprised by Revenue men. But Morland was

29. *The Smugglers' Intrusion* by Sir David Wilkie. R.A.

merely painting beach-scenes in which he thought it would be a nice idea to place a few smugglers for local colour. It was painters like Sir Francis Bourgeois and Sir David Wilkie who realized that danger, urgency, romance and action were what was wanted in a really good smuggling picture.

Bourgeois' finest effect was gained in a pair of paintings' 'The Smugglers Attacked' and 'The Smugglers Defeated', produced in 1793. Roman proportions, intensity of expression worthy of Delacroix, and Turner-like effects in the portrayal of weather and rocks, all add to the rugged effect of this noble pair. Sir David Wilkie, who lived from 1785 until 1841, was an eminent Scottish artist who made his name with large-scale works packed full of human interest and vigour, perhaps the best known of these being 'Village Politicians' and 'Chelsea Pensioners Reading in the *Gazette* of the Battle of Waterloo'. In 1830 he was appointed Painter to the King, and was knighted six years later. It is not known in which year he executed 'The Smugglers' Intrusion', but it was an immediate best-seller as a print, striking a deep popular chord.

It is a real 'story-picture', the genre so beloved of the Victorians. The family is at breakfast, their little bottle of gin and its accompanying jug of hot water on the table, and the husband is just ready to go off to work, his hay-knives and basket hanging ready on the back of the chair. High on the wall poultry and game are hanging and below them is a paper which could be a 'Wanted' poster with details of a smuggler the Philistines wish to interview; while beneath the table crouches the alarmed dog, obviously nervous about intruders, particularly smugglers. The main figure, the Gentleman of the Night, dominates the scene, a powerful giant, with his crafty henchman behind him, perhaps the lander, the brains of the gang. The smuggler has an eastern suggestion about his looks, possibly gypsy in origin, with not a little of the pirate mixed in, and he is very well armed, with ready pistol and cutlass at his side. Great sea-boots complete his ensemble, together with a sort of marine-helmet which looks as if it could be pulled down over his face as a mask to conceal his features, as many smugglers did when capture was in the offing. The two barrels he carries seem to have been brought for the family, but if they are expecting a delivery, why are they so alarmed at his 'intrusion'? Perhaps they know the smugglers are being pursued and will want either to hide in their house or nip through and out the back.... Like all good Victorian pictures, it not only tells a story but poses a mystery as well, giving the viewer an enigma to unravel, a riddle to solve.

It was inevitable, with such eminent painters taking up the smuggler as a subject to the great delight of the public, that one of lesser talent should decide to concentrate almost solely on the genre, almost to the point of obsession. This was Henry Perlee Parker, who became so keen on such paintings that he became known as 'Smuggler' Parker. His most interesting painting is that of Isaac Gulliver, and has already been partly described. This happy gang of smugglers could be lying on the cliffs anywhere from Boscombe to Burton Bradstock: tobacco and drink are being freely consumed, and three of the smugglers, at their picnic-table, improvised from one of the larger tubs they have just brought up from the distant beach and covered with a cloth of real damask which, presumably, also came in the contraband, appear to be enjoying French pâté, which they are spreading on biscuits. There is even an Italian Leghorn straw hat in the right foreground.

It was details like these that made 'Smuggler' Parker's pictures so popular, although they were not all on smuggling themes. Between 1817 and 1863 this incredibly industrious artist, whose main love always remained marine subjects, exhibited eighty-six pictures in London, most of which were reproduced in the *Illustrated London News*. Twenty-three of these were placed in the Royal Academy.

But the smuggler inspired not only pictures. A stream of songs issued from the pens of minor composers in the first part of the nineteenth century, many of them headed by drawings of smugglers. *The Smuggler's Bride* sang of 'A damsel fair that in Kent did dwell'; while *The Female Smuggler* introduced a girl called Jane, who lived, rather vaguely, 'By the rolling sea', and who in the end marries 'a Commodore of the Blockade'. *The Smuggler's Boy* was a real tear-jerker, its hero's father being drowned. However, he is luckily befriended by a lady who conveniently also dies and leaves him an enormous fortune of £20,000, not bad for a smuggler's boy who, to judge from the ballad, had very little indeed to do with actual smuggling. These songs seem to indicate that it was enough merely to mention the word 'smuggler' in a title for the public to be attracted to it. Later in the century, when the Free Trade had completely ceased to exist as such, came novels like *The Preventive Man* and *The Owl's House*, and even plays, the best-known local example being *Billy Coombes' Last Fight*.

Without doubt, the finest smuggling ballad is *Will Watch, the Bold Smuggler*, which stayed popular throughout the late 1830s and 1840s. Its melody is truly lovely, and this is not surprising for it was composed by John Davy, who also wrote the more famous *The Bay of Biscay*; while the words, by Thomas Cory, make it far livelier than most other smuggling ballads. But the most interesting point about Will Watch is that he actually existed, unlike the heroes and heroines of most other works in the genre. It is said that his real name was Gil Brown. Will, or Gil, had a ship which he had named the *Susan* after his beloved Sue, who appears in the song and lived at Leigh near Havant, in Hampshire. The *Susan* was a formidable smuggling vessel, for she mounted eighteen brass cannon which enabled her to see off most Revenue or Royal Naval ships. But one day she was being chased by

30. Will Watch: the Staffordshire pottery figure of the smuggler made famous by the popular ballad *Will Watch, the Bold Smuggler*.

one of these very craft in the Solent, a Royal Naval sloop. Just as she was about to be overtaken, she found herself in a sudden fog-bank, and Will Watch and his crew heaved a sigh of relief. However, it was not a very big bank, for a few minutes later out came the *Susan* into the daylight and there was the King's sloop, which immediately opened fire. Plain truth tells that the *Susan* was captured, but the song says Will was shot down in the fight. His body was taken ashore to his Sue, and his spirit immediately ascended into that serene Valhalla to which all great folk-heroes go. He was then immortalized in song and story, and also in a Staffordshire pottery figure, which sold to all classes of people in its thousands, to stand on their mantlepieces alongside Shakespeare, Wellington and Robin Hood. In this way the smuggler faded gradually into England's folk-mythology, celebrated, mourned and given an extension of life by potters, poets, writers and musicians.

On the Smugglers' Trail

On the Isle of Wight is the Ventnor Museum of Smuggling History, the only museum devoted entirely to the craft; while on the mainland the following Museums have smuggling displays: the Dorset County Museum, at Dorchester and the Poole Maritime Museum, in Poole, Dorset. In the Russell-Cotes Art Gallery and Museum at Bournemouth is the pistol belonging to the famous Dorset smuggler Isaac Gulliver.

In Christchurch you can see Ye Olde Eight Bells in Church Street, the George Inn in Bridge Street, as well as Number Ten in the same street, the residence of Abraham Pike and the other Chief Riding Officers and Supervisors of Customs. You can also visit the Priory Church's own Museum, over the Lady Chapel, which used to house the Christchurch Grammar School from which Richard Warner saw the smugglers' convoys coming over Hengistbury Head. You can actually look out of the very windows through which he peered with his 'tolerable glass'.

Out on Hengistbury Head you can walk from the beach below Double Dykes, on which the smugglers landed their contraband, following their footsteps between the huge earthbanks. Take the second exit on the left, cross the Broadway, and walk along the pavement until you strike the old smugglers' track going off to the right across the Solent Meads Golf Course. As you traverse it you will see Mudeford and the Run, the mouth of Christchurch harbour, and the site of the bloody Battle of 1784. The Haven House Inn and the Black House both show up starkly, and you may make a note to visit Mudeford later, perhaps as the sun sets.

Every so often along this path you pass by thorn bushes which grew far more thickly in smuggling days to provide shelter not only from prying eyes but also the sharp south-westerly winds. The end of the path gives on to pavement: this is Rolls Drive. Go along this road and you will pass into Thornbury Road. Turn right at the end of the Primary School's fence and you are in Wick Lane, which leads down into the village which saw the birth, if legend is true, of Sam Hookey, the 'Wicked Man of Wick', whose amazing career was described in the chapter on Christchurch.

If you wish to follow the smugglers' trail by car in Hampshire and Dorset, then go out to Kinson and find the Parish Church. (You will pass Pelham's on the way, the large house in its park, which was once, it is said, owned by the daughter of Isaac Gulliver, the great Dorset smuggler.) You can still see the grooves made by the smugglers' ropes as they hauled their brandy tubs up to the roof in the stones of the Church tower's parapet. Behind the church you will find the grave of Robert Trotman with its touching epitaph. Have a look, too, at the impressive memorial to Isaac Gulliver's descendants against the building's wall. If you take the road on past the church to Longham you will clearly see how the high rough ground between the village and the River Stour could have been riddled with escape-tunnels from the smugglers' houses in Kinson. Those with a special interest in Gulliver might like to motor on to Wimborne Minster, passing the White Hart, one of the smuggler's properties. In the town will be found Gulliver's House in West Borough; and in the Minster Church, at the west end, his tombstone, much worn, will be seen affixed to the wall.

It is not all that far, and it certainly makes an enjoyable drive, to Burley in the New Forest, the best route being through Ringwood. Again, those interested by Gulliver might like to turn off the road to the left in the direction of West Moors, just after passing through Ferndown, and after some distance along this road Gulliver's Farm will be seen on the left-hand side. If you have the Ordnance Survey map with you, this building will be clearly seen marked. Rejoin the main road and continue to Ringwood.

Once in Burley you will see Warnes Lane, named after the famous smuggling family; and in the Queen's Head you will find the Warnes Bar, as well. The smuggling atmosphere is strong here, and you will discover plenty of information from the walls and from the landlord and landlady. Take the road out of Burley in the direction of Crow. Just before you reach the Warne homestead, Knave's Ash, you will come to the Smugglers' Road Forestry Commission car-park. Here you will be able to explore the remarkable sunken lane and the wide path along which the contraband passed, as well as the many paths over Cranes Moor used by the Gentlemen of the Night. A pleasant walk is up the road to Vereley Hill, with its radio-mast, where the great tree grew which carried the smugglers' lantern, and this is just above Lovey Warne's favourite place when she was on duty, flashing her warning to the smugglers with her bright red cloak.

Perhaps one of the most striking smuggling relics is on the top of mighty Eggardon Hill in West Dorset: the octagonal earthwork where Gulliver planted his grove of trees to act as a sea-mark for his incoming smuggling luggers when he was at the height of his power. And below the hill you will come upon his farm, still working hard, but not at contraband traffic.

Glossary

Batmen: the smugglers' infantry, who stood as sentinels in screens to warn of the approach of the Customs Officers, and who escorted the convoys of tubmen, packhorses and wagons from the beaches and into the country. Their name comes from their holly or ash clubs which were called 'bats', for the penalty was death for any smuggler found carrying a firearm.

Collector: the principal Customs Officer of a port, which included a number of subordinate ports, and directly responsible to the Board of Customs in London.

Comptroller: the Customs Officer under a Collector whose job it was to ensure proper returns of Duties collected being sent to the Board of Customs in London.

creepers: small-fluked grapnels, one above the other, for hooking on to lines connecting sunk barrels.

crop: the total cargo of a smuggling ship, used particularly when it had to be sunk beneath the sea, with floats and weights, to hide it from the pursuing Customs men.

dark: a moonless night, the smugglers' favourite time.

donkey, one-legged: also called a rump-stool, a seat with one leg, rather like a shooting-stick, used by Coastguards on watch, to ensure that they did not 'drop off' to sleep.

Dragoon: cavalryman, armed with sword and carbine, really a mounted infantryman.

East Indiaman: merchant-ship of the East India Company, which received its charter in 1660, granting it exclusive trading rights east of a line from the Cape of Good Hope to the Straits of Magellan.

flaskers: smugglers who specialized in smuggling liquor.

flink: the signal, usually a single flash, sent by the land smuggler looking out when the smuggling ship arrived off the appointed shore. Spout lanterns were used mainly.

Free Traders: the name for the smugglers which signified their role as the country's benefactors.

Genevars: gin, the corruption of the original word.

Gentlemen of the Night: another name for smugglers.

Guard: length of coast looked after by the Coastguards of a particular station.

Hat Duty: this duty of five per cent ad valorem was imposed in 1660 and not repealed until 1860.

Hollands: another name for gin

King's Warehouse: store situated in each major port for holding contraband until it was disposed of.

Lander: the 'beachmaster', who had absolute charge of the tubmen, packhorses and wagons and all other smugglers involved in the complex business of landing a cargo of contraband, including signallers, lookouts and batmen.

Landguard: the force of Customs Riding Officers, who were complementary to the Waterguard, in the patrolling cutters and sloops at sea.

Laggan: contraband which had been sunk, marked with unobtrusive buoys, and collected after the Customs men had left the area.

Owler: originally the traders who smuggled wool out of England after the laws passed by King Edward I to prevent its leaving the country. They were also called caterpillars. This name was used of smugglers generally as time passed.

Preventy Men: one of the many smugglers' names for their enemies, the Officers of the Board of Customs. They were also called landsharks, watersharks, Philistines, pickaroons, gobloos, gobblers, gobbies, gaugers, shingle-pickers, and even bluebottles, (the Coastguards) long before this name was used for policemen.

rummage: to search for hidden contraband in vessels suspected of smuggling, and still used today in the Customs Service.

run: the passage of the contraband from the beach where it was received from the smuggling ship to its destination, either store or selling-point.

Smugglers: also called Free Traders or Gentlemen of the Night.

Spotsman: captain of smuggling ship who was able to arrive, by incredible feats of navigation without modern aids and almost always on pitch-dark nights, at the pre-arranged 'spot' on the coast where the shore-based smugglers were waiting for him and his cargo.

stinkibus: brandy which had been sunk and left in the sea too long.

sweep: long oar manned by two or more men, used for propulsion in shallow waters.

sweeping: dredging up sunken contraband using two boats in concert.

tide-waiter: a shore-based Customs Officer who boarded ships in port and examined them 'on the tide-line'. Today he is called a Preventive Officer.

tub: a keg or small barrel, about four gallons, the standard smugglers' container of spirits; also sometimes referred to as a half-anker.

Index

INDEX

INDEX

INDEX

INDEX